# Aisha

The Wife, the Companion, the Scholar

# Aisha

The Wife, the Companion, the Scholar

Reşit Haylamaz

NEW JERSEY • LONDON • FRANKFURT • CAIRO • JAKARTA

TUGHRA
BOOKS

New Jersey

26 25 24  23  7 8 9 10

Originally published in Turkish as *Hazreti Aişe (r.a) Mü'minlerin En Mümtaz Annesi* in 2009

Published by Tughra Books
335 Clifton Ave., Clifton, NJ, 07011, USA
www.tughrabooks.com

Library of Congress Cataloging-in-Publication Data

Haylamaz, Reşit.
[Hazreti Aişe (r.a), mü'minlerin en mümtaz annesi. English]
Aisha: the wife, the companion, the scholar / Resit Haylamaz
pages cm
Includes bibliographical references.
ISBN 978-1-59784-266-2 (pbk. : alk. paper)
1. 'A'ishah, approximately 614-678. 2. Muhammad, Prophet, -632--Family. 3.
Women--Religious aspects--Islam. 4. Islam--Doctrines. I.Title.
BP80.A52H39 2013
297.6'42--dc23 [B]
2013029311

ISBN: 978-1-59784-266-2

Translated by Tuğba Özer Gürbüz

Printed in Canada

# CONTENTS

# PREFACE

Khadija and Aisha, may God be pleased with them, had a special position among the wives of God's Messenger, peace and blessings be upon him; while the former was like the royal vizier in Mecca for fifteen years before the revelation, the latter fulfilled the same duty during the Medina years and after. When they are considered in terms of their mission, each of them had the proper qualifications. God Almighty provided the Messenger of God with a strong character: in Mecca, where belief, self-sacrifice, and bravery were so necessary, He gave him Khadija; in Medina, where the requirements of knowledge, intelligence and reasoning were needed, He bestowed him Aisha.

Khadija was the sturdiest woman of Mecca. She provided unyielding support to God's Messenger during the hardest days when troubles were at their peak, during his days of suffering when there were consecutive problems and disasters. When he began to call people to Islam, she was his greatest supporter, both materially and spiritually. Khadija was the first Muslim; believing in God's Messenger at a vital moment when he needed her most meant a special place at the side of God and His Messenger.

Aisha's place was different. She was a special vizier to the Messenger of God after the Hijra to Medina, when it was necessary to render service to religion. Aisha, with a bright, inquisitive mind and a quick wit, distinguished herself in the Prophet's house. God Almighty bestowed her with extraordinary brilliance. She had a questioning nature, and did not blindly accept what she heard. She was critical of everything she heard, according to the criteria of the Qur'an and the Sunnah (the Prophetic Tradition). Her eyes and ears were constantly on the alert for revelation. Aisha was like a bridge between the time of the Prophet and the future of Islam.

Aisha represented the vitality of revelation during the half-century after the death of God's Messenger, and did not deprive her students of the light of Prophethood. Like a meeting point for travelers from different directions, her place was by the Four Rightful Caliphs. When possible controversies arose, Aisha was a kind arbitrator. For mistakes on religious issues, she was a dignified corrector, and a decisive and patient example of the straight path of Islam.

Wherever she went, that place would come to life. People who entered into her ambience felt that they became colored with the light of revelation and returned in excitement, almost as if they had visited the Messenger of God. There was no one who came to her with a question who was unable to get an answer. She concluded nearly every matter with revelation, and found solutions to others' problems directly from the Qur'an and the Sunnah. In other matters, she evaluated, compared, and interpreted based on her own vast knowledge of the religion.

Aisha was the mother of all believers. Among the things that passed to us from her, there was certain information that would normally remain private between spouses. Out of necessity, she appeared to convey details of the religion. Many matters would have remained unknown to us if she had not existed. Behind closed doors, she asked the most intimate questions to God's Messenger, as if she was throwing a life ring to us. Aisha invites people of conscience to the Straight Path of Islam. We hope that this book in your hands, like an invitation, will be the means for good deeds.

# Chapter 1

---

## Meccan Years and the Migration

# BETROTHAL

One day, there was a knock on Abu Bakr's door and Mut'im ibn 'Adiy[1] came in to ask the family if they would give their daughter, Aisha, as a bride to Jubayr, his son. Mut'im ibn 'Adiy was a rare person who, like Abu Bakr, was knowledgeable in the field of genealogy; as such, it was natural that he wanted to join families with a person like Abu Bakr. Mecca in those days was so small that people knew each other intimately, and hence Mut'im ibn 'Adiy could foresee the future of Aisha—her nature, attitude and behavior. He dreamed of having a daughter-in-law like Aisha who was intelligent, respectful, polite and pure. That day, Abu Bakr did not decline the request. In those days, to some, not declining a request was equivalent to a betrothal. But Abu Bakr, who considered his statement as a contract, had decided to give special attention to the request. However, as the days passed, suspicions arose. Since no answer was given, the ibn 'Adiy family began to have grave doubts about marrying their son with the daughter of Abu Bakr. Their visits to Abu Bakr's household became less frequent.

The problem was understood later. Assessing the changed conditions, Ibn 'Adiy's family were defeated by their doubts. When Prophet Muhammad's revelation began in the cave of mount Hira, Abu Bakr's family accepted Islam. It was a time when believers started to convey

---

[1]  Mut'im ibn 'Adiy was the leader of the Banu Nawfal tribe. He was the person who gave protection to the Prophet on his return from Taif. Likewise, Ibn 'Adiy was the leading figure in ending the three-year boycott against Muslims.

the message from Ibn Arqam's house, when calling people to Islam became public and worship was not hidden in Mecca as it had been before. As the beloved Companion of the Prophet, Abu Bakr and his family were at the front lines. The visits from ibn 'Adiy's family to Abu Bakr's family ceased as the ibn 'Adiy family watched from afar the trials of Abu Bakr, whose daughter they had insistently requested for their son.

## MECCAN MEMOIRS

But life went on. Every morning, Mecca became luminous with the news of new believers entering the faith. Every night, Mecca became dark with the hardships forced on believers.

Experiencing joy and difficulty together, Aisha watched everything, and would describe these precisely to future generations. Her natural sense of curiosity led her to record every development she experienced, almost like a photographic record of her life. She knew where verses were revealed, who became Muslim and when. One day, many years later, a man from Iraq came to Medina and asked questions about the Meccan period. In her reply, Aisha related an insightful analysis of the time.

The Meccan period was full of unforgettable and sad memories for Aisha. The only brightness in their lives was the Messenger of God. He visited the house of Abu Bakr frequently and comforted them. Aisha expressed her pleasure at this and said:

"Ever since I can remember, I saw my parents as practicing believers. The Messenger of God used to visit us almost every day in the morning or in the evening."[2]

## THE MARRIAGE OFFER

Two years had passed since the death of Khadija, and the Messenger of God was living alone with his three daughters. One day, the wife of

---

[2]    Ahmad ibn Hanbal, *Musnad*, 6/198; Bayhaqi, *Sunan* 6/204.

Uthman ibn Maz'un, Khawlah bint Hakim, came to God's Messenger respectfully and asked:

"Do you not want to marry?"

The Messenger of God was fifty years old, feeling the sadness of Khadija's death together with his three daughters, he responded:

"Alright, but with whom?"

Already prepared, Khawlah answered his question with another question and asked whether he preferred to marry a widow or someone who hadn't married before. Her attitude was that of a woman capable of finding both. God's Messenger asked about the latter option.

"It is Aisha, the daughter of Abu Bakr, a friend whom you love the most among people." Then he asked Khawlah about the other option. It turned out to be Sawdah bint Zam'a, one of the earliest Muslims. Sawdah had accepted Islam during the most difficult days in Mecca and had even migrated to Abyssinia to escape being persecuted. Unfortunately, her husband as-Sakran ibn 'Amr had died in Abyssinia and so she returned. Both of them were possibilities, so he told Khawlah to find out the ladies' opinions.

## FIRST STOP

Khawlah was happy because she hoped to lessen the Prophet's troubles. Sawdah was a mature, trustworthy woman. Though she still mourned for her husband in her heart, this offer was of a nature that could cease her pains. Sawdah had an elderly father and she decided to receive his blessings first. This duty was also given to Khawlah.

So, Khawlah went to Sawdah's elderly father and told him that Muhammad, the son of Abdullah, was asking for her daughter's hand in marriage. When the old man heard the name "Muhammad, the son of Abdullah," he straightened up and said:

"He is a generous man and a good match. But how does your friend feel about this?"

Khawlah quickly responded:

"She likes the idea, too."

Even though Sawdah consented, some of her relatives opposed the marriage. Her brother Abdullah ibn Zam'a, who heard the news later on, protested his father's decision.[3] Sawdah's uncle, too, screamed in poetic verse, objecting to this marriage.

## SECOND ADDRESS

Then Khawlah went to the house of Abu Bakr and spoke to his wife Umm Ruman:

"The Messenger of God sent me to ask for your daughter Aisha's hand in marriage."

Umm Ruman was speechless with pleasure. But she remembered something that threatened to overshadow her joy. She remembered Abu Bakr's promise long-ago to Mut'im ibn 'Adiy. So Umm Ruman suggested that they wait for Abu Bakr. When Abu Bakr arrived home, Khawlah told him the news. He certainly wished to become a relative of the Prophet, but there was a doubt in his mind. According to pre-Islamic traditions, it was not appropriate to marry a child with the child of a close friend. When the Messenger of God heard about that, he said that theirs' was brotherhood in religion, thus there was no problem with this marriage. Abu Bakr was so happy that his eyes overflowed with tears. However, he had not forgotten the other problem. He went to the house of Mut'im ibn 'Adiy to be relieved of a promise that would have caused him misery. As Abu Bakr had thought, it was clear that they expected no betrothal.

Khawlah and Umm Ruman each took a deep breath when they heard the news. Abu Bakr said to Khawlah, "Now, you can go and invite the Messenger of God."

It was the month of Shawwal in the twelfth year of revelation and an engagement was made between the Prophet and Aisha. Four

---

[3]    Later on, Abdullah ibn Zam'a would become a Muslim and express his regret for the reaction he showed that day.

hundred drachma, which was considered a little generous for that time, was settled on as the *mahr* (bridal due).[4]

From that day, a new period began for Aisha. She was the happiest of young women, since she would become the wife of the most beloved servant of God. At the same time, a huge responsibility - being a mother of believers[5] - was placed onto her shoulders at a young age. Let into the secret fold of God's most beloved servant, she was given intimate knowledge that no one else could reach.

Aisha was aware of her responsibilities. The process of revelation, which she had followed carefully until that day, would now be approached even more meticulously, recording every event like a photograph in her mind.

## THE ADVICE GIVEN TO UMM RUMAN

Aisha's mother, Umm Ruman, felt a heavy burden on her shoulders because her daughter was going to become the wife of the Prophet. She became very sensitive to her daughter's energetic behavior. When she saw something she did not like, she condemned Aisha, sometimes quite harshly. God's Messenger, who came to visit after such an incident had taken place, felt the chilly atmosphere in the home and asked the reason for it. Umm Ruman was embarrassed but explained what had happened between herself and her daughter. The Prophet turned to Umm Ruman and said:

"O, Umm Ruman! Treat Aisha properly and preserve her rights, please, for my sake!"[6]

---

[4]   *Nasa'i*, Nikah, 66 (3350); Ahmad ibn Hanbal, *Musnad*, 6/427 (27448)
[5]   It is stated in the Qur'an (al-Ahzab 33:6) that the Prophet's wives are mothers of believers.
[6]   Hakim, *Mustadrak*, 4:6 (6716).

## THE HOLY MIGRATION

Aisha continued to reside in her parents' home. During that time, the Messenger of God visited other tribes and invited them to Islam. He was looking for open hearts that would submit to God and went to Ta'if with that intention but returned with enormous troubles. But then, something happened to the Messenger of God which made him forget all his troubles.

The Night Journey and the Ascension (*Isra* and *Miraj*) were the product of these days of hardship. God's Messenger was taken to al-Masjid al-Aqsa in Jerusalem in one night, where he traveled up through the heavens and came back the same night. When the idolaters of Mecca heard of the Ascension, they rejoiced thinking the impossibility of such a tale was the perfect opportunity to make people disbelieve in the Messenger of God. But the incident pulled a curtain between belief and unbelief, allowing believers to reach a higher level of faith. Abu Bakr reached the rank of loyalty. As a member of Abu Bakr's house and as the future wife of the Messenger of God, Aisha followed what happened very closely.

The idolaters in Mecca continued persecuting the believers. The Prophet and his Companions were close to the end of their time in Mecca. In fact, the Messenger of God had a dream showing his Companions the ways of Medina to overcome the troubles in Mecca. But it was not easy.

For the Messenger of God, Abu Bakr's home was like his own home; hardly a day passed in which he did not visit Abu Bakr's home.

One day, he came in the middle of the day, which was an unusual time. Everyone was surprised and the members of the house quickly told their father about the visit.

Abu Bakr knew more than anyone about the Prophet's character. He knew how sensitive he was about respecting others' rights, how he avoided making anyone uncomfortable by visiting at the normal times of rest. Knowing that the Prophet had visited despite his sensitivities, Abu Bakr felt it must be a significant matter.

As soon as he entered the house, the Prophet expressed that he wished to speak in private. Abu Bakr responded: "May my parents be sacrificed for you, O Messenger of God. They are all from your community."

He was right. Both Asma and Aisha were close to the Messenger of God in the first years of revelation and they could keep secrets.

The two sisters stayed in place to witness this important conversation. The Prophet said:

"I was given permission to leave Mecca and to emigrate."

This was the sentence that Abu Bakr had been waiting for. He was delighted because he knew the persecution in Mecca would finally end. But was he going to be together with the Messenger of God on his trip? Anxiously, he asked:

"Will we be together, O Messenger of God?"

Abu Bakr waited for the answer with bated breath. The Prophet turned to him and the following words came out from his blessed lips:

"Yes, together!"

Abu Bakr shed tears of joy.[7] From that point on, Abu Bakr's household talked of nothing else other than the upcoming migration. Aisha and her sister, Asma, had already started travel preparations with their mother, Umm Ruman.

This meant that Asma[8] and her younger sister by ten years, Aisha, were the first witnesses of the holy migration. They were the first to know the travel plans of their father and the Messenger of God. They followed closely the scheme that included issues such as the route, the arrangement of guides, the places on the Mount of Light where they would hide and wait for three days until everything became calm, as well as information about who would visit them and what responsibilities they would take.

When the unbelievers in Mecca heard that the Messenger's community was migrating to Medina, they attempted to stop it in various

---

[7]   Tabari, *Tarikh*, 1:569; Ibn Hisham, *Sira*, 3:11.
[8]   Asma was twenty-seven years old, and married to Zubayr ibn Awwam.

ways. They kept watch on various routes to Medina and made some emigres return; they physically barred people from leaving, took the wealth of some believers, and even separated some believers from their families. But in the end, they were not able to make the Muslims stay.

In the end, the unbelievers got together and made a final decision to kill the Prophet.

The same day, the pale streets of Mecca, where death had fallen, were preparing to say goodbye to the two travelers. When the time came, a deep sorrow filled the hearts of Abu Bakr's family. Surely, Aisha was experiencing twice as much sorrow as Asma. Everyone felt sad to be separated from the Messenger of God, but Aisha's sadness was very different. From that day on, Aisha's ears pricked up to listen for any news that came from around. Her anxieties were heightened in response to the incomprehensible reactions of polytheists in Mecca; she looked for news from any source. The pagans of Mecca became furious when they could not catch and kill the Prophet, so they promised a reward of one hundred camels to anyone who could bring the travelers, dead or alive. Not surprisingly, the leader of the pagans was Abu Jahl; he went angrily to Abu Bakr's home and asked them where their father was. They did not know, but this was no excuse for Abu Jahl. Furious, he slapped Asma, who was six months pregnant.[9]

The two travelers had left, keeping their destination a secret. But a crowd forming around the Ka'ba attracted the attention of Asma, and she ventured closer to hear what they were saying. A man had witnessed two people with incredible perfections travelling toward Medina. When Asma shared what she had heard with the others of Abu Bakr's home, they all breathed a sigh of relief and thanked God for protecting their father and the Messenger of God despite the efforts of the pagans in Mecca.

---

[9]   Abu Nuaym, *Hilyatul Awliya* 2:56; Ibn Hisham, *Sira*, 3:14.

# HIJRA

Three months had passed and yet there was no news of Abu Bakr and the Messenger of God. One day, Aisha and Asma saw their brother Abdullah, happily coming towards them. Instantly, they understood and ran to him in joy. Their father, Abu Bakr, had sent a letter which invited the family members to Medina.

The letter was brought by Zayd ibn Harithah and Abu Rafi. Abdullah ibn Urayqit, the guide of the holy migration, also joined these two in their journey. At the end of the letter written to his son, Abdullah was told by his father to take his sisters and mother to Medina.[10]

The tasks of Abu Rafi and Zayd ibn Harithah were defined; it was the Messenger of God who had sent them. He had given them two camels and five hundred drachmas and assigned them to bring the Prophet's household, together with Abu Bakr's family, to Medina.

A short time later, preparations were complete and both families started to migrate together while the unbelievers of Mecca were unaware. They were going to Medina, the center of civilization, and to the Messenger of God, with the intention that they would never be separated from him again. They had begun a journey that would leave every problem behind.

Their path was full of different surprises. They had just left Mecca and came to Mina, where they came across Talha ibn Ubaydullah, who was migrating too. Their happiness increased from having found this trustworthy man who had been involved with the mission of the Prophet since the first days. Their joy was apparent in their shining eyes. The group continued going on their way. Then Aisha's camel became nervous, refusing to follow the caravan. This concerned Umm Ruman because the camel was carrying the future wife of

---

[10] It is stated that the Prophet took five drachmas as a debt from Abu Bakr. When they came to the place named Qadid, Zayd bought the three camels to be used during the journey. See Abu Nuaym, *Hilyatul Awliya* 9:227; Dhahabi, *Siyar* 2:152.

God's Messenger. The camel kept going the way it wanted. It seemed there was nothing they could do. Umm Ruman, whose fear increased as, with every step the camel took her daughter further away, screamed:

"Give up its halter!"

She hoped her advice could help where her actions could not. She hoped that the halter would get caught up in a branch while it dragged on the ground, which would keep the camel from going further.[11]

And that's exactly what happened. The camel that Aisha was riding, whose rope she tossed following her mother's advice, stopped without going much further. Its halter had tangled itself in a branch, keeping the intractable camel from wandering away.

Other members of caravan ran over and helped calm the camel. Everything was placed back on the right track and their journey toward Medina resumed once more.

The journey meant a different hardship for Aisha's sister, Asma, who was pregnant. Asma's labor pains increased gradually, and when they came to Quba, she had no more endurance left. Although they were very close to their destination, they had to stop, and Asma delivered a baby boy. They took the baby to the Messenger of God. He held the infant and named him Abdullah.[12]

## THE MEDINA PESTILENCE

Their three-month long journey ended when they arrived in Medina. By this time, the Messenger of God was busy with the construction of his mosque—Al-Masjid an-Nabawi.

Their problems in Mecca seemed to have ended. Yet, they were about to experience a scene that would overshadow their happiness: emigrants, who were not accustomed to Medina's conditions, were suffering from an unfamiliar disease. Abu Bakr was one of them.

---

[11]   Tabarani, *al-Mujamu'l Kabir*, 23: 183 (296); Haythami, *Majmuntu'z Zawaid*, 9:366; Tahmaz, *as-Sayyidatu Aisha*, 27.

[12]   *Bukhari*, Manaqibu'l Ansar, 45 ('909, 3910); *Muslim*, Adab, 25-26 (2146); *Musnad Ibn Hanbal*, 6:54, 206.

He slept feverishly, awaiting a merciful hand that would guide him to health. They had fallen ill with the Medina pestilence. Some of them did not even have the energy to stand, and for this reason, they did their Daily Prayers, which they had never given up, while sitting down. The Messenger of God turned to them and said:

"You should know that the one who prays while sitting gets half of the good deeds than the one who prays while standing."[13]

After that, the Companions used all of their effort to pray while standing.

After getting permission from the Messenger of God, Aisha came to visit her father, who was still very sick. Bilal al-Habashi and Amir ibn Fuhayra were sharing the same room with Abu Bakr. Aisha went towards her father, but her heart was deeply grieved by the scene that she saw: it was as if her father had gone and someone else had taken his place. The active man was now, in turns, writhing with fever or sleeping unconsciously. She came nearer and said:

"O my dear father, how are you? How do you feel?"

Abu Bakr's eyes glittered. It seemed as if a light appeared from inside him, emanating from his daughters' nearness. Yet his soul was far from her question. He gave a meaningful look to his daughter whom he had been away from for months and said:

"Everyone wakes up in their home, but death is closer than one's shoelaces."

Aisha was shocked. Yes, death was always near, but life still continues for a sick man. Abu Bakr wanted to give advice with the language of sickness, first to Aisha, then to everyone else. She thought:

"Surely, my father does not know what he is saying."

Amir ibn Fuhayra and Bilal al-Habashi were not fully conscious either. Homesickness had placed a permanent mark on their hearts, making their sickness in their new home worse.

---

[13] *Tirmidhi*, Salat, 247; *Ibn Majah*, Salat, 141; Ahmad ibn Hanbal, *Musnad*, 2:192, 203, 214; Ibn Kathir, *al-Bidaya*, 3:224.

Aisha left them sadly. She couldn't pretend that something minor had happened. Aisha went to the Prophet and told him what she had seen and heard, for he had always solved every problem. Aisha said:

"They are delirious with high fevers and they are talking to themselves, unconsciously."

The Messenger of God was very upset. He held his hands up to sky and prayed against those who had caused this situation by persecuting Muslims for years:

"My Lord! I leave Utbah ibn Rabi'ah, Shayba ibn Rabi'ah and Umayya ibn Khalaf to you; as they made us leave our city and come to this place where sickness has spread, you too give them what they deserve!"

Then he turned and prayed for his society and said:

"My Lord! Make us love Medina as much as or more than you made us love Mecca. Make this city a land of health and grant abundance. Then take this disease and send it toward Juhfa."[14]

The Messenger of God had a dream that night: a gloomy woman with a messy appearance was traveling from Medina toward Juhfa. The dream meant that his prayers were accepted. After that time, the emigrants never again suffered from high fevers or any other sickness due to the Medinan environment.[15]

---

[14]   *Bukhari*, Fadailu'l Medina, 11, Fadailu's Sahaba, 75, Marda, 8.
[15]   *Ibid.*

# Chapter 2

## A Home Full of Peace and Virtue

# THE MARRIAGE

A isha, who had migrated with her family members, had naturally settled in her father's home. The house was in the Banu Harith ibn Khazraj neighborhood. At that time, the Messenger of God was staying as a guest in the house of Khalid ibn Zayd.

Then Aisha fell ill. Her body was weak; the conditions of the journey and Medina were difficult for her. She had lost a lot of weight and her hair had started to fall out. Her mother, Umm Ruman, tried everything to make her daughter regain her health. Abu Bakr, who was well by this time, visited his sick daughter, and he stroked her head with compassion. He prayed to God for his daughter's health to return.

After a month had passed in sickness, Aisha started to feel better, and she even gained some weight as a result of her mother's special attention.

By this time, the Prophet's Mosque had been constructed and the civilization that would grow around it started to flourish in Medina.

Gabriel came to the Messenger of God and brought the message:

"Marry her, since she is your wife."

Then Abu Bakr came and asked too:

"O Messenger of God, is there a reason preventing you from staying with your wife, Aisha?"

The Messenger of God responded:

"*Sadaq!*"

*Sadaq* was the money that needed to be given directly to the bride upon marriage. For Abu Bakr, no material value could be compared to the Messenger of God. Abu Bakr gave the necessary amount to the Prophet, who gave the money to Aisha without delay. Previously, women's rights were disregarded completely. The money sent by the groom was customarily used by the bride's father and not the bride. With every passing day, the Prophet's practices corrected a wrong and established Islamic principles.[16]

Abu Bakr had more things to do, and he initiated the construction of a one-bedroom house near the mosque, using his own money. Then a small room was finished for Aisha. It was so small that when the Messenger of God stood up, his head nearly touched the ceiling and when Aisha laid down to rest, the remaining area was not enough for prostrating. Physically, it was small and unadorned, but spiritually, the room was large enough to enlighten the entire world.

This meant the end of the Messenger being a visitor in Khalid ibn Zayd's home, which he had been for seven months.

Eight months had passed since the Hijra. Choosing the month of Shawwal for marriage was also meaningful, since people thought marrynng in that month was a cause of ill fortune. Many years later, Aisha recommended Shawwal marriages in order to kill the remains of this pre-Islamic superstition, saying:

"The Messenger of God and I were engaged in the month of Shawwal and again, we married in the month of Shawwal. Now tell me, who among his wives is loved more by the Messenger of God?"[17]

The time had come, and Umm Ruman took Aisha to a place where the women of Helpers (Ansar, the native Medinan Muslims) had gathered. They walked so quickly that both were out of breath. Examining the most treasured bride in the world, the women said:

---

[16]   Tabarani, *al-Mujamu'l Kabir*, 23:25 (60); Ibn Abdilbarr, *Istiab*, 4: 1937; Ibn Sa'd, *Tabaqat*, 8:63.

[17]   *Muslim*, Nikah, 73 (1423).

"May her good deeds and blessings be in abundance and may her happiness increase." [18]

It was two or three hours before noon. With friends such as Asma bint Yazid, Aisha took her first step into her new home, a home that would later be known as 'the school of Prophethood'. Everything was different, and Aisha, who had been nervous and frightened before, felt quite calm. When she entered, the Messenger of God gave her a bowl of milk. Aisha felt shy; she bowed her head, lacking the courage to look at the shining face of the Prophet. Her friends said:

"Take the bowl from his hand; do not turn down his offer."

Hearing that, Aisha took the bowl from the hand of the most beloved servant of God and started to drink. The Prophet told her to give some to her friends.

But they declined, saying:

"We do not want to drink."

The Messenger of God again insisted:

"Lies and hunger cannot be together." Hearing that, Asma said:

"O Messenger of God, if someone says, 'I do not want something', when he does want it, is this considered a lie?" The Prophet answered:

"Yes. While a lie is recorded as a lie, a little lie is recorded as a little lie, too."[19]

Without any ostentation, the simple wedding was finished. According to Aisha's narration, the Messenger of God sacrificed neither a camel or a sheep that day; instead, Khazraj's leader, Sa'd ibn Ubadah, had brought a meal to the Prophet's home, so this became their wedding dinner.

From then on, there was Aisha, a woman in the Prophet's household who would follow the Prophet closely when he was apart from society and attaining decisions for mankind. She was a woman of her time, who helped things progress, a brilliant mind who followed incidents and understood them, and a wonderful storyteller who explained

---

[18] *Bukhari*, Fadailu's Sahaba, 73 (1423).
[19] Ahmad ibn Hanbal, *Musnad*, 6:438 (27511

what she had seen and heard in the home of the Prophet. God's most beloved and merciful Prophet, who was sent as a guide to mankind, was followed closely by a talented person who opened doors that may have stayed shut, particularly about family life and issues related to women. He was a guide for all, male and female, and a gracious adviser everyone should follow.

## HER FATHER'S ATTITUDE AFTER THE WEDDING

In the Qur'an, God stated the privilege of those who were married to the Prophet: *O wives of the Prophet! You are not like any of the other women...* (Ahzab 33:32). This specialty was a merit, but if unfulfilled, carried many risks. While great rewards could be gained for putting forth effort, possible sins would be twice as worse. Yet, the wives of God's Messenger were poised to fulfill their duties, and would die in purity and go to Paradise.

Though Abu Bakr was the father of Aisha, he called her mother and showed even more respect to her than he did to his own mother.

He heard that Mistah ibn Usasa had said negative things about Aisha when she was slandered. He was disappointed and stopped sending the money that he had formerly given to Mistah for his daily needs. A short time later, when the verses (an-Nur 24:22) were revealed about giving charity to needy people in every circumstance, and about forgiving people by blinding yourself to their faults as the most significant invitation for Holy forgiveness, he changed his attitude, repented, and said:

"I swear to God, I surely want the forgiveness of God."

He then started to give Mistah the money that was necessary for his daily bills.

Abu Bakr made an oath to himself:

"I swear to God, I am going to continue to give this money without delay."[20]

---

[20]  *Bukhari*, Shahadat 15 (2518), Ayman, 17.

## THE PHYSICAL CONDITIONS OF AISHA'S HOUSE

Aisha was not living in a large palace. Her room was only big enough for her needs. Her place was on the eastern side of the Prophet's Mosque and its door opened toward the west side. The mosque was like the garden of Aisha's home. When the Messenger of God stayed in the mosque for worship, particularly during Ramadan, Aisha could reach from her place to comb his hair or quickly fetch something for him from her room.[21] The walls of her room, which were plastered with mud, measured six or seven arms' length. Its ceiling, which anyone could touch with one arm raised, was covered by date-palm leaves filled with wool to prevent rainwater from leaking down. The house's only wooden door was never closed to anyone.[22]

Aisha explained the size of her room in this way:

"If the Messenger of God were performing Prayer when I was sleeping, he used to touch my foot when he was about to prostrate, I would pull my legs in and only then could the Messenger of God perform his prostration."[23]

The homes of the other wives were no different than Aisha's, except their doors opened outwards and not into the mosque. Describing the simplicity of their rooms, Hasan said:

"I was visiting the wives of the Messenger of God during the Caliphate of Uthman and when I raised my hand a little, I could reach the ceiling."[24]

When it was necessary to enlarge the Prophet's Mosque and the deconstruction of Aisha's house was discussed, the famous imam Said ibn Musayyab stood up and said to the Caliph, Walid ibn Abdulmalik:

"I wish you didn't have to destroy this room and that people could be content with what they have. Thus future generations could

---

[21] *Bukhari*, Itiqaf, 4 (1926).

[22] *Bukhari*, Adab al-Mufrad, 1:272 (776).

[23] *Bukhari*, Salat, 21 (375).

[24] Ibn Sa'd, *Tabaqat*, 1:506; Tahmaz, *as-Sayyidatu Aisha*.

understand what kind of life the Messenger of God was pleased with, even though he had in his hand the key to the world's treasures."[25]

There was a divan, matting, a leather pillow filled with fiber, a piece of leather hung to a hook, a waterskin, a bucket to put water and dates in, and a bowl for drinking water. There was no light in this little home. Aisha once said:

"At the time of the Messenger of God, we would spend forty nights in succession without a burning lamp or anything to give light."[26]

In those days, the oil used for lighting was also used for cooking. Aisha said:

"Surely if we had an oil lamp, then we would have used it for cooking."[27]

Aisha checked the room whenever she felt worried that the Messenger of God had left. The conditions of the women were consistent with their homes. According to Aisha, the members of the Prophet's household never ate wheat bread three days in a row[28] until he passed away and reached his Merciful Lord. Most of the time, they did not eat bread; they would go over a month without baking food or cooking over fire.[29] Sometimes, three frill moons would pass and they would eat only dates and drink zamzam water.[30]

When they ate, they sat together at the table and ate from the same bowl. Sometimes their relatives shared in what they ate as well. The reality was that nothing changed in this house of felicity; neither the booty received in later years or the gifts sent by his supporters altered the simplicity of his life. When he passed through the veil

[25]  Ibn Sa'd, *Tabaqat*, 1:500, 8: 167; Suyuti, *ad-Durru'l Mansur*, 7:554.

[26]  Tayalisi, *Musnad*, 207 (1472).

[27]  Harith ibn Abi Usama, *Musnadu'l Hadith*, 2:996; Tabarani, *al-Mujamu'l Awsat*, 8:360 (8872); Ishaq ibn Rahuya, *Musnad*, 3:1000.

[28]  *Bukhari*, At'ima, 73 (5059); Muslim, *Zuhd*, 20 (2970).

[29]  Ahmad ibn Hanbal, *Musnad*, 6:217.

[30]  *Bukhari*, Riqaq, 17 (6094).

between this world and the hereafter, the Messenger of God remained the purest and most humble of people.

Regarding the day he passed away, Aisha said:

"On the day that the Messenger of God passed away, there was only a little barley on the shelf for food. There was nothing more. I ate it and thus managed to stand on my feet. But after weighing how little was left over, the blessing of abundance was lost and it finished soon."[31]

While the circumstances of her life with the Messenger of God were difficult, the 50 years she lived as a widow were no different; she distributed charity from whatever she possessed to others, and usually kept herself content with zamzam water and dates. She said:

"I never ate enough to become frill, even after the Messenger of God" [32]

She continued to practice what she had seen and heard from the Prophet. One day, the Messenger of God said:

"O Aisha, save yourself from hellfire, even if it means giving just half a date in charity, since it would both ease one's hunger and serve an enormous need" [33]

A poor and needy person came to Aisha's home and she gave whatever she had as charity. Later, she asked people around her to bring back the person that she had helped. When the Messenger of God saw this, he interrupted and said:

"Give and do not calculate; this is so that calculation will not be made against you"[34]

On another day, she heard the Messenger of God praying:

"My Lord! Enable me to live as a poor man, take my life as a poor man and resurrect me with poor people on the Day of Judgment!"

Aisha asked:

"Why, O Messenger of God?" He replied:

---

[31] *Bukhari*, Khums, 3 (2930).
[32] Abu Nuaym, *Hilyatu'lAwliya*, 2:46; Tahmaz, *as-Sayyidatu Aisha*, 38.
[33] Ahmad ibn Hanbal, *Musnad*, 6:79 (24545).
[34] Ibn Hibban, *Sahih*, 8: 151; Bayhaqi, *Sunan*, 2:38 (3436)

"Because the poor will enter heaven more than forty years before the rich. O Aisha! Love the destitute and needy people and always keep them nearby, because on the Day of Resurrection, God will exalt you."[35]

One day, Prophet Muhammad, peace and blessings be upon him, entered Aisha's room and noticed that she was wearing silver rings. He asked, in a displeased tone:

"What are those, O Aisha?"

Aisha said:

"I wore them to look nice for you, O Messenger of God."

In the same tone, he asked:

"Then did you pay *zakah* (prescribed purifying alms) for them?"

She knew that *zakah* was not obligatory for such rings, which were worth very little. But it seemed this was another situation in which being near to the Prophet meant being different from others; deeply grieved, she replied in the negative.

After her reply, the Messenger of God, who wanted those around him to live an ascetic life like his own, stated that this minor incident could be enough to lead her to Hell.[36]

His words hit her very hard, depriving her of her senses. After that, Aisha never kept any possession, no matter how small, without thinking about the afterlife. She gave away whatever she had. She learnt that her most vital wealth, in this world and the Hereafter, was her closeness to the Messenger of God; to lose this wealth was unthinkable for a woman so clever. One day, God's Messenger asked her to do something after his death:

"If you want to reunite with me, be in this world like a traveler! Keep away from being near the rich and do not think about buying a

---

[35] *Tirmidhi*, Zuhd, 37 (2352); Bayhaqi, *Sunan*, 7:12 (12931)

[36] *Abu Dawud*, Zakah, 3 (1565); Hakim, *Mustadrak*, 1:547 (1437); Bayhaqi, *Sunan*, 4.

new dress before the present one becomes so old that it cannot be used anymore."[37]

The Messenger of God was a man of moderation who balanced the needs of this world and the next in the best possible way. Through the message that was revealed to him, God Almighty made him realize that he must continually seek rewards in the afterlife, without forgetting his duties in this world (al-Qasas 28:77). There is an unsatisfiable degree of ambition in human nature; humans were created to remain dissatisfied with the world and everything in it. This ambition is meant to be used to earn the Hereafter, for the Qur'an indicates that individuals who live for this world and do not consider the Hereafter will lose everything. God's Messenger was well aware of this, and when he came home, he turned to his wives and encouraged them to embrace the same sensitivity:

"If a man had two valleys filled with wealth, he would ask for a third. Only soil can fill up his mouth. Nevertheless, wealth is given to make daily worship possible and to fulfill the requirements of *zakah*. There is no doubt that God accepts the repentance of the people who ask."[38]

While his wives never considered their poverty as a problem, the Messenger of God, too, tried to be comforting about it. When he visited their rooms, he asked:

"Is there anything to eat at home?" Upon learning that there was nothing, he would say "I am fasting" and direct himself towards worship.[39]

The Helpers of Medina sometimes tried to lessen the worries of the Prophet by sending him food and drink.[40] But it was the life that he had chosen; he preferred to live in an ascetic way. What the Companions did, however, was a kindness that would be rewarded. The

---

[37] *Tirmidhi*, Libas, 38 (1780); Hakim, *Mustadrak*, 1:547 (1437).
[38] Ahmad ibn Hanbal, *Musnad*, 6:55, 5:218 (24321, 21956).
[39] Ahmad ibn Hanbal, *Musnad*, 6:49 (24266); Ibn Hibban, *Sahih*, 8, 393 (3630).
[40] *Bukhari*, Hiba, 1 (2428); *Ibn Majah*, Zuhd, 10 (4145).

Messenger of God was sensitive; he never wanted to risk consuming even a tiny blessing in this world that belonged to the Hereafter. He had only a plain mattress filled with rough fibers. When a female Companion from the Helpers noticed it, she presented Aisha with a new mattress filled with wool as a gift. When the Messenger of God came home, he immediately asked:

"What is this, O Aisha?"

Aisha answered:

"O the Messenger of God! A woman from the Helpers saw your bed when she came to our home and sent this after going back to her house."

Although the kindness of the Medinan woman was nice, his preference for the plain bed was nicer. He turned to Aisha and said:

"Send it back. I swear to God, if I wanted, God would put mountains at my disposal and turn them into gold and silver. "[41]

Although silk and gold are allowed for women, the Messenger of God wanted the women closest to him to be more careful and asked them to remain distant even from everyday blessings. One day, he saw two golden bracelets on Aisha's wrist, and said:

"Do you want me to tell you what is better than these? If you take them off and buy two silver bracelets instead and then color them with saffron; that would be better."[42]

The Messenger of God not only gave advice, he also closely followed the changes happening around him. It was obvious from the simplicity he had chosen for himself that he also wanted similar things for the people who were closest to him. He wanted them to keep away from anything that bound them to this world or caused them to forget the afterlife. When he and his army went to Tabuk, the meeting place of the Byzantine empire, the world's supreme kingdom at the time, Aisha procured a piece of cloth that had a picture on it and hung it up

---

[41]  Bayhaqi, *Shuabu'l Iman*, 2: 173 (1468); Tabarani, *Mujamu'l Awsat*, 6:141.
[42]  *Nasa'i*, Zina, 39 (5143).

as a curtain on one side of the house. When the Messenger of God returned from Tabuk and saw it, he ordered:

"Take it away from my sight. Change it, because when I enter the house and see it, I remember this world."[43]

After the Battle of Khaybar, the Messenger of God allocated eighty *wasks*[44] of dates and twenty *wasks* of barley to be given annually to his pure wives. But because of Aisha's generosity and their large number of visitors, the amount was not enough to meet the need.

On the day that God's Prophet ascended to the Exalted Friend (*ar-Rafiq al-Ala*) there was nothing more than half a bowl of barley in his home. And even that had been borrowed from a Jewish neighbor after giving the Messenger's armor as collateral.[45]

Aisha was living in this house under austere conditions. Her simple lifestyle, showing that real pleasure and happiness do not stem from worldly wealth, was sustained meticulously after the passing away of the Prophet. Her room, tiny in terms of area, continued to serve generations of Muslims, like a spring that flows into many rivers. In later days, just like those when the Messenger of God was alive, Aisha's first responsibility was to feed the hearts and minds of people.

## ENDURING AUSTERITY

Aisha's nights were as bright as her days; she spent her nights in Prayer and her days in fasting. Her stance was clear: she observed every detail of asceticism and piety. Some, such as Qasim, one of her closest pupils and a leader of the following generation of Muslims (*Tabiun*), said that she fasted the whole year except *Eid al-Fitr* and *Eid al-Adha*[46] (the feast of Ramadan and the feast of Sacrifice). Aisha spent every day in repentance, asking forgiveness from God, thinking of the previous day with remorse. Her example was the Messenger of God, and she believed in

---

[43] Ibn Hibban, *Sahih*, 2:447 (672); Nasa'i, *Sunanu'l Kubra*, 5:502 (9781).

[44] One *wask* is the equivalent of 165 liters.

[45] *Bukhari*, Jihad, 88 (2759), *Tirmidhi*, Buyu, 7 (1214).

[46] Ibn Jawzi, *Sifatu's Safwa*, 2:31.

her heart that it was necessary to use given opportunities to make progress every day.

Aisha also thought that continuing every single act of worship was obligatory for herself. She was quite determined; no one was able to deter her. When some found her enthusiasm strange, Aisha said:

"If my father rose from his grave, and told me not to do even one supererogatory Prayer that I had begun to perform in the time of God's Messenger, I would still not quit."[47]

Aisha barely met her own needs but she still gave whatever she had to the needy. One day, Jabir came to visit her. She wore a wornout dress, with parts covered in patches. Wanting to fulfill his responsibility, Jabir said:

"Why don't you wear another dress?"

However, as the mother of believers, Aisha did not think like Jabir and said:

"One day, the Messenger of God said, 'If you seek a reunion with me, do not change your dress until it becomes unusable, and do not think about what you need more than a month in advance.' Tell me, do you think I should change what he ordered me to do until the time I will meet with him again?"[48]

Still not content, whenever Aisha saw the heart-wrenching state of the poor and needy, she gave whatever she had, or sold something of some worth at the market, and sent the money to them. While she was giving, she never thought about her own needs, but always tried to lessen the troubles of others. One day, she literally gave everything she had to the poor, and had no more money for that day. She still did not quit giving; she sold some of her belongings at the market, and without hesitation, gave that money as charity. In the evening, when the time came to break her fast, she only had a piece of barley bread to eat.

Aisha's intentional humility represented a singular type of lifestyle for the people around her and she continued to live the same way after

---

[47]   Ahmad ibn Hanbal, *Musnad*, 6: 138 (25122).

[48]   Tabarani, *al-Mujamu'lAwsat*, 7:113 (7010).

the Messenger of God passed away. Genuine freewill is that of a person who is powerful and has limitless opportunities; it was this will-power that Aisha, until the end of her life, chose to carry in the same humble way that she had shared with the Prophet, living with delicacy and sensitivity until her last breath.

Aisha could have lived however she wanted. Yet, she chose the Messenger of God. This choice led to her other choice: to live humbly, just as he had.

Surely, this was a voluntary choice. Aisha was one of the closest people to the Messenger of God, yet their closeness was different to others. Even after his death, Aisha followed his ways, even though she had many opportunities to do otherwise. Yet she never changed the lifestyle they had shared. Her wealth was in her Muslim asceticism and piety.

## WOMEN'S REPRESENTATIVE

Aisha considered life from this humble perspective and lived plainly in every detail. Her responsibility stemmed from the time she married the Messenger of God. Undoubtedly, the serious responsibility she carried on her shoulders had different repercussions. She became a representative for women when she entered the Prophet's home, acting as an intermediary between the Messenger of God and women of every kind. Her situation made her a vital confidant, especially for female Companions.

The women of that society had been second-class citizens, the result of many centuries of tradition. Aisha's sensitivities to women, including her attempts to impart meaningful information to her close friends in her home and the allocation of most of her time to women, were aimed at providing solutions to these age-old traditions.

The Messenger of God sometimes witnessed her efforts. In fact, when he arrived home, Aisha's friends would try to run away, but the

Messenger of God would call them back. Not wanting to disturb them, he would leave the women alone together.[49]

Aisha sometimes kept toys in her house to allow children to amuse themselves. One day, the Messenger of God saw a two-winged horse and asked:

"What is this, O Aisha?"

She replied, without hesitation:

"A horse."

The Messenger of God asked:

"Does a horse have wings?"

Aisha had an answer prepared, one which showed that she considered the Qur'an even in mere children's games and entertainment:

"Didn't Solomon's horses have wings too?"

The Messenger of God responded with a smile to this witty reply.[50]

From the day she joined the house of felicity, Aisha was at the center of eliminating the ignorant pre-Islamic habits of their ancestors formed during the Age of Ignorance (*Jahiliyya*). Her closeness to the Messenger of God, her knowledge of the Qur'an, and her amiable attitude toward the troubles of women, both before and after her marriage, were an advantage to all women.

In the Age of Ignorance, women were generally treated with contempt; they were barely even considered human. Though many were converting to Islam, the old attitudes in society were not entirely erased overnight. Many women had neither rights or value, and remained in a state worse than slavery.

However, women now had an influential representative at the side of God's Messenger. Aisha was like a consultant for women. They came to her, confessed their secret problems, and returned home with solutions. They had been reluctant to share intimate details. One woman came to Aisha with great sorrow and said:

---

[49]   *Bukhari*, Adab, 81 (5779).
[50]   *Abu Davud*, Adab, 62 (4932); Bayhaqi, *Sunan*, 10:219 (20771).

"My husband neither divorces me or leaves me on my own, or has marital relations with me."

The woman wept, unable to suppress the tide of emotions erupting inside her soul. Crying, she explained the heartbreaking condition that she had lived in for many years. She was nothing more than a toy under her husband's control. First, he said that he was divorcing her ,but before the waiting period finished, he returned to her claiming to have changed his mind. From that point on, he persisted in going back and forth, playing with her emotions. His real intention seemed to be to prevent his wife, whom he wanted to divorce, from being married to someone else.

When the Prophet came home, Aisha informed him of the situation. He felt uneasy. It seemed like a marriage of tyranny; however, no holy verse or decision on this issue had come forth from the Angel Gabriel. So he decided to wait.

Then Gabriel appeared and brought a verse that warned believers that marriage was a serious matter, not to be trifled with:

*"Divorce must be pronounced twice and then (a woman) must be retained in honor or released in kindness"* (al-Baqarah 2:229).

It then became clear that a second statement of divorce meant that the husband and wife separated. This matter was more serious than suspected, for a man was now forbidden from returning to a wife that he had divorced three times. Even if he felt regret, that possibility would be closed to him. The only exception was if the wife married and divorced another man; only then could she be married once again. This put an end to arbitrary divorce practices.[51]

Another day, Khawlah bint Tha'labah visited Aisha. She was miserable. Years of suffering and hardship were apparent from her appearance. She explained her troubles, one by one. Her husband had divorced her, according to a pre-Islamic custom. A husband would say to his wife, "You are henceforth as my mother's back to me," thus forbidding himself from marital relations with her. Under this condition,

---

[51] *Abu Dawud* ,Talaq, 9 (2194); *Ibn Majah*, Talaq, 13 (2039).

a woman was not allowed to re-marry. The only one who could solve her problem was the Messenger of God. When he came home, Khawlah turned to him and said:

"O Messenger of God, he exhausted my youth; I gave him whatever I had. When I got older and was unable to give birth, he divorced me by saying 'be as my mother's back to me.'"

It was a difficult situation. She said that her children had grown up and she lived alone with her husband. So if her husband left her, she would have been left alone, without any protection. She added that her husband would have agreed to re-accept her as his wife, but according to custom he was not able to do so. Holding her arms up, she prayed about what was weighing on her heart:

"O my Lord! I am complaining to you about my situation!"

The merciful Prophet's heart ached. But her oppression would not last forever; even as Khawlah prayed, God sent verses to clarify the matter. A message carried by Gabriel explained frilly the situation of Khawlah and solved similar problems for all women. The verses explained that these wrong practices belonged to the pre-Islamic era of *Jahiliyya* and were entirely renounced. It also explained what women in this situation should do and what the punishment for anyone who persisted in this kind of behavior was:

> God has indeed heard the words of the woman who pleads with you concerning her husband and refers her complaint to God. God hears the dialogue between you. Surely God is All-Hearing, All-Seeing. Those among you who declare their wives to be unlawful for them by using against them the expression, "Be as my mother's back to me," (should know that) their wives are not their mothers. Their mothers are none other than the women who gave them birth. Such men certainly utter a word abhorred and a falsehood. Yet God is surely All-Pardoning (He overlooks the faults of His servants), All-Forgiving. Those who declare their wives unlawful for them (by using against them that abhorred expression) and thereafter wish to go back on the words they have uttered must free a slave before they (the spouses) touch each other. This is what you are urged to do. And God is fully aware of what you do (so do not

seek to evade this act of penance and expiation for your wrong).
Whoever does not find (means to do that), let him fast two (lunar)
months consecutively before they (the spouses) touch each other.
And he that is not able to do so, (his penance shall be) to feed sixty
destitute ones (two meals). This is in order that you may perfect
your faith in God and His Messenger (so that you believe in
the n-uth of whatever God has enjoined and His Messenger has
conveyed to you, and live accordingly). These are the bounds of
God. And for the unbelievers there is a painful punishment. (al-
Mujadilah 58:1-4)

On another occasion, Thabit ibn Qays' wife, Habiba bint Sahl,
came to visit Aisha, saying that she wanted to divorce her husband and
asked for Aisha's help. Habiba was the daughter of Abdullah ibn Ubayy
ibn Salul, the leader of hypocrites; she married Thabit ibn Qays one
day after the death of her husband, Hanzalah, in the Battle of Uhud.
She was distinguished both in beauty and manners, and was treated
with great care by her family. Although Thabit was well-known for his
speaking abilities, he was short and unattractive. Most likely, Habiba
felt social pressure to divorce her husband. When the Messenger of
God came, Habiba explained:

"O Messenger of God. I am not criticizing my husband for his
religion or his character. Yet I am afraid of forsaking my belief, after
having accepted Islam. I want to divorce my husband."

Habiba seemed very decisive. The Messenger of God asked:

"Are you going to give his garden back to him?"

Without any hesitation, she replied:

"Yes."

After that, the Messenger of God called Thabit and asked him
about the marriage. Thabit had no solution either. Apparently, the
unrest had grown and the wound had festered and become incurable.
The marriage could not be sustained under these circumstances.
Although divorce was known to be the permissible act that God hates
the most, there was no other solution. Thabit's opinion was the same.
The Messenger of God said:

"Take the garden and divorce her." [52]

Considered within the context of the time, the incident meant an important expansion of women's rights—a woman could exercise her will and choose to divorce her husband.

When it was seen that such matters were resolved with authority, the number of people knocking on the door of the Prophet with similar reasons increased. Khawlah bint Hakim, the wife of Uthman ibn Madun, who was among the first believers of Islam, found her way to Aisha's door. She was distraught. The Messenger of God knew Khawlah; years before, she had arranged the marriage between himself and Aisha. When God's Messenger came home and saw her in such a state, he turned to Aisha and asked:

"O Aisha, what made her become this way? What has happened to her?"

Aisha, explained the following about Khawlah's husband, Uthman ibn Madun:

"O Messenger of God, it is as if she is unmarried; in fact, she is a married woman without a husband. For her husband spends his days in fasting and his nights in Prayer. Therefore she is unable to control herself, and as you can see, she is ruined."

Uthman ibn Madun had devoted himself to worship entirely and thus had neglected his family's rights over him. Though, like a shepherd, he was responsible for the people under his control, he had neglected his wife. But these sad circumstances became a cause for a revelation of truth from God.

The Messenger of God then sent a message to Uthman ibn Madun. He came to God's Prophet soon afterwards. The Messenger of God said:

"O Uthman, we are not ordered to live as monks. Am I not enough for you as an example? Or do you break off from my Sunnah?"

---

[52]   *Ibn Majah*, Talaq, 22 (2056); *Muwatta*, Talaq, 11 (1174).

Uthman ibn Madun was confused. His aim, in performing so much worship, had been for a religious life, and he thought that what he did was for the Hereafter. Uthman replied:

"No, O Messenger of God. On the contrary, I am trying to practice your Sunnah, letter by letter."

But of course there could be no doubt that the Messenger of God knew exactly what the Sunnah was. Upon Uthman's words, God's Messenger gave the following advice:

"I am the one who, at the highest level, fears God and observes the boundaries of God's religion among you. Yet I pray and sleep, fast and break my fast, and at the same time, I am married to women. Be afraid of God, O Uthman. Because your family members have rights over you. Your visitors have rights over you. Your own self has rights over you. Therefore you should fast some days, but do not fast others, and you should pray at a certain part of the night, but also sleep at certain parts." [53]

There were female Companions, too, who never slept during the night; they attracted the attention of others and were talked about in society. Khawlah was one of them. When she came to Aisha, Khawlah mentioned her habits and Aisha shared them with the Messenger of God. When he heard that she prayed all night, his reaction was negative—such habits could not be sustained indefinitely, and small but constant worship was more pleasing to God.

"What? Does she not sleep at night?" He asked again, as if he did not want to believe what he had heard. Then he said:

"Oh why do you burden yourself with more than you can bear? Do not forget, you become tired and exhausted; it is only God who never needs rest." [54]

---

[53] Ahmad ibn Hanbal, *Musnad* 6:226 (25935); Ibn Hibban, *Sahih*, 1:185, 2:19.

[54] *Bukhari*, Tahajjud, 18 (1100).

One day, a young girl came to Aisha with great sorrow and said that her father wanted her to marry his cousin even though she did not want to.

In those days, girls were not permitted to state their opinion on whom they were going to marry; their feelings were considered irrelevant. The final decision always belonged to the father; what he said, happened. But another wrong custom would be changed by God's Prophet—this was what the girl hoped for.

Aisha listened to her, and as she had said to many others, said:

"Wait here until the Messenger of God returns." Aisha was going to inform the Prophet of the situation and through this young girl, a widespread problem from the era of *Jahiliyya* was going to be clarified.

When the Messenger of God came, Aisha explained the girl's situation to him immediately. Prophet Muhammad, peace and blessings be upon him, then sent a message to the girl's father, calling him to his home. When the Messenger of God invited someone, it was unthinkable not to respond to his request.

The Messenger of God asked the father about the issue. What the girl had related turned out to be accurate and God's Messenger gave advice to the father. When he spoke to him, it was as if he was speaking to society at large. Listening to the Messenger, the father began to understand what he had done wrong and announced that he would not force his daughter to marry against her wishes, and the matter was settled pleasantly. For the first time, a young girl's wish had been treated seriously. The two would not marry - at least that's what everyone expected. However, the situation ended differently. When the Messenger of God turned to the girl and told her that the decision was her own, the girl, contrary to what was expected, said:

"O Messenger of God, I do accept the marriage that my father arranged. By asking you to intervene, I was trying to show women that fathers did not have any right to force their daughters into marriage."[55]

---

[55] *Ibn Majah*, Nikah 12 (1874); Ahmad ibn Hanbal, *Musnad*, 6:136 (25087).

Certainly, these were not the only women who came to Aisha and, through her, shared their problems with the Messenger of God. Many of these women ultimately learned of a solution to their problems, and went home pleased and at rest.[56]

Hers was not a useless and blind justification of women; Aisha defended them because they were right. She did not refrain from admonishing women who were wrong, who went too far, who were trying to force the boundaries of religion. Justice and equity were the essence of her decision-making. When it was necessary, she criticized women sharply and did not hesitate to warn them, helping them see and correct their faults.

After many years had passed, and with newly conquered territories, believers had come into contact with different societies and ideas. Many women were also affected by the new situation. In particular, some women did not protect their former sensitivity and began to show different attitudes. Poignantly, Aisha summarized her grief as follows:

"If the Messenger of God saw the current state of women, he would prohibit them like the women of the children of Israel and ban them from coming to the mosques."[57]

Her words show how well she knew the Messenger of God. At the same time, her words were an indication that time can change decisions; the conditions in the time of God's Messenger were perhaps more suitable for women to attend congregational Prayer and it was recommended for them. But the situation in later days was different.

Aisha was very sensitive on the issue of *hijab* and she admonished women who did not show the necessary concern. Meticulous and critical, she wanted everyone to show the same care on religious issues and often underlined that there should be no sluggishness about a religious practice.

---

[56] *Bukhari*, Libas, 23 (5825).
[57] *Bukhari*, Sifatu's Salat, 79 (831); *Muslim*, Salat, 144 (445).

One day, the daughter of her brother, Abdurrahman, came to visit her. As soon as she saw the sheer headscarf of Hafsah bint Abdurrahman, she took it and folded it in half. Then she brought Hafsah to her side and warned her:

"Do you not know what God revealed in the chapter An-Nur?"

From the people nearby, Aisha asked for a thicker scarf and covered her niece's head with it, showing her how to cover, and thus putting an end to the matter.[58]

Aisha explained how they used to cover in the time of the Messenger of God by relating personal memories:

"At the time of God's Messenger, if horsemen rode toward us while we were wearing pilgrim's garments, we covered our faces right away, and when they passed by, we uncovered our faces again."

Pilgrim's garments are worn for the *Hajj* (pilgrimage), and distinguished scholars, such as Abu Hanifa, said that a woman could uncover her face while in pilgrim's garments, because they are worn in a place of worship and the possibility of evil thoughts are low compared to other times. Yet, Aisha was very sensitive, explaining that they covered their faces when they saw a stranger coming, even though they were wearing pilgrim's garments. Furthermore, she mentioned the difficulties that she encountered while she wore the *hijab* and stated that a fearless struggle was necessary. When she became ill during the Farewell Pilgrimage and had no choice but to go to Tanim with her brother in pilgrim's garments, she had many difficulties, but never lost her sensitivity. She showed people that what she said was what she believed—not fiction but real life.[59] Her life was a kind of lesson, from beginning to end. Aisha did as much as she could for those who visited her, but when there was a male visitor, she separated herself behind a curtain, as approved in the Qur'an, even though she was the mother of believers.[60] When she witnessed social changes, she remember the

---

[58]    *Muwatta*, Libas, 4; *Bayhaqi*, Sunan, 2:235; ibn Sa'd, *Tabaqat*, 8:72.
[59]    *Bukhari*, Hayd, 15 (310, 311, 313).
[60]    Ahmad ibn Hanbal, *Musnad*, 6:219 (25883).

era of God's Messenger with yearning; she would tell her female Companions about how deep their belief was, how sincere their practices. She would sigh and say:

"May God bestow mercy to the immigrant (*muhajir*) female Companions of former days! They competed to fulfill the order as soon as God commanded them to draw their veils over their bosoms, wrapping themselves up in their garments."[61]

She heard that some women in the recently conquered provinces walked around unrestrictedly compared to the past and that they acted rather carelessly outside their homes. She started to grieve. One day, when a group of women from Homs came to visit her, Aisha scolded them saying:

"Are you one of the women who go to public baths? Do not forget that I heard the Messenger of God saying that 'a woman who takes her clothes off in a place other than her husband's home means to tear the curtain between her and God'."[62]

Witnessing that the clothing of the woman who visited her had changed and become less covered, Aisha warned:

"A woman who believes in the chapter An-Nur cannot cover like this. If you are believer, do not forget that the garments you are wearing are not the garments of believing women."[63]

When someone came to visit her, Aisha could decipher their intentions from their behavior and attitude. Before they even asked a question, she knew their real purpose and answered with that perspective. One woman who visited her asked the opinion of the Prophet about henna and she replied:

"God's Messenger liked its color but not its smell!"[64]

Her dialogue with women not only consisted of such details; she directed them to a state with which God and His Messenger would be

---

[61] *Bukhari*, Tafsir, 31 (4480).

[62] Ahmad ibn Hanbal, *Musnad*, 6:41, 173 (24186); *Tirmidhi*, Adab, 43 (2803).

[63] Qurtubi, *al-Jami*, 14:57.

[64] *Abu Dawud*, Tarajjul, 4, (4164); Ahmad ibn Hanbal, *Musnad*, 6: 117 (24905).

content and advised them to establish peace within their homes. She believed that harmony within the home consisted of peace in this world and the next. She said that both husband and wife should fulfill their responsibilities and expect to make sacrifices. Aisha showed the proper respect to the ones who were close to the Messenger of God and supplied them with what they needed. Though she tried her hardest to please everyone, she expected the women who visited her to show the same concern as herself — expecting other women to behave towards their husbands the way she had behaved towards the Messenger of God. When a woman came and asked for advice, Aisha said:

"If you had the opportunity of removing your irises to replace them with more beautiful ones in order to please your husband, do it without hesitation."[65]

To Aisha, family happiness was to be regarded above everything else, and to meet this objective, the wife played an invaluable role. A wife is the source of family contentment, and for this reason, she ought to act more carefully when fulfilling her responsibilities toward her husband. To the women who had questions regarding these issues, Aisha gave longer and more thoughtful answers than they expected. If they asked related questions, she gave other advice as well. One of them asked:

"I have hair on my face; should I pull it out in order to be attractive to my husband?"

Aisha answered:

"Just as you wear jewelry and adorn yourself when you visit someone, clean up whatever troubles you and make yourself beautiful to your husband. When he orders you, obey him; if he asks you for something, do not neglect his request. Moreover, do not accept someone that your husband does not like inside your home."[66]

---

[65]   Ibn Sa'd, *Tabaqatu'l Kubra*, 8:70-71; Dhahabi, *Tarikhu'l Islam*, 1:537.
[66]   Abdurrazzaq, *Musannaf*, 3: 146 (5104).

## HER LOVE FOR THE MESSENGER OF GOD

Aisha loved the Messenger of God very much. He was the most beloved servant of God, and God had asked His servants to love his faithful Messenger: *"Say (to them, O Messenger): If you indeed love God, then follow me, so that God will love you and forgive you your sins. God is All-Forgiving, All-Compassionate."* (Al-Imran 3:31).

She was not keen to share her time with the Messenger of God with others and wanted to spend all that time with him alone. However, he was a Messenger and everyone's Prophet. The Messenger of God wanted to reach all people, however inaccessible, and aimed to open doors that had not been entered before. His later marriages probably happened for this reason. Aisha had understood that. People lined up to sacrifice their lives for the sake of his mission. They were devoted to him, and their devotion made Aisha anxious. Her anxiety persisted until the following verse was revealed: *"... you can defer the turn of visiting any of them (your wipes) you please, and take to you whomever you please. There is no blame on you if you give precedence to one whom you deferred before"* (al-Ahzab 33:51).

After the revelation of the verse, she turned to the Messenger of God and said:

"As I see it, your God always bestows on you what your heart wants."

Hers was a reflection of love, an expression of intimacy. She wanted to be with him all the time, but conditions did not allow it, and again, it was she who made the sacrifice. Each wife of God's Messenger took her husband away from her for a day. The Messenger of God made a schedule for his wives and divided his days equally among them. While she had enjoyed the opportunity to be with him fairly often, now her turn came only every nine days.

The Messenger of God did not change his attitude after these verses were revealed. Even if he had a preference that deviated from the planned schedule, he always got permission from his wives. Aisha specifically focused on this point when she reiterated the attitude of God's Messenger:

"The Messenger of God continued to ask for permission about our schedule even after the verse (al-Ahzab 33:51) was revealed: *you can defer the turn of visiting any of them (your wives) you please, and take to you whomever you please.*"

Aisha, on her day, wanted to spend all of her time with the Messenger of God and was sensitive to anything that interfered with their togetherness. One night, she woke up and realized that the Messenger of God was not with her. Since there was no light, Aisha was not able to see. She was worried that he had left her to visit one of his other wives. She fumbled around with agitation. Then her hand touched one of his feet; she was relieved to discover that he was prostrating. She calmed down and took a deep breath. The Messenger of God had not left her; he was in tears praying to God on the other side of the room. Aisha was touched, and as she listened, she heard his sincere supplications:

"O Lord, I seek refuge in Your pleasure from Your wrath, and in Your forgiveness from Your punishment; I also seek refuge in Yourself from You. I cannot praise You as You praise Yourself."

Aisha was ashamed of her worries; turning to the Messenger of God, she said:

"May my parents be sacrificed for you. How did I think about you when you were busy with this?"[67]

Aisha was faced with the same situation another day. When the Messenger of God was going to bed, he left his sandals near it and hung his clothes nearby, as if he would be getting up and leaving immediately. Normally he got permission from his wives even to get up for the Night Prayer, since he considered other people's rights over

---

[67] *Muslim*, Salat, 221 (485, 486, 512); *Tirmidhi*, Da'awat, 76 (3493), *Abu Dawud*, Salat 152 (879).

him as essential.[68] He was acting differently that day and Aisha did not understand why, and so she became suspicious. He started to rest.

After some time had passed, the Messenger of God slowly got up from his bed. He walked quietly on tiptoe, in order to not awaken Aisha. But Aisha was not sleeping; she was watching him with curiosity. The Messenger of God put on his sandals and clothes with careful movements, then opened the door and left. Aisha was upset.

She rose instantly and covered her face with her veil. Then she started to follow God's Messenger. He went to the Medina cemetery (Al-Baqi Cemetery) and raised his palms to the heaven and started to pray with longing. When his arms grew tired he lowered them, and then a little while later, he raised them to continue praying.

Then the time came to leave the cemetery and he started to return home. Aisha started to walk too in order to hide herself. When the Messenger of God walked faster, so did she. When he walked even faster, Aisha ran.

She arrived home before God's Messenger, but she was out of breath. She laid down immediately trying to pretend she had never left the room.

But when the Messenger of God came in soon after, he noticed her agitation and asked:

"What happened to you, O Aisha?"

She replied, "Nothing."

As God's Messenger, he knew better, so he asked:

"Are you going to explain yourself or do you want God the All-Knowing and the Gracious to tell me about it?"

Her heart pounded. Turning to the Messenger of God, she said:

"O Messenger of God, may my parents be sacrificed for you."

It was an indirect way of confessing her guilt. The Messenger of God asked:

"Were you the indistinct figure I saw in front of me while I was walking?"

---

[68] Bayhaqi, *Shuabu'l Iman*, 3:383 (3837).

"Yes," she confessed.[69]

These incidents showed her that the Messenger of God was beyond reproach and that she had nothing to fear.

Her love for him ran so deep that she could not allow anything negative to be said about him. One day, someone said:

"May God grant death[70] over you."

When Aisha heard this she stood up immediately and said:

"Who would dare to wish for the death of God's Messenger? On the contrary, may God bring both death and curses on you."

God's Messenger understood her sensitivity and appreciated the generous motive behind her words, but as a Prophet, he needed to consider everyone as a potential believer. A potential believer's unkindness should not be repaid with unkindness. So the Messenger of God turned to Aisha and said:

"Be calm, O Aisha! God the Almighty is the most Gentle (Rafiq) and He loves us to be kind in all matters. He does not bestow His blessings to those who act without kindness."[71]

Aisha was not able to say no if someone asked her for something. Though she fretted inwardly about being away from the Prophet, she could not have acted differently.

When the Messenger of God prepared for a military expedition, he drew lots among his wives to determine who would accompany him. One time, Hafsah and Aisha were drawn. Their journey began, and they made much progress on their first day. When night fell and they took a break, the Messenger of God sat and began to chat with Aisha. Hafsah took this to mean that the first night would not be hers, but Aisha's instead.

After some time had passed, Hafsah approached Aisha and suggested:

---

[69]  *Muslim*, Janaiz, 102 (974); *Nasa'i*, Janaiz, 103 (2037); *Ishratu'n Nisa*, 4 (3963- 3964).

[70]  Instead of saying "salaam" (greeting, peace) be upon you, certain adversaries of Islam deliberately greeted the Prophet by saying "saam" (death) be upon  you.

[71]  *Bukhari*, Adab, 38 (5683).

"You mount my camel and I will mount yours and let's see what the Messenger of God will do."

It seemed like a fine joke. Aisha was sure that the Messenger of God would choose her camel and she would have bragging rights so she agreed.

When the army began to depart, the Messenger of God went to Aisha's camel, though Hafsah was inside of the palanquin instead of Aisha. Thus Aisha, who had received proof of her worth to God's Messenger, was actually deprived of traveling with him.

She had said yes to the game, but it was not easy to tolerate the result. The Messenger of God had chosen her, but she was not with him. She felt miserable and did not know what to do. Digging her feet into the grass, she felt sorry for herself and unburdened herself to God:

"O My Lord, send a scorpion or a snake to bite me! Your Messenger is going and I am not able to say anything to him."

Inside her home with the Prophet, which was warm and full of mutual love, there was not even the smallest problem that could damage their relationship. Every passing day increased their love by two and every incident served to feed their affection for one another. Aisha did not abuse her love for the Prophet, and thus, he didn't feel the need to take certain measures into his hands. This was the Prophet's general state; his affection for his other wives was similar. He understood their wishes before they expressed them, and fulfilled their requests as he always had. Aisha said:

"The Messenger of God neither hit a woman or a servant or anyone else with his hand."[72]

Her love for him continued even after his death. The mother of believers, who sustained the humble lifestyle she had shared with the Prophet after his death, reacted against anyone who brought endowments into her home, and kept herself far from worldly blessings. Those who viewed her as the mother of believers were competing to

---

[72] *Muslim*, Fadail, 79.

do good deeds, too, and so she gave away what was given to her as a gift to the needy; most of the time, she kept nothing for herself. At first, Aisha wanted to return the gifts when they were given, but a phrase that she had heard from the Messenger of God made her unable to do this, and so she was obliged to accept whatever was offered.

One day, Abdullah ibn Amir's emissary came to bring clothing and food to Aisha. She turned to him and said:

"O dear son! I accept nothing from anyone."

She returned the gifts to him. Even though he was only the envoy, he was sad. Their intention was merely to do good, because when they gave something to Aisha, they felt as if they had given to the Messenger of God. They respected her as their own mother and wanted to meet her needs, but it was necessary to respect her choice. As Abdullah walked home, he felt desperate, worrying about what he would say had happened.

At the same time, Aisha was reconsidering what she had done. Immersed in deep thought, she wondered whether she had acted in opposition to the Messenger of God. Rashly, she said to those around her:

"Call him back!"

When they reached him, the envoy was shocked, He returned to Aisha's home with anxiety, wondering what she was going to say.

Aisha's former anger had disappeared, as if blown away by a sea breeze. In the gentlest manner she said:

"I remembered something that the Messenger of God told me. He said, 'O Aisha, if someone gives you something without you asking, never return it; always take it. For it is a blessing God has offered to you!' "[73]

The meaning of the hadith was clear and the envoy returned with a smile.

---

[73]    Ahmad ibn Hanbal, *Musnad*, 6:77 (24524).

## THE PROPHET'S LOVE

The love Aisha had for the Prophet was not one-sided; the Messenger of God, who set an example for society on every issue, also loved Aisha deeply. As he did in every arena, the Prophet of God lived with excellence in terms of family relations. He said:

"The best among you is he who behaves best toward his family. I am your leader in this."[74]

The basis of this was mutual love. The Messenger of God helped Aisha understand his love for her and made it clear to others. Of course, the Prophet represented justice, but love cannot be constrained by human will. His love for Aisha was a reflection of human nature. He never discriminated against any wife, equally cared for each one's provisions, and behaved with kindness to them. Yet, he could not help how he felt. Because of this, after spending a day with any wife, the Messenger of God turned to God and prayed to Him to erase any deficiency that may have arisen from his differing emotions:

"O my Lord! This is the share that I can do; do not judge me by the share that You can do which I am not able to do."[75]

This prayer was about Aisha. God's Messenger had a rare intimacy with her compared to his other relationships, The Messenger of God, the most sensitive of people, wanted to be perfectly just, but took refuge in the most Merciful God from any injustice that might occur. A revelation that God sent shed light on this matter:

> (O husbands!) You will never be able to deal between your wives with absolute equality (in respect of love and emotional attachment), however much you may desire to do so. But do not turn away altogether (from any one of them), so as to leave her in a dangling state (uncertain if she has or does not have a husband). If you act righteously (between them) and act in piety (fearful of doing any deliberate wrong to any of them), then surely God is All-Forgiving, All-Compassionate. (an-Nisa 4: 129)

---

[74] *Tirmidhi*, Manaqib, 64 (3895); *Ibn Majah*, Nikah 50 (1977).
[75] *Tirmidhi*, Nikah, 41 (1140); *Abu Dawud*, Nikah, 39 (2134).

Some Companions began calling Aisha the "darling of God's Messenger." When something negative about Aisha was said in the presence of Ammar ibn Yasir, he got angry and shouted:

"How could you talk about the 'darling of God's Messenger' like that and hurt her?"[76] Ammar commanded the person who had said the negative remark to get out of his sight. Their love for each other was so obvious that the Companions preferred to give gifts to him on the day that the Messenger of God was with Aisha, since the smile on his face was more special on those days.[77]

It was a situation well understood, and in order to avoid problems, everyone warned and tried to help one another. One day, Umar advised his daughter, Hafsah:

"O my dear daughter! I hope the state of your companion does not mislead you if she is more graceful and dearer to God's Messenger than you."[78]

Umar was trying to impart to his daughter the special status of Aisha and hoping he could convince her to avoid competing for the Prophet's affection.

A Persian neighbor of theirs cooked very delicious soup and one day, he invited the Messenger of God for a meal. God's Messenger never thought of accepting the invitation by himself and wanted to take Aisha, who was suffering greatly from hunger. Indicating Aisha, God's Messenger asked:

"Are you inviting her, too?"

The man replied in the negative. Perhaps he had only a small amount of soup to share or perhaps he did not understand that the Prophet wanted him to invite Aisha. So the Prophet declined the invitation.

After awhile, the man returned and repeated his invitation. God's Messenger gestured to Aisha and asked:

---

[76] *Tirmidhi*, Manaqib, 63 (3888); Hakim, *Mustadrak*, 3:444 (5684).

[77] *Bukhari*, Hiba, 6, 7 ((2435-2441).

[78] *Muslim*, Talaq, 30 (1479); *Tirmidhi*, Tafsiru'l Qur'an, 387 (4629).

"Are you inviting her, too?"

Again, the man said no, and again, the Messenger of God said no.

Finally, the man came for the third time and repeated his invitation once more. Finally, the man understood that God's Messenger did not want to attend without Aisha. So he invited her, too, and the Messenger of God and Aisha went to the Persian man's house together.[79]

The love between Aisha and the Prophet was so clear that people sent Aisha to him to help him forget conflicts and make him happy again. One day, Safiyya took Aisha aside and said:

"O Aisha, can you make the Messenger of God pleased? If you can, I will give you my day."

Aisha replied in the affirmative and then went and sat down near the Messenger of God. Knowing this day was not hers, and that he never changed the schedule, he found the arrival of Aisha strange, and told her to go to her room.

Since he had started the conversation, she continued it by saying:

"O Messenger of God, this is a blessing which is bestowed from God to the ones He wants."

She had gained the undivided attention of God's Messenger. Aisha explained to the Messenger of God a detailed account of the talk she'd had with Safiyya, sharing the grief the latter had felt. It was an attempt at peace and Aisha's sensitivity delighted the Messenger of God. The serenity he felt inside was reflected on his face.[80]

Once, on a trip together, Aisha's camel lost its way and departed from the others, becoming lost in a place called Kharra. The Messenger of God became anxious and immediately everyone started to look for her. Worried about losing the one closest to him while she was under his care, he shouted, *"Wa arusah,"* an expression of sadness used by someone who has lost his wife.

Another time, a well-known Companion, Amr ibn al-AS, came and asked the Messenger of God:

[79] *Muslim*, Ashriba, 139 (2037); Ahmad ibn Hanbal, *Musnad*, 3:123 (12265).
[80] *Bukhari*, Hiba, 14; Shahadat, 30 (2542).

"Whom do you love most among people?"

He had hoped to find out his own significance in the eyes of the Messenger of God and expected to hear himself named. But God's Messenger, without hesitation, replied:

"Aisha."

Amr ibn al-As continued, expecting to hear his own name and asked:

"Then among men?"

And he replied:

"Her father."

Amr ibn al-As discerned that he was not the Prophet's top priority, and that asking further questions was risky. Considering the possibility that he could be last, Amr ibn al-As gave up asking any questions like this again.[81]

The events witnessed by everyone were embedded in their memories; every preference of God's Messenger made people love him even more. When he went to an expedition and stayed away from his wives for a month, he would first go to Aisha's home.[82]

Similarly the Messenger of God asked Aisha's opinion first during the incident of *tahyir*:[83]

When the Muslims of Medina began to extricate themselves from the poverty that they had been suffering for years, some of his wives (there were four at that time) asked him: "Couldn't we live a bit better, like other Muslims do?"

The Messenger reacted to their question by going into retreat. He excused himself, saying: "I cannot afford what they want." The Messenger was preparing them to be exemplars for all present and future Muslim women. He was especially worried that they might enjoy the rewards for their good deeds in this world, and thereby he included in the verse:

---

[81]   *Bukhari*, Fadailu's Sahaba, 5 (3462).

[82]   *Bukhari*, Nikah, 83 (4895).

[83]   *Bukhari*, Mazalim, 26, (2336).

> You consumed in your life of the world your (share of) pure, wholesome things, and enjoyed them fully (without considering the due of the Hereafter, and so have taken in the world the reward of all your good deeds). (al-Ahqaf 46: 20).

Thus, these special women were put to a great test. The Prophet allowed them to choose his poor home or the world's luxury. If they chose the world, he would give them what he could afford and then dissolve his marriage with them. If they chose God and His Messenger, then they had to be content with their lives. This was the peculiarity of his family. Since this family was unique, its members had to be unique. The head of the family was chosen, as were the wives and children. Thus, the Messenger first called Aisha and said: "I want to discuss something with you.

"It's best if you talk with your parents before making a decision." Then he recited the verses:

> O (most illustrious) Prophet! Say to your wives: "If you desire the present, worldly life and its charms, then come and let me make the necessary provision for you (in return for divorce), and release you with a handsome release. But if you desire God and His Messenger, and the abode of the Hereafter, then it is a fact that God has prepared a tremendous reward for those among you who act in a good manner, aware that God is seeing them." (al-Ahzab 33:28-29)

Aisha's decision was exactly what would be expected from the truthful daughter of a truthful father: "O Messenger of God, do I need to talk with my parents? By God, I choose God and His Messenger."[84] Aisha herself tells us what happened next: "The Messenger received the same answer from all his wives. No one expressed a different opinion. They all said what I had said."

---

[84] *Bukhari*, Mazalim, 26 (2336); Tafsiru's Sura, 276 (4507); *Muslim*, Talaq, 22 (1475).

All these incidents made society more careful when it came to Aisha. His preference would continue until the day he died. On the day his fatal illness started, he asked:

"Where am I now? Who will I will be with tomorrow?" and he expressed his wish to be with Aisha during his sickness. It was the last proof of his intimacy with Aisha, which she described in this way:

"He died on the day when the turn was mine. God took his soul when his head was on my bosom."[85]

It was with all this in mind that Anas ibn Malik said that the first great love in Islam was the love of God's Messenger for Aisha. When Imam Masruq narrated a hadith transmitted by Aisha, he would say:

"This was narrated to me by the beloved one of the most beloved servant of God and by the woman whose chastity was approved by the heavenly revelation, and who was the truthful daughter of the most truthful one."[86]

## THE REAL REASON FOR THIS LOVE

One cannot help but wonder about the reason for the Prophet's abundant love for Aisha compared to his love for his other wives. First of all, the Messenger of God often reminded the others that Aisha was his closest friend, Abu Bakr's, daughter.[87] Without a doubt, Aisha was an attractive woman. Her mother Umm Ruman, once consoled her when she was grieved, saying:

"Wait a little while! God will give you ease. I swear to God that there is no woman who is as beautiful as you, and who is loved by her husband as you are, and has such good relations with her fellow wives,

---

[85] *Bukhari*, Janaiz, 94 (1323).

[86] Bayhaqi, *Sunan*, 2:458; Ibn Sa'd, *Tabaqat*, 8 (66); Ibnu'l-Athir, *Usdu'l-Ghaba*, 1 (1384).

[87] *Muslim*, Fadailu's Sahaba, 83, (2442); Nasa'i, *Ishratu'n Nisa*, 3 (3944); Ahmad ibn Hanbal, *Musnad*, 6:88 (24619); Bayhaqi, *Sunan*, 7:299 (14526).

and who no one aims to defame. A woman in your situation is normally slandered often!"[88]

It was like the warning Umar had given his daughter Hafsah about never competing with Aisha or making her sad: a result of the same sensitivity towards Aisha, who had a special place at the side of God's Messenger.[89]

When the narrations are analyzed generally, the cause of the Prophet's overflowing love for her was her religion. Aisha led her family in brilliance and knowledge, and was the distinguished teacher of the members of the Prophet's family.

While many witnessed the public behavior of God's Messenger, Aisha saw both his public and private sides. She became the most important interpreter of the Qur'an and the main teacher of hadith, becoming the foremost transmitter of Islam. The Messenger of God advised Muslims to learn the details of religion from her. In a hadith that Aisha narrated, the Messenger of God said:

"A woman is married for three things—her wealth, her beauty and her religion. Yet, you should prefer the religion aspect so that you could attain serenity."[90]

The Messenger of God first practiced and then advised what people ought to do in any given situation.

Several other wives of his were also known for their beauty. So clearly, his particular affection for Aisha cannot be explained only by beauty. Their beauty was narrated to us by Aisha herself. For example, when Aisha saw Juwayriya during the War of Banu Mustaliq, her beauty grabbed her attention and she became anxious. Aisha said:

"She was a very beautiful and nice person with an attractive posture. She came and asked the Messenger of God to determine a ransom for her emancipation. I swear that when I first saw her, I had a

---

[88]  *Bukhari*, Shahadat, 15.
[89]  *Bukhari*, Mazalim, 25 (2336).
[90]  Ahmad ibn Hanbal, *Musnad*, 6:152 (25232)

gnawing suspicion, and I was concerned from the moment she walked up to God's Messenger."[91]

Aisha also felt a similar concern when she first saw Safiyya. Safiyya, who came to Medina after the conquest of Khaybar and who stayed as a guest in the house of Haritha ibn an-Numan, quickly attracted the attention of women of the Helpers and they rushed to see her. Covering her face with her scarf, Aisha was among them. Sometime after she had left the house, the Messenger of God left too. While the Messenger of God had planned to marry Safiyya, and thus please a large number of people with whom he had fought, he did not want to hurt his wives. He asked Aisha her opinion, and she expressed disapproval about her traditions.

In order to avoid problems similar to those of the past arising in the future, it became necessary to think and behave differently. Whatever the thoughts and attitudes of a group were, it was not correct to judge individuals according to the thoughts and attitudes of others. Just as there were good and virtuous people in society, there were also people who had been deprived of these values. Even if this was the case, they were still the children of Adam. It was necessary to make a clean break from the prejudices of the past. Goodness begets goodness, and goodness ultimately softens the hardest heart, like stones reshaped by rushing water. Every incident was an opportunity to make progress among the Companions and the mothers of the believers. Turning to Aisha in a compassionate manner, the Messenger of God said:

"O Aisha She became a Muslim and her conversion was wonderful."[92]

Aisha was special in all respects. It was as if she was created to accomplish this mission in the Prophet's house. She saw Gabriel twice and received greetings from him through the Prophet. Revelation came when God's Messenger was alone or when he was with Aisha, in her room.[93] Considering the status of God's Messenger and

---

[91]   Hakim, *Mustadrak*, 4:28 (6781); Ibn Sa'd, *Tabaqat*, 8:116, 117.

[92]   Ibn Sa'd, *Tabaqat*, 8: 126; Dhahabi, *Siyar*, 2:227.

[93]   *Bukhari*, Fadailu's Sahaba, 30.

the fact that he was directed by revelations from God, it is possible that the basis of their love was the Divine. We must not deny her role in the time of God's Messenger or in the time after his death. Aisha was so invaluable to the Messenger of God that he once said:

"There are many men who attained spiritual perfection; however, no women, save Imran's daughter Mary, and Pharaoh's wife Asiyya, reached that point. Comparing Aisha's virtue to other women is like the superiority of meat *tharid* to other meals."[94]

## AISHA INSIDE THE HOME

The house of felicity was a place of serenity and reciprocal love. In that house, there was a tenacious bond constructed on sacrifices. Relationships did not exist merely in the present and future, but considered the journey toward eternal life.

In her home, Aisha sacrificed herself to fulfill every wish of God's Messenger. Hers was absolute obedience; she was satisfied only in fulfilling his wishes, and at the same time, tried to anticipate his feelings before he stated them. She continued to do this, even after his death and until her last breath. Aisha evaluated every step before she took it and made decisions according to what she knew of him. One day, she bought a pillow for the Prophet to sit on. Yet she did not know his opinion about its decorative painting, or perhaps the painting on the pillow did not grab her attention. But everything that happened had a purpose. Through this incident, an unknown fact would be revealed and his thoughts on the issue would be clarified. When the Messenger of God arrived, he stayed in front of the door and did not enter. The mother of the believers became anxious and asked immediately:

"O Messenger of God! I repent God and ask forgiveness from His Messenger; did I commit a sin?"

---

[94] *Bukhari*, Ahadithu'l Anbiya, 33 (3230). Tharid is a special dish in Arab cuisine and the Prophet liked it very much.

The tone of her voice indicated that her heart was melting with worry. She feared she had done something that God and His Messenger were against. The Messenger of God stated that he did not like the new pillow she bought and explained:

"The painters of these pictures will be tormented and be asked to bring to life what they tried to create. Angels do not enter into a house in which there are such pictures (depicting living beings)."

When his feelings became clear, Aisha took away the painted pillow that prevented angels from entering their house.[95]

Aisha did housework on her own. With effort and hardship, she would grind flour by hand and cooked her own meals. She lifted all the bed linens and pillows, and prepared the water for the Prophet's ablution on her own. Aisha spun the string used for his sacrificial camels, laundered his clothes, combed his hair and would sometimes sprinkle a fragrant odor on it. She softened and prepared the *minvaq* (a special stick or root from the arak tree that is used to cleanse the teeth) that the Messenger of God used and always kept it clean.

She hosted their visitors, trying to supply their necessities and please the Messenger of God. One day, the Messenger of God took some of the people of the Suffah[96] to Aisha's home, the house of felicity. Then he asked Aisha:

"O Aisha, why don't you offer us something to eat?"

The only thing cooked in the house was from the *hashisha* plant and she offered it to the visitors. The Messenger of God addressed her again:

"O Aisha, bring some more things to us."

Pleasing the visitors meant pleasing the Messenger of God, and pleasing God's Messenger meant pleasing God. How could she not do whatever the Messenger of God wanted? But it was like trying to create a meal from nothing. Finally, she made a meal by mixing cottage

---

[95]  *Muslim*, Libas, 87 (2107).
[96]  The people who stayed in the antechamber of the Prophet's Mosque, devoted to mastering religious knowledge.

cheese, dates and oil. When the people of Suffah had satisfied their hunger a little, the Messenger of God said:

"O Aisha, serve us something to drink."

Aisha brought milk to the visitors in a large bowl. But it was clear there wasn't enough milk for all of them. So God's Messenger asked for more milk. There was a tiny amount remaining, and it would be odd if she served it in the large bowl. So she served it in a small bowl to the visitors.[97] Aisha came from such a home where she knew very well that giving the little amount in one's possession for the sake of God would be a means for an eternal reward, and so she behaved accordingly.

The Messenger of God joined in his family members' social lives and watched their entertainment. He took them on social outings. From time to time, he encouraged playful competitions among them. The Messenger of God was the ideal husband and father. One day, Aisha was narrating something to the Messenger of God and she used the word *hurafa* (superstition). He asked:

"Do you know what *hurafa* means?"

But he knew that she did not know and added without waiting for her response:

"*Hurafa* was a man from the Uzra community, he was kidnapped by demons during the era of Ignorance. He stayed with them for a long time and one day they set him free. He started to explain the strange things that he had witnessed while among the demons and the people who heard his stories began to call them 'Hurafa's statement.'"[98]

In the days before God's Messenger passed away, his head started to ache. He knew he would leave this world soon. He began to make amends for all that had passed, not only with those who were living, but also with those Companions he had buried before. Visiting their graves in the cemetery, he returned with the hope that he would meet

---

[97] *Abu Dawud*, Adab, 103 (5040); Ahmad ibn Hanbal, *Musnad*, 5:426 (3666).
[98] Ahmad ibn Hanbal, *Musnad*, 6:157 (25283).

them the next day. One day, Aisha's head also started to ache and she moaned, "Oh my dear head!"

God's Messenger responded, "Why are you moaning like that?" which meant: "compared with my ache what can yours be?"

His words rang true. The Messenger of God continued:

"What will you gain if you die before me? I will wash you, shroud you, perform your Funeral Prayer and bury you in your grave."

Hearing such unexpected words, her eyes opened wide. Was he telling a joke or was he expressing a truth? Seeing that his attitude was gentle and frill of mercy, she understood that he was teasing her. So she teased him back saying:

"Yes, I should die so that when you are done with my burial, you could do whatever you want with your other wives after I am gone, right?"[99]

Her words made the Messenger of God smile, as they conveyed the depth of her love.

Aisha sometimes felt distressed. On one such day, her father Abu Bakr came to her room. She was cranky and spoke loudly. Although Abu Bakr considered her as the mother of the believers since the time she had been betrothed to the Messenger of God, he could not consent to anything she might do that would hurt the Messenger. As soon as he saw her state, he took her aside and scolded her:

"O so-and-so's daughter, how can you talk so loudly in the presence of God's Messenger?"

As Abu Bakr spoke, he held up his hand to indicate that she must endure his lecture. He felt he had the right to scold her since she was his daughter; for nothing could hurt him as much as his own daughter causing sadness to the Messenger of God. Then Abu Bakr realized that the Messenger of God had witnessed his scolding, and he felt ashamed for intervening in the private matters within the Prophet's home. He knew that he had been wrong, but he felt he had to do it

---

[99] *Bukhari*, Marda, 16 (5342).

to prevent something worse. Still, the anger he felt towards Aisha did not lessen—how could she talk to the Messenger of God in such a tone? He remained annoyed but the presence of God's Messenger prevented him from saying anything else. He presumed this from the Prophet's attitude, and he left quietly.

After his departure, the Messenger of God went to Aisha, who was feeling ashamed. Her father had told the truth; nobody should raise their voice in the presence of God's Messenger. She looked at him with embarrassment.

It was time to end the moment happily. Since the matter had been understood, the Messenger of God took a step to turn grief into pleasure. Indicating where Abu Bakr had recently stood, he said:

"See how I interfered with the issue between you and this man and how I rescued you from his anger?"[100]

That day, Abu Bakr left full of sadness, but when he came back a short time later, he saw a different situation entirely. The Messenger of God and Aisha welcomed him with smiles on their faces. The previous situation had been temporary and had left only pleasure. Abu Bakr was an expert on expressions and guessed how the mood had softened but he wanted to hear it from them. With a smile on his face, he said:

"Why not share your pleasures with me just like you shared your troubles?"[101]

Sometimes, there were arguments among the wives which the Messenger of God reconciled with humor. But sometimes verbal quarrels turned into physical attacks. One day, Aisha cooked a meal using flour and milk and offered it to the Messenger of God while Sawdah was sitting next to him. But Sawdah did not want to eat her food. Aisha threatened:

"You will eat this meal or I will spread it on your face."

Sawdah still refused to eat, possibly because they were of a similar age. It was the perfect chance to turn the threat into a joke. So

---

[100] *Abu Dawud*, Adab, 92 (4999); Nasa'i, *Sunanu'l Kubra*, 5: 139 (8495).
[101] *Ibid.*

Aisha did what she had threatened and spread some of the meal on Sawdah's face.

This made the Messenger of God smile. Then he, who always tried to heal the disagreements that sometimes happened between his wives, used the scene as a pretext for solidarity. He took some of the food into his hand, and holding it toward Sawdah, he said:

"Why don't you do the same thing to her?"

So Sawdah spread the flour meal on Aisha's face, which made everyone smile.

Outside, they heard Umar's loud voice calling his son:

"O Abdullah! O Abdullah!"

Umar, who was nearby, would never leave without seeing the Prophet. Since the Messenger of God thought he might come inside, he said:

"Let's get up so you both can wash your faces."

Although it was a joke, it had happened in the privacy of their family and did not need to be shared with anyone else, even with Umar, who had a special place at the side of God's Messenger. Aisha made the following remark about this memory:

"After I saw the attitude of God's Messenger toward Umar that day, I hold Umar in awe."[102]

There were even times when the Messenger of God was angry, and sometimes, the reason for his anger was Aisha. One day, he came home with a captive who he left in Aisha's room. At that time, there were other women visiting and talking with Aisha. As their conversation deepened with time, they forgot about the captive. Seizing the chance, the man escaped.

Sometime later, the Messenger of God came back and the slave was missing. He became very angry. Granting slaves their freedom was his normal behavior, and he had probably planned to set this one free as well, but the timing was important. Turning to Aisha, he asked:

"O Aisha, what happened to the captive? Where is he?"

---

[102] Abu Ya'la, *Musnad*, 7/449; see also: Tahmaz, *as-Sayyidatu Aisha*, 42, 43.

There was nothing Aisha could say. With enormous sadness, she said:

"I was lost in conversation with the other women."

As there was no chance to catch the captive, the Messenger of God said:

"Shame on you; may your hands break."

The Messenger of God's anger was enough to make Aisha distraught. She knew she should have been more careful with what had been entrusted to her, no matter the circumstances. Then the Messenger of God left and started to ask people to find the captive. He was found and brought to God's Messenger. The problem was resolved. Sometime later, the Messenger of God came home, Aisha was gazing at her upturned hands and then flipping her palms down over and over again. When God's Messenger saw Aisha in that state, he asked:

"What is wrong? Do you need to take ablution?"

"You cursed me so I am waiting to see which of my hands will break."

It was like the return of a child to his mother after he was chastised. She was both scared of his curse but at the same time, hoping to turn his curse into a prayer for herself. The Messenger of God opened his hands to heaven and after many prayers exalting God, added:

"O My Lord! I am human and I become angry like a human. Whichever believer, man or woman, that I have cursed; please consider the curse as a reason for them to be cleansed of their material and spiritual sins."[103]

Like any family, there were times when Aisha was discontented or times when the Messenger of God was angry. God's Messenger understood her displeasure and immediately intervened to settle the matter amicably. One day, he said:

---

[103] Ahmad ibn Hanbal, *Musnad*, 6:52 (24251).

"You understand immediately whether I am pleased or angry with you and I understand immediately whether you are pleased or angry with me."

Aisha was surprised and asked:

"How do you know that?"

The Messenger of God said:

"You use the expression, 'I swear to Muhammad's God' when you are pleased with me; you prefer to say 'I swear to Abraham's God' when you are angry with me."

Aisha responded:

"That's true. O Messenger of God, I swear to God, you tell the truth. I promise you that from now on I will not take any name other than yours to my mouth."[104]

One day, eleven women sat down and they promised to tell each other their real opinions of their own husbands. Each of them, in order, talked first about the most well-known feature of her husband. Some honored their husbands while others listed their bad habits. Aisha listened carefully, sometimes smiling, and other times feeling sad. When Umm Dharr's turn came, she explained that she was the daughter of a shepherd when Abu Dharr married her. She said that he had done many kindnesses for her and that she had tasted every type of pleasure with him. She also listed the favors of her mother-in-law as well as the virtues of her stepson from Abu Dharr's previous wife, and of her maid. But her beloved husband had divorced her and she was now married to another man. Her new husband was good and generous, but his kindness and generosity did not equal Abu Dharr's. Although Abu Dharr had divorced her, she still could not forget him, for her new husband's benevolence did not overshadow that of Abu Dharr.

Though the other women told their stories, what Umm Dharr said stuck with Aisha and she later shared it with God's Messenger.

The Messenger of God turned to Aisha and said:

"You see, you and I are like Abu Dharr and Umm Dharr with one difference; he divorced his wife but I will not do that."

It was a compliment that pleased Aisha and she said:

"May my mother and father be sacrificed for you. You are better for me than Abu Dharr."[105]

## ENTERTAINMENT

The Messenger of God allowed moderate levels of entertainment. When he saw Aisha came to his place without any show or ceremony on the day they were married, he asked:

"O Aisha, haven't you got any amusement? The Helpers like amusements."[106]

There were certain instances where the Prophet let his family members watch some games. Later Aisha explained:

"I remember God's Messenger was screening me with his clothes when the Habashi (Abyssinian) people came to do a display in the mosque. I watched them until I got tired."[107]

On the festival of *Eid*, a group came with shields and spears to entertain the crowds. People gathered and were watching and Aisha came near to see what was going on. Because she was at the back, she wasn't able to see the action. Turning to God's Messenger, Aisha said she wanted to see what was happening. The Prophet asked:

"Do you really want to see?"

Aisha nodded.

So the Prophet lifted her behind his shoulders, her cheek resting against his cheek, and the Messenger of God called:

"Come on, O Banu Arfida!"

After some time had passed, the Prophet asked:

"Are you satisfied?"

---

[105] *Bukhari*, Nikah, 82 (4893).
[106] *Bukhari*, Nikah, 63 (4868).
[107] *Bukhari*, Iydayn, 2 (907).

Aisha had become tired and replied in the affirmative.

So God's Messenger said:

"Then you can go."[108]

However, it is true that the Messenger of God also intervened when limits were exceeded, and kept to the boundaries of reasonable entertainment. One day, a female musician came to play for Aisha. The Prophet asked:

"Aisha, do you know her?"

Aisha looked at the unknown woman and responded in the negative.

He explained that she was a musician from some tribe and added:

"Do you want her to play for you?"

Naturally, as no one says no to an offer from God's Messenger, she said yes.

Taking out her instrument, the woman started to play and Aisha noticed some signs of discontent on the Prophet's face. Aisha had seen this look before when the Messenger of God found two girls dancing in Aisha's room. When people got out of hand, a warning came. Today, both the voice and the attitude of the musician did not coincide with the seriousness of belief. Soon, the Messenger of God turned to Aisha and said:

"Satan has made his way to the vocal cords of this woman."[109]

## COMPETITION

The Messenger of God sounded out the people around him and took steps according to theirs. It was his general attitude and he advised his people to do the same:

"Walk in step with the weakest among you."[110]

---

[108] *Ibid.*

[109] Ahmad ibn Hanbal, *Musnad*, 3:449 (15758); Tabarani, *Mujamu'l Kabir*, 7: 158 (6686).

[110] Ajluni, *Kashf al-Khafa*, 2:503.

He was a person of moderation and knew how to act in every environment. As a Prophet, he was occupied with the most sensitive work and carried out his duty with care. He did not however, hold his family to his own standards of sensitivity. As regular people, it would have been impossible for them to endure. And he was there to make life easier.

Once, when there was a military expedition, Aisha was drawn by lots.[111] At a certain point in the journey, the Messenger of God told his army to continue on while he stayed back with Aisha.

Then the Messenger of God said:

"Let's race."

Aisha was small and naturally more agile so she won the race. Years later, they were on a different journey together. The time that had passed had made her forget their earlier competition. But the Prophet had not forgotten, and again told the others to keep going while he stayed behind with Aisha. He said:

"Let's race."

As before, Aisha accepted the challenge. They started to run again but this time, the Messenger of God won. Aisha had gained some weight and lost some of her speed. God's Messenger turned to Aisha and, with a smile, said:

"This is pay-back for our earlier race!"[112]

## REQUEST FOR A NEW NAME

One day, Aisha asked for a new nickname from God's Messenger. Mature people in Arabian society were not called by their birth name, but were named in relationship to someone else. It was common practice and an important sign of rank and honor. There was competition in virtue among people in terms of their names. Some people became so well-known by their nicknames that people forgot their real

---

[111] When there was a military expedition, the Prophet decided which wife would accompany him by drawing lots, in order not to break their hearts.

[112] *Abu Dawud*, Jihad, 68 (2578). Ahmad ibn Hanbal, *Musnad*, 6:39 (24164).

names. Generally, these names were given in relation to their first-born child; a father became Abu (father of) so-and-so, and a mother became Umm (mother of) so-and-so. People without children were called *ibn* (son of) so-and-so or *bint* (daughter of) so-and-so.

Actually, the Messenger of God called her by a number of names, such as Humayra, Uwaysh, Aish, Bint Siddiq, Muwaffiqa and Binta Abu Bakr. But none of them could be a permanent nickname. Since everyone she knew had a nickname, Aisha expected to have one too. Depressed, she wailed:

"O, Messenger of God, all of my friends have nicknames!"

Though this was all she said, the Messenger of God understood her silent request for one of her own. Most likely, this was the polite way to ask for something. Perhaps Aisha was asking for a baby, who would automatically supply her with a new name, and who would continue the progeny of God's Messenger.

But perhaps the Prophet had concluded from his own poignant experiences that having a child was not his destiny. All three of his sons had died in early childhood, and three of his four daughters would precede him in death—Ruqayyah had died during the Battle of Badr, and neither Umm Kulthum nor Zainab would outlive him.

A discerning and wise person such as God's Messenger would have drawn a conclusion from such events: perhaps God did not want any of his children to live on the earth after him.

It was necessary to explain it to Aisha in a kind and delicate way. He chose a response that neither made Aisha sad or avoided a reply, and said:

"Then you should take the nickname of your sister's son, Abdullah."

His words probably meant 'that path is closed to you.' The astute Aisha understood immediately and never made the same request again. From that time, Aisha was called by the nickname of her sister's son Abdullah ibn Zubayr and was known as Umm Abdillah.[113]

---

[113] *Abu Dawud*, Adab, 78 (4970). Ahmad ibn Hanbal, *Musnad*, 6:260 (26285).

## SENSITIVITY

The Messenger of God was sent to perfect morality. His wives were influenced by his moral instructions the most. Witnessing all of his directions and declarations, and all his actions and behavior, they learnt his good manners and shared them with others. They gained new wisdom and learnt a new path for high morals. Every person who came to the house of felicity, every gift that was brought there, or every incident that happened, resulted in novel judgments from God's Messenger, the representative of the morality of the Qur'an.

One night, Aisha had baked a small bun of barley for the Messenger. But when he came, he closed the door as soon as he entered, which meant he wanted to rest. He always covered the rim of the water jug, covered the top of the food bowl, and turned off any lights that were on.

As he rested, Aisha also became sleepy and fell asleep. Then the Messenger of God felt a little cold and came near to Aisha, warming himself by putting his head in her lap and falling back asleep.

Meanwhile, a sheep that belonged to their neighbor came inside the room and took the barley bun. Aisha tried to frighten the sheep from where she was sitting, but it did not work. Her movement awakened the Prophet, so Aisha jumped up and started to run after the sheep. Looking on, the Messenger of God shouted after her:

"If you catch it take only the bun, don't hurt our neighbor for what the sheep did?"[114]

In those times, many ate the meat of *kalar*, a type of lizard the Messenger of God did not choose to eat because of its nature. However, eating lizards was *halal* (permitted) and the Prophet made it clear to his Companions that it was permissible.[115] One day, a gift of *kalar* meat was brought to their home which the Prophet did not eat. Aisha asked:

---

[114] *Bukhari*, al-Adabu'l Mufrad, 1:54 (120).
[115] *Bukhari*, Tamanni, 15; *Muslim*, Sayd, 42.

"Should I give it to needy people?"

Her intention was sincere; others could eat what they chose not to, since there was no statement that banned the meat's consumption. But the Messenger of God did not share Aisha's opinion, because he thought of aspects that Aisha was not considering. He felt he should not discriminate against others because if it was to be known that he disliked this meat, other people would not like it either. He would be giving meat that he did not like to someone else. So he turned to Aisha and said:

"No, never give the things that you do not eat to others."[116]

## HER WORSHIP

Aisha was living an exemplary life in every regard. She was at the height of her service to God. Aisha was consistent during the life of the Messenger of God and after his death. She saw God's Messenger as a man who loved worship and who served with the attitude of a lover. Aisha spent the most fruitful times of her life with the person who was closest to God—a man who reached new heights in his knowledge of God, who was the most beloved servant of God. He prayed during the nights until his feet were swollen—during just one *rakah* (Prayer cycle), he stood long enough to recite hundreds of pages of the Qur'an. His bows and prostrations at Prayer were as long as the time he spent standing. Aisha said:

"Neither can you ask or can I explain the beauty of his Prayers."[117]

Aisha witnessed hundreds and thousands of miracles; she even saw the revelation of the Qur'an where God's Messenger and Gabriel met. She considered the life of the world like the shade under a tree where people rest for a while, and then continue on their way. She directed her earthly life toward the life of the Hereafter. The world and everything in it held no value for her, for God's Messenger had taught

---

[116] Ahmad ibn Hanbal, *Musnad*, 6: 123 (24961); Bayhaqi, *Sunan,* 9:325 (19208).

[117] *Bukhari*, Tahajjud, 16; Manaqib, 21.

her to value the other world. During the nine years that she lived with the Messenger of God, Aisha followed him and attempted to put his example into practice.

The Prophet went to his room after he finished the *Isha* (Night) Prayer, brushed his teeth and went to bed. At midnight, he got up and performed the *Tahajjud* Prayer, which was obligatory only for him. After two-thirds of the night passed, he awakened Aisha and asked her to pray. Aisha also got up and performed the *Tahajjud* Prayer followed by the *Witr* Prayer.[118]

Sometimes, Aisha joined the Messenger of God and prayed with him all night until sunrise. On such a night, God's Messenger recited the chapters Al-Baqarah, Al Imran, and An-Nisa in just one *rakah*. When he recited a verse that made someone quiver with fear, he prayed to take refuge from God's wrath and when he recited a verse of good news, he again turned toward God and asked for mercy.[119]

Before the Morning Prayer, the Messenger of God performed a short two-unit Prayer and slept on his right side if he needed rest, or talked with Aisha until the *muezzin* called to Prayer. Aisha followed the congregational Prayer from her room adjacent to the mosque. Basically, her nights were brighter than her mornings.

Aisha joined the Messenger of God in fasting too. God's Messenger spent the last ten days of Ramadan on retreat in the mosque (*itiqaf*) and Aisha joined in the Prayers from her room. Sometimes, he placed a tent inside the mosque and after he led the congregational Prayer, he continued his retreat inside his tent.[120]

At the Farewell Pilgrimage, Aisha was with him and witnessed the large crowd where the Messenger of God said farewell to his society. During the pilgrimage, he fell ill and his society learnt how to perform the pilgrimage rites in illness.[121]

---

[118] Ahmad ibn Hanbal, *Musnad*, 6:55 (24320).
[119] Ahmad ibn Hanbal, *Musnad*, 6:92 (24653).
[120] *Bukhari*, Itiqaf, 18 (1940).
[121] *Bukhari*, Hajj, 76 (1557).

Having learnt how to worship directly from the most beloved servant of God, Aisha knew, explained, and continued to perform all the recommended Prayers.

One day, Aisha took Abdullah ibn Qays to her side and said:

"Do not neglect to get up at night and pray. The Messenger of God never abandoned the Night Prayer. When he was sick or very tired, he prayed while sitting, but he never gave it up."[122]

Even for non-obligatory, recommended Prayers, Aisha made them up if she missed performing them on time. After witnessing God's Messenger performing the *Duha* Prayer, she considered it indispensable and would not abandon it.[123]

Very early one morning, Aisha's nephew, Qasim ibn Muhammad, came to her home while she was praying. It was not yet time for the Morning Prayer and the time for the Night Prayer had passed. He asked:

"What is this Prayer?"

With the attitude of one who seeks to hide their good deeds, she replied reluctantly:

"I missed my habitual Prayer tonight so I am performing a compensatory Prayer."

Abdullah ibn Abu Musa once came to ask her the principal points about Islam; again, he arrived while she was performing the *Duha* Prayer. When he said, "I will wait until you are finished with your Prayers," in a voice loud enough to be heard by others, the other residents of the house who were familiar with the length of her Prayers said:

"Alas!"[124]

The one who intended to wait for the end of Aisha's Prayer should expect to wait for a very long time. When she started to pray,

---

[122] Ahmad ibn Hanbal, *Musnad*, 6: 125 (24989).

[123] Ahmad ibn Hanbal, *Musnad*, 6: 138 (25112), Nasa'i, *Sunanu'l Kubra*, 1: 181 (482).

[124] Ahmad ibn Hanbal, *Musnad*, 6: 125 (24989).

absorbed in her deep reverence for God, it was as if she lost connection with the world and everything in it.

Aisha led an ascetic life. She performed the Night Prayer until morning and spent her days fasting. When Aisha recited a verse that included a warning or threat, she hesitated, then went back to the beginning and recited it again in order to feel deeper grief. The people around her witnessed that her scarf often became wet with her tears.

One day, when Aisha recited the verse *"Then God bestowed His favor upon us, and protected us from the punishment of the scorching fire,"* (at-Tur 52:27) she could not hold back her tears and began to sob. It was an explanation of the state of those who had left the world and lived in the peace of salvation in the hereafter. But Aisha remained concerned about her position in the afterlife and never thought of herself as guaranteed such mercy. When she recited the verse, she took refuge in her Lord and begged:

"O Lord, please bless me and keep me away from the hell fire!"[125]

Her nephew and student, Urwa, who saw this and was waiting for her to finish, grew tired of waiting and left to work at the bazaar. He said:

"When I came back from the bazaar after finishing my business, I swear to God, I found her continuing the same Prayer in tears."[126]

Aisha always tried to perform her Prayers in congregation, following the *imam* (the leader in the Prayer) from her room which was adjacent to the mosque or praying with women who came to her room.[127] Other times, she asked Zakwan, her emancipated slave, to lead her in Prayer.[128]

Her sensitivity about fasting continued; she spent almost everyday in fast.[129] On the Day of Arafa one year, which was the day before *Eid*

---

[125] Ibn Abi Shayba, *Musannaf*, 2:25 (6036).
[126] *Ibid.*
[127] Tahmaz, *as-Sayyidatu Aisha*, quoted in Abdurrazzaq, *Musannaf*, 2:82, 126, 141.
[128] *Bukhari*, Jama'a, 26 (659).
[129] Ibn Sa'd, *Tabaqat*, 8:68.

*al-Adha*, the weather was suffocatingly hot. Aisha was fasting. Her brother, Abdurrahman, visited her, and when he saw that she was fasting despite the weather and that she was tired and soaked in sweat, he said:

"Why do you not break your fast?"

But Aisha, who aimed to follow the Messenger of God, replied:

"How could I break my fast when I heard God's Messenger say: 'Certainly, the fast of the Day of Arafa is atonement for the sins of the year before.'?"[130]

Aisha fasted during the days in Mina; though eating and drinking during those times were permitted,[131] she never gave up her fast, even during journeys when breaking one's fast was allowed.[132]

Aisha once performed the pilgrimage with the Messenger of God —it was his last. She went to Mecca several times after he died and showed a different sensitivity on those pilgrimages.

During the early years, the Ka'ba was not crowded. In later years, because of the increasing crowd of believers, Aisha circled the Ka'ba very carefully to avoid mixing with men, doing her rotation on a wider scale. It took longer and increased her hardships, but despite that, she looked for chances to be alone. When she saw that it was crowded around the Ka'ba, she left and circled Ka'ba from as far away as the middle of Sabir Mountain.[133]

Following God's Messenger was her goal. In the early years, she took a break in Mina, in a place called Namira, but later, because of the crowds, she set up her tent in a deserted region called Arak. Sometimes, she even set up her tent in the region of Sabir Mountain.

Aisha was meticulous about the minor pilgrimage, too. Before she saw the moon for the month of Muharram, she went to Juhfa and waited there until moonrise. When she saw the moon, Aisha started

---

[130] Ahmad ibn Hanbal, *Musnad*, 6:128 (25014).

[131] *Bukhari*, Sawm, 67 (1893).

[132] Abdurrazzaq, *Musannaf*, 2:560-561 (4459-4461); Bayhaqi, *Sunan*, 4:301 (8266).

[133] Malik, *Muwatta*, Hajj, 13 (750).

to prepare for the minor pilgrimage by reciting the invocations and then, without losing time, she went to Mecca.[134]

When it was time to break her fast on the night of Arafa, she requested only water.[135]

## HER ASCETICISM AND HUMILITY

Aisha did not meddle in any issues other than those which had religious decrees and did not spend time nagging other people for their mistakes. Among the hundreds and thousands of hadiths that she narrated from the Prophet, it is impossible to find a distorted or negative expression. She warned those who abused others, and did not shy away from pointing out what was clearly wrong. When Hassan ibn Thabit was charged by a religious law and started to condemn himself, Aisha consoled the old Companion by saying:

"Yet you are not as bad a person as you are saying."[136]

She comforted him even though Hassan had hurt her years ago with similar statements. Aisha did not return slander and did not hold grudges. Until her death, she was an example of forgiveness toward those who openly worked against her. One day, when her nephew and student, Urwa, denounced Hassan ibn Thabit, Aisha became angry and said:

"Do not condemn him; he was an important man who defended the Messenger of God."[137]

When people around her engaged in gossip or backbiting, particularly about someone who was deceased, Aisha flew into a rage and then prayed to God for the forgiveness of the person that had been talked about. Aisha would say:

"The Messenger of God said, 'only speak well of your dead.'"

---

[134] *Ibid.*

[135] *Ibid*, Hajj, 43 (836).

[136] *Bukhari*, Maghazi, 32 (3915).

[137] *Muslim*, Fadailu's Sahaba, 155 (2488).

She practiced her religion precisely. One day, while walking on a road, she heard a bell ring and stayed where she was. The ringing of a bell was an unwelcome sound and so she tried to avoid it. A little while later, she heard it behind her and began to walk faster to escape the sound disliked by God's Messenger.[138]

One day she heard that the orphans staying with her in her home had brought a game similar to backgammon. She became angry and sent a message saying:

"Either you throw it out or I will come and take you out."[139]

Aisha felt anxious, even about her dreams. She never thought they were meaningless and thought perhaps they contained important messages about the interpretation of hadiths. A single nightmare either made her give *sadaqa* (voluntary charity) or emancipate a slave the next day.[140]

She habitually used any small excuse to emancipate a slave. Once, she gave in to the demands of others and broke a certain oath; she emancipated forty slaves as expiation, instead of just one, but she still did not forgive herself and shed tears over it for the rest of her life. Upon realizing that her female slave was of the Tamim tribe, which God's Messenger had said descended from the lineage of Prophet Ishmael, she gave her her freedom.[141]

There was no one who did not know of her unwavering resolve on this issue; Aisha emancipated a total of sixty-seven slaves.[142]

She spoke to everyone and did not look down on anyone. One day, she gave a small bag of bread to a man who had asked for food. After he had gone, another man, who was destitute and who appeared to be mentally ill, came. Aisha called him near and offered him her own food. When the man had satisfied his hunger and left, Aisha was asked why she behaved this way, and she answered:

---

[138] Ahmad ibn Hanbal, *Musnad*, 6:152 (25229).

[139] *Bukhari*, Adabu'l Mufrad, 1:435 (1274).

[140] Haythami, *Majmuatu'z Zawaid*, 1:484 (419).

[141] *Bukhari*, Itq, 13 (2405).

[142] San'ani, *Subulu's Salam*, 4:139.

"How could I act differently when the Messenger of God said 'Treat people in accordance with their condition'?"[143]

Despite every hardship she experienced, Aisha lived frugally and never thought of obligating someone for a kindness she rendered. She hesitated to waste anything. Aisha wanted the people around her to exercise the same discipline. She never complained about her ascetic life because she had chosen it out of her own free will and lived a life that centered on the Hereafter.

This choice wasn't a result of poverty, because even in times of plenty, she chose the same lifestyle. When Umar sent a bag of gold to her, she could not hold back her tears, and gave away the gold to those around her immediately. She still did not think she had done enough, so she prayed to God that she would never be subjected to such a blessing again.[144]

A special student of hers, Aisha bint Talha, said:

"Those of us who were close to her, based on our positions, young and old, came from all around and wrote letters and brought armfuls of gifts. I would present them to her saying: 'O dear aunt! This is so-and-so's letter and this is her gift,' and she would tell me: 'O my dear girl! Write a letter and send a gift in response. If you do not have a gift, I will give it to you.' And then she would give me a gift to send."[145]

Aisha had amazing willpower. Neither the people around her or the changing times were able to change her. She never gave up treating others justly, even those who hurt her, oppressed people around her, or gossiped about her. She never based her actions on the wrongdoings of others.[146]

Aisha had only one dress. When it was dirty, she would wash and dry it, and then wear it again. This was a general practice among the wives of God's Messenger.[147] But during her first years in Medina, when

---

[143] *Abu Dawud*, Adab, 23 (4842).

[144] Hakim, *Mustadrak*, (6725).

[145] *Bukhari*, Adabu'l Mufrad, 1:382 (1118).

[146] *Muslim*, Imara, 19 (1828).

[147] *Bukhari*, Hayd, 11 (306).

she first began to live in the house of felicity with God's Messenger, Aisha owned a high-quality garment worth five drachmas. She made Medinan women happy by lending it to them, temporarily, for weddings or special occasions.[148]

She never thought to buy a new dress until the one she wore became completely worn-out. Her nephew, Urwa, confirmed this:

"Aisha did not replace the garment that she wore with a new one until the one she had was threadbare and covered in patches."

In those days, many people said to her:

"God gives you much; why do you not benefit from it?"

Aisha gave a short and direct answer:

"The new will not fit the ones who are not created for the new."[149]

Aisha said she would not give up her habits. When a gift was sent to her, Aisha remembered the plain lifestyle of the Messenger of God and his statements on the issue, so she would shed tears and allocate the gifts to the needy. During his Caliphate, Muawiya sent her garments, silver, and other things that she could use. When she saw them, she started to weep and said:

"The Messenger of God was not able to have any of these."

Aisha separated them into parts and gave them to needy people. By night time, nothing remained of what the Caliph had sent.[150]

One day, baskets full of grapes were brought to her as a gift. Aisha immediately started to give them to the poor. The female slave who helped with her housework accompanied her. By nightfall, the woman came over to her with some grapes. Aisha was surprised, because she thought that she had given away all the grapes. She asked:

"What is this?"

The slave did not know what to say. She had kept the grapes without Aisha's knowledge in order to offer her to them at night. Aisha scolded her and said:

---

[148] *Bukhari*, Hiba, 32 (2485).
[149] *Bukhari*, Adabu'l Mufrad, 1:166.
[150] Abu Nuaym, *Hilyatu'l Awliya*, 2:48.

"One bunch, huh?"

Her attitude surprised the slave, who then understood the sensitivity of her mistress. Aisha added:

"I swear to God that I will neither touch or eat it," and she went away.[151]

Aisha continued to give away gifts that were brought to her throughout her life, always helping the poor. Aisha knew that when she gave even a little, she would receive abundant blessings from God, Who has infinite treasures to bestow. Aisha never thought of her own benefit. Caring for the destitute, she hoped to supply their needs. There was nothing that pleased her more than a smile from a needy person.

At the times when she had no money, Aisha sold her belongings and gave the money as charity. Aisha's nephew, Abdullah ibn Zubayr, said:

"I swear to God, either our beloved mother Aisha will give up her attitude or I will stop her."

Aisha heard this from someone and asked:

"Did he really say this?"

Then she said:

"I swear not to talk with ibn Zubayr until the afterlife."

So she did not speak to him. This hurt Abdullah ibn Zubayr and he looked for a solution to restore their past relationship. Although he came to Aisha's door many times, he did not hear anything other than:

"No! I swear that I will neither go back to this issue or give up my promise."

The passing of time hurt his conscience. Abdullah asked two leaders, Miswar ibn Mahrama and Abdurrahman ibn Abd al-Aswad, to intercede on his behalf. It was a duty for every believer to make peace between two believers.

They made a plan and went to Aisha's door and said:

---

[151] *Ibid.*

"May God's mercy and blessings be upon you. Are we allowed to come inside?"

Abdullah ibn Zubayr was with them but the two did not say that.

A voice from inside said:

"Welcome, come in."

They were happy, and said:

"All of us?"

"Yes, all of you."

Their plan got Abdullah ibn Zubayr inside. As soon as he entered, he implored her for forgiveness from the other side of the curtain. Miswar ibn Mahrama and Abdurrahman ibn Abd al-Aswad supported him and asked Aisha's forgiveness for him. Despite all their pleading, Aisha did not change her mind and forgive Abdullah, who was in tears.

The two intercessors, as part of their plan, said:

"You know that The Messenger of God said 'It is not allowed for one Muslim to stay angry at another Muslim for more than three days'."

Then Aisha started to cry, remembering the statement of God's Messenger, and replied:

"But I swore an oath, and you know that swearing an oath is serious."

Her heart was softening and she had no option but to follow the Messenger of God's statement. She did not reject the requests of the intercessors and accepted Abdullah ibn Zubayr's apology. From then on, she spoke to him but this cost Aisha forty slaves because she had broken an oath. Aisha cried when she remembered her oath and what she had experienced; people witnessed that her scarf became wet with tears.[152]

One day, during the lifetime of the Prophet, a woman came to Aisha with her two daughters in her arms. It was apparent that they were needy and that their life was full of hardships. Aisha did not have much in her home, but it was her nature to be content with what she

---

[152] *Bukhari*, Adab, 62, (5725).

had and to not worry about what she did not have. She brought three dates from her home to them. The mother gave two of the dates to her daughters. The children, who had long felt the absence of food, ate the dates with pleasure. Their mother watched them with grief, as Aisha looked on. When the children had finished their dates, their eyes focused on the remaining date in their mother's hand. With maternal love, she divided the date that she had kept for herself into two and gave half to each daughter. They ate happily. Nothing remained for the mother, who was satisfied with her daughters' joy, whose eyes were shining.

As soon as the Messenger of God came home, Aisha shared the incident with him. She was touched and expressed the mother's sacrifice. Then God's Messenger gave the following good news:

"For what she did, God bestowed heaven to that woman or saved her from hell!"[153]

Most of the time, Aisha's eyes were filled with tears and her heart was delicate. She was not able to keep herself from crying and wept until her tears dried up. She always sobbed when she did not do her duty or when she was not able to keep her word, and she always paid its atonement. Aisha spent her day and night in lamentation when she was treated unjustly.

But her tears were not restricted to herself. Disappointed with Muslim society, she wept for future generations as well. One day, she remembered the Antichrist (Dajjal) and started to weep thinking of the troubles and disasters that Muslims would experience. Aisha cried so fervently that she did not realize that God's Messenger had come to her side, and he asked:

"Why are you crying?"

Aisha turned to God's Messenger and said sadly:

"O Messenger of God! I remembered the Antichrist!"[154]

---

[153] Ahmad ibn Hanbal, *Musnad*, 6:92 (24655).
[154] Ahmad ibn Hanbal, *Musnad*, 6:75 (24511).

# HER GENEROSITY

Aisha lived for others. Whenever she saw needy people, she forgot her needs and gave whatever she had to them. She knew well the hadith of the Messenger of God:

"Save yourself from the hell-fire even by giving half a date-fruit in charity."[155]

Aisha was also the daughter of Abu Bakr, the most generous of men. Being generous was a general characteristic of her family. When Aisha's nephew, Abdullah ibn Zubayr, described the characteristics of his mother, Asma, and his aunt, Aisha, he said that they were like competitors when it came to giving charity.[156]

When Aisha had nothing to give, she sometimes borrowed from someone else and gave it as charity. Some found this strange and asked:

"Where did you get this idea to borrow and give as charity?"

She referred to a hadith of the Messenger of God, who said:

"Any servant of God, who had the intention and effort to repay his debt, will be given help by God Almighty." [157]

Her nephew, Urwa, said:

"I witnessed that she gave seven thousand drachmas of charity while she was wearing a patched garment."[158]

Aisha sold her house to Muawiya for one hundred and eighty thousand or two hundred thousand drachmas. Before getting up from where she sat, she had given it all to the poor, with nothing remaining for herself.[159]

One day, a needy person came to her and asked for a bite of food. Aisha had some grapes and asked a woman nearby to give them to the person at the door. The woman looked at her strangely, implying

---

[155] *Bukhari*, Zakah, 8, 9 (1347, 1351).

[156] *Bukhari*, Adabu'l Mufrad, 1: 106 (280).

[157] Ahmad ibn Hanbal, *Musnad*, 6:99 (24723); Hakim, *Mustadrak*, 2:26 (2202).

[158] Ibn Sa'd, *Tabaqat*, 8:67; Dhahabi, *Siyar*, 2:187.

[159] Ibn Sa'd, *Tabaqat*, 8: 165; Abu Nuaym, *Hilyatu'lAwliya*, 2:47, 48.

that Aisha needed the grapes herself. Aisha reminded her that even the tiniest of good deeds will be rewarded:

"Why are you hesitating? Do you know how many atoms are in this grape?"[160] alluding to the verse *"whoever does an atom's weight of good will see it"* (az-Zilzal 99:7).

One day a needy woman with two daughters came to Aisha and asked for something to eat. There was nothing; Aisha looked everywhere but found only one date, which she gave to the woman with embarrassment. Then her eyes were caught by the woman's reaction —she divided the date into two and gave half to each of her daughters. Aisha was reminded of the mother who had divided her own share into two for her daughters.

Aisha was deeply moved by what she saw. After the woman left, she continued to think about her. When the Messenger of God came home, Aisha shared the story with him. The Messenger of God was also affected and said:

"There is no doubt that such daughters will be a shield against Hellfire for those who treat them kindly."[161]

Another day, a poor woman came to Aisha, who searched everywhere and found only one piece of bread. It was the bread she was going to break her fast with, but Aisha gave it to the woman without hesitating. Aisha's housekeeper tried to warn her:

"But there is nothing for you to break your fast with."

Still, Aisha ordered:

"Give the bread to the woman."

The housekeeper had no choice but to give. Close to sunset, some gifts of lamb meat and bread were brought to Aisha. God blesses those who give for His sake. When it was time to break the fast, Aisha joked with the housekeeper:

"Take this and eat; it is better than your dried bread."[162]

---

[160]  Malik, *Muwatta*, 2:997 (1811).
[161]  *Bukhari*, Adabu'l Mufrad, 1:59 (132).
[162]  Malik, *Muwatta*, 2:997 (1810).

Something similar happened when one of her nephews, Abdullah ibn Zubayr, brought gifts valued at one hundred thousand *drachma*, and saw her giving it all away. It was a day of fasting for Aisha, but she gave until nothing remained. When it was sunset, Aisha asked her housekeeper, Umm Dharr:

"O Umm Dharr why don't you bring something for us to break our fasts?"

Umm Dharr brought some olive oil and bread and said:

"O mother of the believers, why didn't you keep something, even just one drachma from what you gave away so that we could buy some meat?"

In the housekeeper's words were embarrassment about being unable to set a good table for Aisha and bewilderment that she never benefitted from so many opportunities. Aisha understood her and said gently:

"Do not pressure me. If I had remembered at that time, I might have done that."[163]

Aisha knew that she would benefit from what she gave away and so she gave endlessly. She had learnt this from God's Messenger.

One day, they sacrificed an animal and Aisha gave away meat from the entire animal until only its shoulder blade remained in her hands. When the Messenger of God came home, he asked:

"What did you do with the sacrificed animal? What remains for us?"

"I distributed all of it, only its shoulder blade remains," Aisha said. It was what the Messenger of God expected, because God the Almighty had promised that He would increase the value of anything given for His sake. The good deed that is recorded for charity given for God's sake will never be removed and is permanent. The Messenger of God said:

"No dear Aisha, on the contrary, every part of it except its shoulder blade remains (as an eternal reward)."

---

[163] Ibn Sa'd, *Tabaqat*, 8:67; Dhahabi, *Siyar*, 2:187.

## HER ATTENTION TO HIJAB

While Aisha warned others about *hijab*, she too paid strict attention to it. As a wife of the Prophet, she was a mother to other Muslims. In spite of this, she behaved carefully and kept a distance between herself and men who were not close relatives.

She covered even around blind men. One day, Ishaq, a leader of the Tabiun, came and Aisha removed herself to the other side of the curtain. Ishaq, being blind, found her behavior strange and said:

"Are you covering in order to protect yourself from me? But I am not able to see you."

Aisha responded:

"It may be true that you are not able to see me, but I can see you."[164]

Aisha felt uncomfortable even when her wet nurse's husband came inside, though he was considered an uncle near whom she did not have to wear *hijab*. To those who found this odd, she said:

"His wife was the one who breast-fed me, not him."

Perhaps the decision on this issue had not been made clear yet, so Aisha was erring on the side of caution. When the Messenger of God came and she asked him, he told her:

"He is your uncle. Allow him into your place."[165]

It was said by ibn Abbas that Aisha used to cover even when the Prophet's two grandsons, Hasan and Husayn, visited her home. Hasan and Husayn, because of her caution, did not always go near the wives of the Messenger and behaved more carefully as well.[166]

Even while worshipping, she did not mix with the crowd and circled the Ka'ba at more serene times. Once, when Aisha was circling the Ka'ba, a woman asked her to go together to the Hajar al-Aswad (the Holy Black Stone):

---

[164] Ibn Sa'd, *Tabaqat*, 8:69.
[165] *Bukhari*, Shahadat, 7 (2501).
[166] Ibn Sa'd, *Tabaqat*, 8:58.

"O mother of the believers, why do we not kiss or touch the Hajar al-Aswad?"

Aisha told the woman to stay away from her and expressed that it was improper for women to move into such a crowd.[167]

Knowing her cautious ways, people often tried to make her more comfortable while she was circling the Ka'ba, by clearing the area of men. The circling area was prepared for Aisha in this way. She even covered her face while circling the Ka'ba, never wanting anyone to see her face.[168]

She was meticulous even during a visit to the cemetery. After Umar was martyred and buried, Aisha conducted her visits more carefully to the graves of the Messenger of God and her father, Abu Bakr.[169]

Her sensitivity was even reflected in her lectures. Aisha allowed everyone to come and benefit from her knowledge and had students from every region. Her foremost students were her nephews and her relatives. Though it was easier for them to visit her home, she kept a curtain between herself and distant relatives and strangers, and taught her lessons from the other side of that curtain. If she had to interfere, Aisha corrected mistakes by signaling with her hands. Her disciple, Imam Masruq, said:

"I used to hear the noise of her clapping from the other side of the curtain."[170]

With care, Aisha constructed a beneficial environment for classes. She made sure the ones who always came to take lectures had been breast-fed by her closest relations so she could see them more for the sake of knowledge. She knew that the Messenger of God had given similar permission to Abu Hudayfa's wife, Sahla bint Suhayl, and although Salim had been an adult, she had given milk to him so they became close relatives.[171]

---

[167] *Bukhari*, Hajj, 63 (1539).
[168] Ahmad ibn Hanbal, *Musnad*, 6:85 (24592).
[169] Hakim, *Mustadrak*, 4:8 (6721).
[170] *Bukhari*, Adahi, 15 (5246).
[171] *Muwatta*, Rada, 2 (1265); *Abu Dawud*, Nikah, 10 (2061).

If it was necessary, she taught what she knew through practice to her students, who were her relatives. One of her close relatives had a servant named Salim, who wanted to learn how to perform ablution. She taught him how the Messenger of God had - by performing ablution herself. Since Salim was the slave of one of her close relatives, she also accepted him like a relative.

After some time had passed, the same man came to Aisha again and told her:

"O mother of the believers, please pray for me."

Aisha asked why.

Wanting to share his happiness with her, he said:

"God Almighty bestowed me freedom."

She responded:

"May God give you blessings."

As soon as she had said this short prayer, Aisha hid herself behind the curtain. From then on, he did not have the status of a close relative, and so she talked with Salim from the other side of the curtain.[172]

## GUIDING OTHERS AND CONVEYING THE MESSAGE

Conveying the message and guiding others truly constituted the center of Aisha's life after the days of God's Messenger; she intervened in mistakes she witnessed to explain how an issue was resolved during his lifetime. Aisha enjoined the good and forbade the evil in every circumstance; she did whatever she could to guide her people. The motive behind her efforts was her serious concern for putting the teaching of the Qur'an and the Sunnah into practice.

Aisha once saw a woman while she was walking between Safa and Marwa wearing a *hijab* painted with pictures. Aisha warned her:

"Get rid of these pictures on your clothing. The Messenger of God got angry when he saw clothing like that."[173]

---

[172] *Nasa'i*, Tahara, 83 (100).
[173] Ahmad ibn Hanbal, *Musnad*, 6:225.

Aisha insisted on sharing the knowledge that she had and felt anxious that something would remain restricted only to her. Among them were things that she felt ashamed to share because of her modesty, so Aisha told wives to share them with their husbands. One day she said:

"Since I feel ashamed to say this to them, tell your husbands that they should use water to clean themselves after using the rest room. This is what the Messenger of God did."[174]

She warned girls, even little ones, who wore jewelry on their hands and feet when they visited her, explaining that excessive adornment would invite Satan and their house would be deprived of angels.[175]

Whenever she saw a fault, she wanted it to be corrected. One day, she saw her brother, Abdurrahman, performing ablution in a hurry to attend the Funeral Prayer of Sa'd ibn Abi Waqqas, and warned him:

"Abdurrahman, be more careful washing your feet while performing ablution. I heard the Messenger of God say: 'what a pity for heels (burning) in fire!'"[176]

## AISHA'S ATTENDANCE TO MILITARY CAMPAIGNS

Aisha's bravery was immense and she did not shy away from being on the front lines, even when others withdrew. Though she was a woman, she was often found on the battlefield with the Messenger of God. She never hesitated, even in fierce battles.

Aisha was beside the Messenger of God during significant turning points at Uhud, al-Khandaq, Banu Qurayza, Banu Mustaliq, Hudaybiya, and the Meccan conquest.[177] She supported the ones who were fighting in battle, and at the same time, served God's Messenger. Anas ibn Malik said:

---

[174] *Tirmidhi*, Tahara, 15 (19); *Nasa'i*, Tahara, 41 (46).
[175] *Abu Dawud*, Hatam, 6 (4231).
[176] *Muwatta*, Tahara, 35.
[177] Nadawi, *Siratu's Sayyidati Aisha*, 170.

"At the Battle of Uhud, I saw Aisha bint Abu Bakr and Umm Sulaym carrying water on their shoulders; they competed with each other to carry water in a hurry for wounded veterans. They went back and forth to Medina from Uhud to refill their waterskins."[178]

Aisha was on the battleground of al-Khandaq when the Meccans laid siege on Medina. She served the Prophet and carried water for men together with other Muslim women.

Close to the conquest of Mecca, the Messenger of God said:

"O Aisha, something important happened with the Huza'as!"

When Muslims made the peace treaty of Hudaybiya with the Meccans, the Huza'a tribe was among the Muslims' allies. Immediately Aisha guessed that the Quraysh had violated the treaty of Hudaybiya. Yet she knew that the Meccans were not powerful enough to do that with impunity; it would be foolish of them. So she asked whether the Prophet thought that the Quraysh would venture to violate the treaty. But it was true: the Meccans had attacked the Huza'a tribe by night and killed twenty-three people, including children. It was a gross violation of the Hudaybiya treaty. Still, the Messenger of God drew attention to the divine wisdom behind the happenings and stated that the Quraysh violated the treaty because God willed something else to be realized.

Aisha knew that if God willed something to happen, its result would be good. Still, she asked:

"O Messenger of God, will the result be good?"

"Yes, it will be good."

After some time had passed, God's Messenger told Aisha to prepare for journey and keep the issue secret.

This journey would be different than the previous ones—it would be to their birth home, a place God Almighty gave particular value. As she was preparing for their journey, Abu Bakr came and asked the reason for her activity. Since Aisha was determined to do as the Prophet told her, she did not say one word, even to her father.

---

[178] *Bukhari*, Fadailu's Sahaba, 48 (3600).

Aisha also strived to find financial support when necessary. The Muslim women gave whatever jewelry they had - earrings, anklets, bracelets, and gold - as charity to serve God and his Messenger's cause.[179] Before Tabuk, Aisha laid a blanket in her room and the women competed to bring valuable things from their houses to place on the blanket.

## PERFORMING ABLUTION WITH SAND OR EARTH

Because of Aisha, the verses about *tayammum* (using earth for ritual purity in the absence of water) were revealed. During a halt while the army was returning from the Banu Mustaliq campaign, Aisha realized she had lost a necklace belonging to her sister, Asma. She felt she should do whatever she could to find it and return it to its owner. She looked around in the darkness, but could not find it. She went to God's Messenger and together, they started to look for it. When others saw that God's Messenger was looking for something, they joined in the search.

But the necklace was not there. When everyone understood that they would not be able to find it, they started to rest again. The Messenger of God put his head on Aisha's lap and closed his eyes.

Some went to Aisha's father, Abu Bakr, and said:

"Do you see what your daughter did? She kept God's Messenger and his people in this place without even a sip of water!"

It was true. There was no water in their waterskins, or any sign of a well or spring nearby. They would rise at dawn to perform the Morning Prayer, but how could they perform their ablutions without water? They thought about it and were not able to solve the problem.

Abu Bakr became angry. If his daughter's necklace had not been lost, they would not have stayed there, and would have likely rested near a spring. With anger, he entered Aisha's tent, prepared to lecture

---

[179] Waqidi, *Maghazi*, 1:992.

her. Then he saw that the Messenger of God was resting in her lap, so he stopped, and then came closer slowly. Angrily, but quietly, he said:

"You made people and God's Messenger stay here, and they neither have a sip of water nor a chance to find water."

Aisha was in a difficult situation, as she had no reply and could not move because the Messenger of God was still resting. But suddenly, he woke up and quickly realized there was no water. He thought of his people who were suffering and who had to pray but did not have any water. Just then, the state of revelation descended on God's Messenger. From Gabriel came a verse declaring a different way of performing ablution in the absence of water:

> "...if you are ill, or on a journey, or if any of you has just satisfied a call of nature, or you have had contact with women, and can find no water, then betake yourselves to pure earth, passing with it lightly over your face and hands (and forearms up to and including the elbows). Surely God is One Who grants remission, All-Forgiving." (an-Nisa 4:43)

The new revelation had solved their problem. Now, when they were without water, they would not feel anxiety, knowing they could perform ablution with clean dust and do their Prayers until water was found.

Abu Bakr witnessed what God had bestowed on them, and where he had scolded and been angry, he now looked with great admiration. It was her mistake that had created an opportunity for revelation. Abu Bakr said:

"O my daughter, what a blessed person you are. As a result of the delay that you caused, God bestowed Muslims with ease and blessings."[180]

Others too, understood this superiority. A short time later, Usayd ibn Khudayr came to Abu Bakr and said admiringly:

---

[180] Ahmad ibn Hanbal, *Musnad*, 2:272 (26384); Ibn Majah, *Tahara*, 90 (565).

"This was not your first blessing, dear family of Abu Bakr."[181]

After the Prayer was performed, their journey started again. As Aisha's camel stood up, she noticed a shiny object that had been underneath it. She bent over and looked closer, and saw with joy that it was the necklace she had borrowed from Asma.[182]

---

[181] *Bukhari*, Tayammum, 1 (327, 329).
[182] *Bukhari*, Fadailu's Sahaba, 5 (3469).

# Chapter 3

Aisha the Immaculate

# THE SLANDER

It was also during the same expedition that Aisha experienced her greatest sadness. Abdullah ibn Ubayy ibn Salul, the leader of the Hypocrites, was on the lookout for an opportunity to reinstate the esteem he felt he had lost by the migration of the Muslims to Medina. He sought revenge against the Muslims, especially God's Messenger and Abu Bakr. He had thought of many different scenarios, but without the right opportunity, he had not been able to succeed. The Meccans had sent many letters to provoke him against the Medina Muslims and Ibn Salul had replied that he was prepared to give support, in the form of the soldiers and weapons that they wanted. He had planned to shatter the spirits of the Muslim army during the Battle of Uhud by leaving the battleground with a throng that constituted one-third of the army. He had helped and harbored the Meccan army by joining with several Jewish tribes, such as Banu Qurayza. Many of his plans had been executed but he had not been able to reach his goal. Every passing day worked against him and his followers. His allies, such as Banu Nadr, Banu Qaynuqa, and Banu Qurayza, had not obeyed the Medina treaty and had been forced to leave Medina. In short, Abdullah ibn Ubayy started to lose his base of support, and day by day, he saw his power diminish.

These events had deeply affected the Hypocrites, and seeing the success of their enemies produced hatred and rancor in their hearts, and directed them toward traitorous thoughts. Although unexpressed in words, Ibn Salul's real goal was to weaken the reputation of the Messenger of God and keep people away from him. Abu Bakr, the closest Companion of God's Messenger, was his first target. Ibn Salul found his chance in the region of the Muraysi Spring.

Abdullah ibn Ubayy and his closest friends voluntarily attended the Battle of Banu Mustaliq, though they had looked for excuses to stay in Medina during previous battles. They hoped to exaggerate small tensions that had erupted by chance at the Muraysi Spring to cause a rift in the bond between the Helpers and the Emigrants. Still not satisfied, Abdullah ibn Salul then took careful steps to offend the Messenger of God. The Helpers and the Emigrants, who had sacrificed their lives for each other without hesitation, were nearly made into enemies because of their plotting. If the Messenger of God had not intervened, an unending feud would have been ignited.

Ibn Salul, seeing that his first attempt had failed, continued to plot. About the Emigrants, among who was the Messenger of God, he went so far as to talk about biting the hand that fed them.[183] He also made threats, both publicly and privately:

"I swear to God, when we return to Medina, the dignified one will get the despicable one out of Medina."[184] This meant himself and the Messenger of God.

When some perceptive Companions recognized his plotting, and it seemed as if he could not continue, he denied what he had said and behaved as if he were as pure as snow. It came to the point where Umar proposed to kill him, but the Messenger of God said:

"No, Umar! Why? Then wouldn't people say, 'Muhammad is killing his friends'? Never!"

So it was best to set off immediately on their journey and the Prophet ordered so. Despite the high temperatures, they would return to Medina without having rested.

Then Gabriel came and informed the Messenger of God, one by one, about what the hypocrites had done and said, and then revealed the chapter al-Munafiqun (the Hypocrites).

---

[183] Ibn Hisham, *Sira*, 2:290; Ibn Sa'd, *Tabaqat*, 2:107.
[184] Al-Munafiqun, 63:8.

Ibn Salul, who had thought he would walk away with all his plotting, was then ostracized by his tribe and he abandoned all hope after the verses were revealed. Sincere people from his tribe, whom he had convinced to follow him, reproached him sharply and left him. His own son, Abdullah, was among them - he felt ashamed of what his father had done. But when a man told him that his father was going to be killed, Abdullah became upset. He waited for a time and then came to God's Messenger with sorrow and said:

"O Messenger of God, I heard that you want to kill Abdullah ibn Ubayy ibn Salul because of the information you got. If you plan to do that, please order me to kill him instead, and I will bring you his head. The Khazraj tribe knows that no one is as sensitive as I about doing good to his father. If you give this order to a man other than me, I could not endure seeing he who executed Abdullah ibn Ubayy ibn Salul living among my people, and I might kill him. Then I would be killing a believer in exchange for an unbeliever, and I am worried that I would be thrown into the hellfire."

It was a suggestion to freeze blood in one's veins. Even though he was his father, he would kill the man who had hurt God's Messenger. But the Messenger of God was merciful and said:

"No! On the contrary, as soon as he is among us we will treat him well and try to make him content."

Despite the reassurance from God's Messenger, his heart was not yet satisfied. He waited for his father, and first made his father's camel lie down, and then held his father by the shirt and said:

"I will not let you go until you say, 'The Messenger of God is dignified and I am despicable'."[185]

After this chain of negative events, they continued on their journey without resting until they were exhausted by the severity of the heat. Finally, a break was given, but it did not last long, and soon after, the Messenger of God gave the order to keep going. They rapidly approached Medina.

---

[185] *Bukhari*, Manaqib, 9 (3330).

Nothing disturbed God's Messenger or his Companions until they saw Safwan ibn Muattal[186] catching up from behind with Aisha atop his camel. Aisha had been forgotten in the region where they had rested. She had left to answer the call of nature, and again noticed her sister's necklace was lost and had searched for it. Because Aisha was very slender, the palanquin that she traveled in had been replaced on her camel without anyone noticing the difference in weight. When she had come back, there was no sign of the army. At first, she called for them but no one could hear her and she heard no one. She had no choice, so she squatted and started to wait for her people to notice her absence and come back for her. Before much time had passed, Safwan ibn Muattal, who had lagged behind the army came. When he saw an indistinct figure in the distance, he led his camel near it and was surprised to see she was the mother of the believers, Aisha. He said:

"God's Messenger's family has been left behind!"

Startled at the voice, Aisha quickly covered her face with her veil. But she was happy, since someone had come to guide her back to the army.

Safwan could not understand how the wife of God's Messenger and the mother of the believers had been left behind alone. He asked:

"May God grant His mercy on you. Who left you here?"

As he asked his question, he led his camel close. For the Companions, the mother of the believers deserved respect beyond their own mothers. In order to help her get on the camel comfortably, he jumped off, lowered the camel, stepped aside and said:

"Please, you can get on."

He held the halter of the camel while Aisha rode it. In this way, they approached the rear of the army.

Ibn Salul had seen the scene of Aisha's arrival with Safwan; it was precisely a scene that someone could use to cause discord. His eyes met

---

[186] Safwan ibn Muattal was praised by the Prophet with the words: "I know nothing but goodness about him" and "The person God clothed in clothes of Paradise."

with the eyes of others and together they started to slander Aisha. It was not the first time that a monument of chastity had been vilified—now Aisha was like the Virgin Mary.

The Hypocrites planned to wear out the Messenger of God by attacking him indirectly. Whispering furtively, they spread the slander secretly, hoping to cause a new rift among the Muslims. Ibn Salul's fear had grieved him deeply but now his eyes were shining with pleasure. It was his chance to take revenge on the Messenger of God and to cover his own mistakes by keeping people busy with the slander of Aisha. He hoped too, that it would confuse people about the message of God's Prophet and shake their faith in him. All at once, he was brazen and peeling back the shame that had covered him; his real personality shone through.

It was a systematic slander. Before they had reached Medina, there was no one left who had not heard it. If the same lies were spoken everywhere, people would not know what to believe. In this way, the Hypocrites thought to take the revenge they had sought for years, and dreamed of the pleasure they would experience in the future from the opportunity that had fallen into their hands.

## THE SICKNESS OF AISHA

Twenty-eight days had passed since they had started the journey for the Battle of Banu Mustaliq. When they returned to Medina, Aisha's weak body, unable to endure a month of privations, became sick. She alone remained unaware of the slander circulating about her. But the Hypocrites worked with speed. The Messenger of God and the family of Abu Bakr had heard the slander and were grieved. Perhaps because neither the Messenger of God nor Abu Bakr's family believed what had been said, they did not feel it was necessary to tell Aisha about the slander. But Aisha felt a difference in the behavior of God's Messenger. In her illness, he had not fussed over her as he had during previous sicknesses. Once, when her mother Umm Ruman was with her, he asked slightly about her health.

Aisha felt hurt and said:

"O Messenger of God, why don't you let me go to my mother's during my illness so she may take care me?"

The Prophet said:

"You know what is best."

Though Aisha did not understand why the Prophet was behaving coldly, her feelings led her to her family's home. She stayed with her mother, Umm Ruman. Twenty days later, she was able to pull herself together. She rose from bed, but remained ignorant of what was being said about her.

Some people came to visit her during her illness and one night she went outside with one of them, Umm Mistah, a close relative, to answer the call of nature. Just then, Umm Mistah's foot got stuck and she stumbled and fell. When she got up and tidied herself, she cursed:

"Damned Mistah!"

Aisha was shocked, wondering how a woman could curse her own son, who was virtuous. Aisha, known for the depth of her Islamic knowledge, felt she should intervene about the mistake. She said:

"For God's sake! What a terrible thing to say about a man who is among the Emigrants and the soldiers of the Battle of Badr."

Umm Mistah looked with confusion and surprise at Aisha. Her son, Mistah, was among those who was spreading the slander. A moment later, she replied:

"O daughter of Abu Bakr, don't you know what he said about you? It is possible that you are among the believing women who consider situations naively. Or do you really not know what happened?"

Even the question was confusing. Aisha was genuinely ignorant of all that had happened. She asked:

"What has he said? What situation? I am not informed about anything."

And she looked into Umm Mistah's face. Her look said, 'Tell me as soon as possible what is going on.' So Umm Mistah began to speak:

"There are some rumors about you."

And at length she explained the slander and resulting discord from the beginning.[187]

It was impossible to believe. The sickness which had been about to end was doubled; her eyes were filled with tears and her heart was filled with sorrow. She had difficulties breathing, and her sobs were suffocating.

She didn't have the energy to move her legs, and she was about faint. She asked:

"Is it true that all this has happened?"

It was her last sentence before she fainted.

After some time, with great effort, she regained consciousness. Yet she was not fully in control of herself. She said:

"Glory be to You O God! How can people talk like that?"

She got up with the help of Umm Mistah and went back to her father's house. She was exhausted, and though she wanted to arrive quickly by taking fast steps, her legs did not comply.

When she arrived home, she went to her mother and reproached:

"May God bestow mercy on you. Why didn't you tell me people were talking amongst themselves about me?"

Umm Ruman was a calm and mature person with a strong character. Under these circumstances, it was necessary to be cool-headed. She began to console her daughter tenderly:

"O my dear child, slow down a little. God will show you ease. I swear to God there is no woman as beautiful as you, who is as loved by her husband, and who also has fellow wives: are there not people against her and who slander to disgrace her? Of course there is much gossip in such a situation."[188]

Umm Ruman had a point, but the slander that was circulating was not the kind that could be tolerated. Many nights passed, but Aisha was unable to sleep.

---

[187] Ibn Hisham, *Sira*, 4:464.

[188] *Bukhari*, Shahada, 15, (2518).

Safwan had heard the slander of which he was accused and had learnt that some Muslims believed it. He went to one of them, Hassan ibn Thabit, and they argued. Their disagreement escalated to the point that it was shared with the Messenger of God.

Abu Bakr, who had helped and given charity to Mistah, changed his mind. When he heard that Mistah had spread the slander, he said that he would never give charity to him again.

The Hypocrites, following the progress of events, were very pleased; in the near past, while coming back from Banu Mustaliq, they had been a target, but now they were forgotten.

## THE COMPANIONS' REACTION AND BELIEF

The gossip confused the Companions as well, though very few of them even considered believing the slander. The overwhelming majority said:

"Glory be to God! This is terrible slander."

Many did not even comprehend the notion that Aisha could have committed adultery. Those who believed in the chastity and purity of Aisha in their hearts defended her constantly. At the end of a busy day, Abu Ayyub al-Ansari's wife asked him:

"Did you hear what people are saying about Aisha?"

Though he had heard, he behaved as if he had not heard anything because he knew who had started the slander and why. He knew that a woman who had become the wife of God's Messenger would never attempt such a thing. He said:

"I heard, but it is a lie!"

Perhaps he thought his wife could be affected by the slander, or perhaps he wanted her to fight against it. He said:

"O Umm Ayyub, for the sake of God please tell me, would you do such a thing?"

She was horrified, for those who believe in God and the Hereafter would never fall into such depravity, and she replied vehemently:

"I swear to God, I would never do that."

Abu Ayyub, with a sharp look, said:

"Do not forget that Aisha is more auspicious than you."

In the verses that would later be revealed, God the Almighty expressed that He was pleased with those, like Abu Ayyub, who firmly spoke against the slander, and that believers should always react strongly against slander.

The Messenger of God was worried about the absence of Gabriel; he was deeply sad because revelation had still not come. Usually divine revelations came quickly under circumstances such as these, and fully explained everything. Perhaps God Almighty was preparing the ground for the revelation to come, so that the message would be cemented in their minds.

The silence encouraged the slanderers and they even convinced some believers. The situation necessitated intervention. One day, after the Prayer, the Messenger of God turned to his Companions and said:

"O my people, society of believers, what excuse could a man have who has caused such trouble to me because of his slander about my family? I swear to God, I do not know anything but goodness about my family. The man who was also slandered never came to my house when I was not there."

The Messenger of God was hurt deeply and the Companions did not want to tolerate it anymore, but not everyone knew who the man was. The leader of the Aws, Sad ibn Muadh, stood up and said:

"O Messenger of God. I can solve this problem and bring you relief. If this man is from my tribe, I will cut off his head! If he is from Khazraj, who are our brothers, we will do whatever you order."

Affected by a statement that implicated his tribe, Sad ibn Ubada became tense and stood up, apparently knowing who was guilty. He replied to the leader of the Aws:

"You don't have the power to kill a man! You only say this because you know the guilty one is from Khazraj. If he were of your tribe, you would not say this."

The Messenger of God had delivered his sermon at the Friday Prayer, and now a quarrel was breaking out. Then Sad ibn Muadh's cousin, Usayd ibn Khudayr, stood up and replied to Sad ibn Ubada, accusing him of protecting the hypocrites:

"We would surely kill them! I swear to God that the ones who did this deserve to be beheaded!"

The atmosphere became tense, as if a hundred years of tension had built up. The real issue was nearly forgotten as tribal pride appeared among the Aws and the Khazraj. It was impossible for people to think clearly when feelings were so heightened. That day, no one could tolerate such statements, even briefly; sides were chosen and a quarrel began. It would be another war between the Aws and the Khazraj which, of course, was the real aim of the Hypocrites.

Calming them down was the duty of God's Messenger. He told both sides to be silent. Then he concluded his sermon and went home.

He called Usama and Ali to his house to consult with them. He was not confused about the innocence of his wife, Aisha, because it was as open and clear as the light of the sun. But the Messenger of God wanted to include the beliefs of others in his decision, because he wanted her purity to be acknowledged in front of everyone. Usama spoke decisively:

"O Messenger of God. We do not know anything but good deeds about your wife Aisha. These are definitely baseless lies and slander!"

God's Messenger's gaze then fell on Ali. Ali understood that God's Messenger was awaiting his response, but was not able to think of anything other than the sadness the Prophet was feeling, which he wanted to relieve. He felt the pleasure of God's Messenger was more valuable than the world and everything in it, and said:

"O Messenger of God, why are you giving yourself a hard time? May God Almighty protect you from experiencing more difficulties. There are many women other than her. Why don't you ask this servant girl, I am sure that she will say something that makes you feel better."

His words also included the meaning, "I am thinking only of you, not myself; perhaps you can ask about Aisha with the ones who know her better." So the Messenger of God called over the servant, Barira, and asked her:

"Did you see anything that made you suspicious about Aisha?"

Barira felt burdened to be the object of such an inquiry and her face turned red. She responded quite seriously:

"I swear to the God who sent you in justice, no. I do not know anything about her but goodness. I never witnessed even a tiny imperfection that I could criticize her about. The only thing I know is that one day, I left dough with her and she fell asleep near it, and a sheep came and ate that dough. For the sake of my ear and eyes, I swear that Aisha is as pure, clean, and unadulterated as gold!"

It was a perfect testimony, but the Messenger of God did not allow himself to be satisfied; he would seek other opinions too.

The Messenger of God decided to consult with his other wives, and he chose Zaynab bint Jahsh, with whom Aisha had a bit of rivalry. He also selected Zaynab because her sister, Hamnah, had believed the rumors about Aisha. He asked:

"O Zaynab, what do you say? Have you ever seen anything negative about her?"

She also replied that she knew nothing but goodness about Aisha.[189]

## THE GOOD NEWS

After some days passed, the Messenger of God came to the house of Abu Bakr and sat down after expressing his greetings. It was his first visit to them after he had returned from Banu Mustaliq.

At that time, Aisha was in the other room with her mother, crying and praying to their Merciful Creator about the slander. A woman from the Helpers was with them, from whom Aisha was trying to get details which she was unable to get from her mother and father.

After performing his Prayer there, the Prophet turned to Aisha and spoke.

---

[189] *Bukhari,* Shahada, 15 (2518).

He asked her to tell him the truth and that if she really did such a thing, he would ask forgiveness from God for her. He also said that if such a thing never happened and there was no doubt, then God Almighty would send news confirming her purity. He concluded by saying that if a servant accepts his fault, and repents to God, the Almighty accepts his servant's repentance.

Each word of God's Messenger hit Aisha like a sledgehammer. Although his speech emphasized the good news, it devastated her that he could mention adultery as even a possibility when she would willingly sacrifice her life for him. She felt exhausted. No tears were left to shed, and the blood in her veins felt dried up.

Aisha wondered who she could talk and share her problems with if the Messenger of God considered the matter this way.

Tongue-tied, Aisha felt numb and thought her heart might stop. She looked at the faces of her father and mother, silently begging them to defend her. But they remained quiet, and only said:

"We swear to God, we do not know how to respond to God's Messenger."

Even her own parents were affected by the slander.

Finally, Aisha turned to the Messenger of God, and mustering her bravery, she said:

"I swear to God, I will never repent or ask for forgiveness on this matter; God knows the slander is not true and I am innocent of all of it. If I repented for what people said about me, I would be repenting for something that did not happen. If I deny it, saying, 'this incident did not happen,' you will not believe me either. Nothing comes to my mind but the situation of Joseph's father, so I will say what he said: '*So (the proper recourse for me is) patience. God is Whose help is sought against (the situation) you have described*'" (Yusuf 12:18).

She had only one option. She begged to the One, Who is everyone for those who have no one. She wanted her innocence to be known by the Prophet. She believed completely she would not return empty-handed, so she kept supplicating to God.

A short time later, the change in God's Messenger caught her attention; beads of sweat appeared on his face. It could be understood from his state that he was receiving a message from Gabriel, who had not spoken for one month. He looked as if his soul would be crushed by the burden of receiving the message. Aisha started to hope. The door of the firmament had opened; a new message to settle the issue was coming. She couldn't look at her parents, whose faces had become pale with anxiety. Their hearts were skipping beats, worrying that a declaration confirming the truth of the slander would be revealed. But Aisha was relaxed because she knew that divine justice would be manifested.

Then the state of God's Messenger returned to normal and he looked at Abu Bakr's family, wiping away the sweat droplets that had gathered on his forehead. The grief that had filled the house until then would be replaced by pleasure, and they would watch the dark clouds overhead disperse because the Messenger of God was smiling. He had the serenity that had been absent since the Hypocrites had tried to set the city in an uproar. He addressed Aisha in a kind voice:

"I have good news for you, Aisha! God the Almighty revealed a verse that you are pure and that the slander is not true. Get up and praise God!"

A month of trouble was ending; what she had expected was revealed. Aisha's eyes shone with joy. She said:

"Glory be to God!"

Both Abu Bakr and his wife Umm Ruman felt relieved. Witnessing the delight of God's Messenger, Umm Ruman turned to Aisha, her daughter and the mother of the believers, and said:

"Come on! Get up and give thanks to the Messenger of God."

But at that moment, Aisha was full of tumultuous feelings. Her chastity and honesty had been announced directly by God Almighty and would remain permanent until the end of the world. The verses directly disproved the slander that had been spread about her for about a month. She felt thankful for the help of God alone, and said:

"No, I will not thank him. I thank only God the Almighty and praise Him."[190]

From then on, there were verses in the Qur'an acquitting Aisha, informing the believers of every era about the purity of her life.

The Messenger of God, excited to share the revealed verses with his people, recited them as follows:

> Surely those who invented and spread the slander are a band from among you. However, do not deem this incident an evil for you; rather, it is good for you. (As for the slanderers,) every one of them has accumulated sin in proportion to his share in this guilt, and he who has the greater part of it will suffer a tremendous punishment."(An-Nur 24: 11)

The Companions took a deep breath, because everyone knew who was in the band. But they had held their tongues and never dirtied their hearts. But the verses that followed were concerning them too: *"When you heard of it, why did the believing men and women not think well of one another and declare: 'This is obviously slander!'?"*

Apparently, choosing a good opinion was essential. It was necessary to close your ears to a rumor before its veracity was known. The safest route for Muslims was to believe in innocence unless guilt was proven. The continuing verses addressing the slanderers were like a slap in the face:

> Why did they not produce four witnesses (in support of the accusation) Now that they have not produced witnesses, it is indeed they who are the liars in God's sight. (an-Nur 24: 13)

In order to accuse a woman of adultery, one should have at least four witnesses or the accuser is assumed to be guilty of slander, which would be punished in this world and the next. Even on the Day of Judgment, an indelible mark on his brow will indicate that he is a liar, to be remembered as a liar forever. Though Aisha had suffered greatly

---

[190] *Bukhari*, Shahada, 15

for one month, she had gathered heavenly blessings for her undeserved grief. Through this incident, many injunctions of the religion were revealed, particularly for Muslim social life. Basing judgments on suspicion would be eliminated, and a new social model based on virtue would be established.

It was important for the Companions to show solidarity in controversial environments because God's Messenger was among them. For the Prophet's sake, they were safe from the natural disasters that befell other rebellious societies. The verses continued as follows:

> Were it not for God's grace and favor upon you, and His mercy in the world and the Hereafter, a mighty punishment would certainly have afflicted you (who got involved in circulating rumors) on account of what you indulged in. (an-Nur 24: 14)

Then the Companions understood that they should praise God for those blessings that had been bestowed. They also perceived that all sins should be taken seriously and never considered insignificant; they should be stopped in their infancy, before they reached adulthood.

The Qur'an addressed those who had heard the slander but paid little attention:

> Just think how you welcomed it with your tongues from one another and uttered with your mouths something about which you had no knowledge. You deemed it a trifle whereas in God's sight it was most grave. Why did you not say, when you heard of it, "It is not for us to speak of this. All-Glorified are You (O God)! This is an awesome slander." God admonishes you lest you ever repeat anything like this, if you are (truly) believers. He clearly expounds to you His instructions and the signposts of His way. God is All-Knowing, All-Wise. (an-Nur 24: 15)

The Qur'an describes both Joseph and Mary as examples of chastity and purity who were slandered. Aisha was similar. She was called 'the loyal woman' and addressed as 'the loyal daughter of the loyal man' referring to her father, Abu Bakr. Her disciple, Imam Masruq, gave her the latter title. Others called her "the loyal woman (Siddiqa), Aisha."

As with Joseph and Mary, Aisha was tested by being accused of adultery, despite her chastity, and showed she deserved her title with her loyalty and patience. Like Mary, Aisha was born in a home where the worship of God was woven into the daily fabric of life. Then she became the wife of God's Messenger, the most beloved servant of God, and never married any man other than him, even after his death. She was the target of Hypocrites and their allies, who wanted to soil her spotless reputation. Her troubled month ended with an acquittal. Like the others, her innocence was made clear by God Almighty —though in the case of Joseph, he was justified by one close to him, and in the case of Mary, she was acquitted by her infant son; Aisha was declared innocent by the direct words of God in the Qur'an. It bestowed on her a particular significance as the wife of God's final Messenger.

## THE WIVES OF GOD'S MESSENGER AND AISHA

The women who had the good fortune to become the wife of the most beloved servant of God were the mothers of believers, a title bestowed on them directly by God Almighty. But the wives were human beings too. They sometimes thought differently from each other and their relations with each other were thus affected. But each had a reason for her behavior and each should be considered within her time and situation. Otherwise, everything—from how people addressed each other, to how they communicated, to manners and more—could all be misunderstood, and the worth of these fortunate women cannot be perceived.

These blessed women were the confidants of God's Messenger and voluntary comrades on God's path. There was wisdom in their speech, as well as in their silences. Any evaluation which does not recognize their value, or any interpretation that does not draw from a full contextual understanding, has no benefit other than to show the ignorance of such evaluators and interpreters. Now, when we analyze Aisha's conversations and relationships with the wives of God's Messenger, two separate situations arise—one with Khadija, and the other with the rest of the mothers of the believers.

## KHADIJA

Khadija passed away before God's Messenger married Aisha, so they did not live a joint life, and they never shared his days. Despite this, Aisha envied Khadija most among the wives of God's Messenger because she was the sweetheart of his youth and his only means of consolation during those difficult years. During the fifteen years they shared before revelation, she was his loyal partner. In the chaotic environment of the first revelation, she was his greatest supporter. At the end, being a strong and unshakable woman, she was his helper. Her death coincided with the end of the difficult period. The Messenger of God never forgot his first wife, with whom he was so close and with whom he spent his most troubled days. Every chance he got, he turned a conversation toward Khadija, even during critical times.

Once, he hesitated when he saw the necklace that his daughter, Zaynab, had sent to save his son-in-law, Abu'l-As, who was among the captives of the Battle of Badr. The Prophet was moved because he remembered that it was a wedding gift to them from Khadija. The sight of the necklace took the Prophet into a reverie, and he remembered Khadija as she was in those days. After a little while, he turned to the people around and suggested they set Zaynab's husband free and give the necklace back to her.[191] Abu'l -As was set free for the sake of a memory from Khadija.

The situation did not change in later years. During the conquest of Mecca, while he was walking with thousands of people to the city, people realized that he had changed his direction and was going to Khajun. The people watched him curiously and again witnessed an example of his fidelity, because the Prophet was visiting the grave of

---

[191] *Abu Dawud,* Jihad, 121 (2692); Ahmad ibn Hanbal, *Musnad,* 6:276.

his dear wife Khadija. Before the conquest of Mecca, an event that changed history, he prayed before her grave at great length.

His love and fidelity continued until his death. When a gift was given to him, he first sent it to Khadija's relatives. He honored them and showed them respect, giving them even the pillow on which he was sitting. When someone asked why, he replied:

"I love the ones she loves, too."[192]

He never allowed anything to be said against her and immediately interfered if someone said something negative. One day, when the conversation turned to Khadija, Aisha coyly said:

"As if there is no one in this world but Khadija!"

These words offended the Messenger of God, and he turned to Aisha and swiftly started to recount Khadija's qualities, one by one. Then he added that, at the same time, he had children who reminded him of her.[193]

One day, while God's Messenger was sitting at home, someone knocked on the door. He ran and opened it, saying:

O my God, Halah, Khuwaylid's daughter, Halah, came!"

He had recognized the voice of Khadija's sister, Halah. Again, the Messenger of God was taken into the past by the sound of her voice and her way of asking permission; apparently he saw Khadija in the personality of her sister.

Aisha, who had witnessed his excitement, watched with wondering admiration. The Messenger of God still loved Khadija so wholeheartedly. If he'd had such worthiness at his side, would she ever need to worry in this world or the hereafter? It was a love worth striving for, so there had to be a way to gain it, which would be possible if the real reason behind his love was known. So Aisha asked:

"What is the reason for your concern for this woman, who died years before and left you? God the Almighty has bestowed on you even more auspicious ones than her since then!"

---

[192]  Yamani, *Ummu'l Muminin*, 13
[193]  *Bukhari*, Fadailu's Sahaba, 50 (3607).

Her question explained what was going on in her mind; Aisha wanted him to explain his love for Khadija. It was impossible that someone as acute as herself would not know how he felt, so likely she was aiming to hear Khadija's worth directly from the Messenger of God's tongue.

The Messenger was again displeased with her words, and in a voice indicating his discontent, he asked:

"Was there someone like her? I swear to God that He never bestowed me one better than her! When people persisted in unbelief, she came and believed me. When people accused me of lying, she confirmed what I said. When people withheld their possessions from me, she brought whatever she had and gave it to me. And God granted me children with no one but her."[194]

Aisha got the answer she expected. At the side of God's Messenger, everyone had a special place, and loving one of them did not mean that he did not love the others. Because of Aisha's question, Khadija became known by all of Muslim society as a woman about whom nothing negative should be said.

Then it fell to Aisha to apologize to God's Messenger and ask forgiveness. She promised to never again say anything about Khadija.[195] God the Almighty bestowed the merit to Khadija of enjoying a love the others could never attain. She remained with the Messenger of God even after her death. Aisha would express her feelings about Khadija as follows: "Although I did not share the same days with Khadija, I did not envy any other wives of God's Messenger as I did Khadija. The Messenger of God mentioned her so often and spoke of her always with praise and admiration. Whenever he slaughtered a sheep, he would send some meat to Khadija's friends."[196]

---

[194] Ahmad ibn Hanbal, *Musnad*, 6:117 (24908).
[195] Tabarani, *Mujamu'l Kabir*, 23: 11.
[196] *Bukhari*, Nikah, 107 (4931).

## OTHER WIVES OF GOD'S MESSENGER

Years after Khadija passed away, Sawdah was the first woman to have the honor of becoming the Prophet's wife. Actually, the woman who arranged the marriages mentioned the names of Aisha and Sawdah at the same time. Sawdah married God's Messenger ten years after the revelation; Aisha married him four years after that marriage...

All the women he eventually married joined his household after the Emigration. They became the mothers of the believers as follows: Hafsah was in the third year; Umm Salama in the fourth year; Juwayriya and Zaynab bint Jahsh in the fifth year; Umm Habiba in the sixth year; Maymuna and Safiyya in the seventh year. God's Messenger was fifty-four when he married Aisha, fifty-six when he married Hafsah, fifty-seven when he married Umm Salama, fifty-eight when he married Juwayriya and Zaynab, fifty-nine when he married Umm Habiba, and sixty when he married Maymuna and Safiyya.

These fortunate women, who shared a home with God's Messenger, became the mothers of believers. Once, Sawdah was afraid that the Messenger of God was displeased and planned to divorce her, and she said:

"I beg you, do not divorce me and do not leave me far away from you. My time is not important; assign my days with you to Aisha."[197]

But the Prophet did not divorce her, and she would keep her title as mother of believers until the Day of Judgement.

## AISHA'S STATUS

But fate placed extraordinary roles on some of the Messenger's wives. Aisha's status, in particular, was special and acknowledged by the other wives.

It was because of Aisha that the Qur'an revealed the punishment for slander, and the sentence was applied directly by the Messenger of God. In other ways, too, Aisha was different than the other wives.

---

[197] *Bukhari*, Nikah, 97 (4914).

Because of Aisha, the verse about *tayammum* (performing ablution with sand or earth) was revealed, and Muslims learnt how to cleanse themselves in a place where there was no water. In Mecca, she was shown to the Messenger of God in a dream, and he was told directly by Gabriel that she would be his wife.

Aisha was the only wife of God's Messenger who was a virgin when they married. His other wives were widows.

Aisha was also the only one whose mother and father were Emigrants. Another distinction of her family was that four generations of the same family—including her grandfather, father, brother and two nephews—believed in God's Messenger and became Companions.

Aisha was the only wife who witnessed a revelation as it came to the Prophet. The Companions who wanted to bring a gift to the Messenger of God preferred to give it on his day with Aisha, believing he would be happier and more likely to accept it.

Aisha was the only one who saw Gabriel (in human form) and Gabriel greeted her as well.

Aisha's bridal due was higher than the others. Years later, she explained this and accepted only Umm Habiba, whose wedding was held in Ethiopia:

"Her marriage ceremony was done by a king."

After the day that Sawdah gave her turn to Aisha, the time that Aisha spent with God's Messenger was double that of the others.

Aisha had a different kind of relationship with the Messenger of God, who wanted to make her content. Sometimes, she behaved coyly as a result of her favored position, and enjoyed how the Messenger of God tried to please her.

The Messenger of God raced against her twice during his life.

God's Messenger said that he had seen Aisha in heaven, and described the shining whiteness of her palms. She was surely the best among the mothers of believers, with whom God's Messenger was content when he died.

Aisha became distinguished in knowledge—no other wife, and no woman among the Companions, narrated as many hadiths as she. The depth of her knowledge had a stronger influence than any other woman, including the other wives of God's Messenger. When those who were unable to decide on an issue came to ask her about the matter, they left her place without worry and with an answer.

When his sickness worsened, God's Messenger wanted to spend his last fourteen days with her. He passed away with his head in her lap. Aisha continued to share the same room with God's Messenger after his death. After he passed away, God's Messenger was buried into the soil in Aisha's room, where the soil was the most auspicious on earth. After his death, Aisha became the best source for information about his behavior. Everyone, even the leading Companions, applied to her, and everyone left with an answer.

Her submission in worship, her sensitivity in fasting and Prayer, her asceticism and devotion to God, and her desire to give away whatever she had were the unique characteristics that showed her virtue.

People who considered her according to her innate superiority respected her more, and competed with each other to please her in order to receive her prayers on their behalf. Umar treated her even more respectfully than the other mothers of the believers, including his own daughter, Hafsah, and reserved more for Aisha than anyone else when he divided the spoils during his Caliphate.

Considering her situation from the outside, and taking feminine characteristics into account, it would have been normal for Aisha to envy Sawdah, whom the Messenger of God had married four years before her. But this was not true; on the contrary, Sawdah was one of the mothers of the believers with whom Aisha found intimacy and friendship. Aisha said:

"What a noble woman she was! I did not see a more likable woman than Sawdah, whom I desired to be."[198]

Umar's daughter, Hafsah, became Aisha's closest friend, almost as if the alliance between their fathers was reflected in them, as well. They

---

[198] *Muslim*, Rada, 47 (1463).

spent time together, consulted each other, and understood and respected each other's opinions.

Umm Salama was known for her clever, keen intellect. Her role in decreasing the tension at Hudaybiya was so crucial that it cannot be undervalued.[199]

Aisha praised the good fortune of Juwayriya:

"I do not know anyone but her who was so beneficial to her society."[200]

Aisha used many similar kind expressions to speak about the other mothers of the believers, but of course each of them kept the Messenger of God away from the others for one day. Under normal circumstances, someone in her position could have considered those who kept the most beloved servant of God away from her with displeasure. With the exception of some minor incidents, Aisha's attitude did not change, and she never had difficulty accepting the preference of God's Messenger.

Before God's Messenger even expressed his desire, she understood what he wanted. Aisha cared about meeting his needs before he asked. She knew there were various reasons for each of his marriges—with some, he aimed to create ties with the Meccans; with others, he hoped to solve problems with Jewish tribes; and with others, he wanted to help some tribes warm to Islam. His aim was often successful, too partly due to his marriages, there were mass conversions to Islam.

Some of his marriages resulted from revelation, such as his marriages to Umm Habiba and Zaynab. It is possible to say that the conquest of Mecca started on the day when the Messenger of God married Umm Habiba[201], and that as a result of his marriage with

---

[199] *Bukhari*, Shurut, 15 (2581).

[200] Abu Dawud, ltq, 2 (3931); Ahmad ibn Hanbal, *Musnad*, 6:277 (26408).

[201] It is known that the Prophet married Umm Habiba after the revelation of the verse meaning: *"...it may be that God will bring about love and friendship between you and those of them with whom you are in enmity."* (al-Mumtahana 60:7)

Zaynab[202], many erroneous problems and practices were eliminated without strife and replaced by the beauty of Islam.

Their home was like a school; it was continually producing answers to questions that people might come across in the future. Examples of all the feelings that could arise in women were shown, and people examined the Messenger of God's life to determine their own approach. From a visionary perspective, perhaps it should be said that these occurrences in the house of felicity needed to happen to be an example for future Muslims. Otherwise, it would have been impossible to find the best way to solve similar problems among women, whose sensitivity is innate. Their feelings were the temporary and transitory results of a variety of situations. God's Messenger was the object of jealousy and envy, too.

It was not forbidden to point out a distinction approved by God. Aisha sometimes did this to win God's Messenger's approval for herself. One day, she went to the Messenger of God and coyly said:

"O Messenger of God, if you came to a valley full of fruit trees and saw some trees in which their fruits had been eaten and others that had never been touched, where would you choose to take a break and tie your mount?"

Her meaning was clear, and God's Messenger understood her; she was his only wife who was a virgin upon their marriage. The Messenger of God gave her the answer she expected:

"Near the trees whose fruit still had not been touched!"[203]

The women of the Prophet's home each had a different nature, and of course some preferred the company of each other. While Aisha was close to Hafsah, Sawdah, and Safiyya, Zaynab was closer to Umm Salama and a few others.[204]

Next to Aisha, Zaynab had perhaps the most influence in the house; she was the daughter of the Prophet's aunt on his father's side,

---

[202] *"We united you with her in marriage…"* (al-Ahzab 33:37).
[203] *Bukhari*, Nikah, 9 (4789
[204] *Bukhari*, Hiba, 7 (2442).

and the sister of Abdullah ibn Jahsh, a loyal Companion. Her marriage with the Prophet was arranged directly by revelation.

The preferences of some wives over others were not like cliques. Being close to someone did not mean being distant from someone else. Though they held different opinions and had different feelings, all it took was remembering the preference and attitude of God's Messenger, and their issues were resolved peacefully.

Despite everything, there was mutual respect among them. Zaynab was the foremost among those who prepared Aisha for her wedding after Hijra and among those who defended her when she was slandered.[205]

Most of the time, the Prophet's wives competed to earn good deeds and heavenly rewards; they wanted for themselves as many good deeds as the others, but without lessening the others' good deeds.

When the Messenger of God wanted to seclude himself in the mosque (*itiqaf*), a tent was pitched in the Prophet's Mosque and he stayed in the tent during the last ten days of Ramadan. Once, a tent was pitched for Aisha in the courtyard of the mosque, too. Then the desire to worship similarly appeared in the other mothers of believers, who wanted to be close to God and His Messenger, and they also asked for tents. First Hafsah, and later Zaynab, requested permission to have tents, too. When the Messenger of God saw the tents in the courtyard of the mosque, he asked:

"What are these?"

After he heard the answer, God's Messenger was somewhat unhappy and asked:

"Now, do all of you intend to create good deeds with all of these tents?"

It was impossible for the women to enjoy worship if their competitive feelings were piqued. Intervening, God's Messenger ordered

---

[205] *Bukhari*, Tafsir, 18 (4473, 4479)

them to dismantle the tents, and quit his seclusion in the middle, intending to complete it in the next month (of Shawwal).[206]

On one of God's Messenger's journeys, Zaynab and Safiyya drew lots to accompany him. The journey was long and conditions were severe, and the camel that Safiyya was riding became tired and unable to walk. Since Zaynab had an additional camel, God's Messenger said:

"Since Safiyya's camel is not able to walk, I want you to give her a camel."

It was a perfectly reasonable suggestion. But the Arabs harbored grievances against the Jewish tribes, primarily those of Banu Qaynuqa, Banu Nadr, Banu Qurayza, Khaybar, and Wadi al-Qura. Safiyya's father, Huyayy ibn Akthab, had led many campaigns against the Muslims, which had led to deep-seated prejudices against Jews. Without thinking, she said:

"Me? Give to that Jew?"

Her thoughtless words injured the Messenger of God deeply and he became angry. He determined that this was not the attitude of a believer and it belonged to the dust of history. He adopted a very serious stance against Zaynab, and to make his feelings even more evident, he avoided her for several months. Zaynab was in great distress, and paid severely for what she had said. She lost the pleasure of being together with God's Messenger, her greatest happiness in the world. Zaynab repented and asked for forgiveness to God, and prayed to return again to the past days. When the period of estrangement had lasted so long, she began to think it was only a dream that they could ever be reconciled. She even started to pack up her pillow and mattress. As a last resort, she visited Aisha and, to save herself from the gloomy situation, asked Aisha to mediate between herself and God's Messenger.

It was a suitable idea, and Aisha's mediation was sure to result in a solution because Aisha pleased God's Messenger. One day, not long after, the Messenger of God came to Zaynab in the middle of the day.

---

[206] *Bukhari*, Itiqaf, 6 (1928).

Thus ended her gloomy days, and the black clouds over her home dispersed as the shining face of God's Messenger appeared in her place again. But there would be one difference—there would not be any discriminatory talk against anyone from then on.[207]

Although Aisha was envied without malice because of her favored position at the side of God's Messenger, Aisha said the following praising Zaynab:

"I did not see any woman more sensitive to religious issues than Zaynab. Surely, she was the most pious and fearful of God; her conversation was the most truthful, and she cared the most for her relatives. Zaynab led in giving *sadaqa* (voluntary charity), sacrificed herself the most to help others, and was the most unreachable in her closeness to God. Though she had a hot-tempered nature, her anger subsided very quickly."[208]

One day, the Messenger of God told them:

"The one among you who will first reunite with me is the one who has the longest arm." After he passed away, his wives remembered his words and came together to figure out who would be the first to die after God's Messenger. They stretched their arms and tried to measure whose arm was the longest, but were unable to reach a conclusion. Aisha explained:

"We continued to measure our arms until Zaynab bint Jahsh died. When she passed away, we understood that the one who had the longest arm was Zaynab, and the real meaning of 'the longest arm' was the charity she gave to help needy people. We all gave to the needy, but she gave so much with her own hand, saving any money she had little by little, to give for the sake of God as charity."[209]

One day, Aisha indicated the petite height of Safiyya to God's Messenger, and coyly said:

"What you spare to her is enough for her."

---

[207] Abu Dawud, *Sunan*, 4 (4602); Ahmad ibn Hanbal, *Musnad*, 6: 131 (25046).
[208] *Muslim*, Fadailu's Sahaba, 83 (2452); Nasa'i, *Ishratu'n Nisa*, 3 (3944).
[209] *Bukhari*, Zakah, 10 (1354).

Her meaning was that he did not need to allocate more time for her. Her attitude angered God's Messenger and he said:

"If what you said was poured into an ocean, it would surely become turbid."

Upon hearing this, Aisha became sad. She had not meant to make God's Messenger angry, or to criticize Safiyya. She said:

"I only wanted to describe her."

But the Messenger of God turned to her and said:

"Even if the world were given in return, I would never be pleased with that kind of description!"[210]

After that, to keep her heart away from any kind of negativity, Aisha took Safiyya into her room and became her friend, and they worked together on important things.

Safiyya, who was known for her talent at cooking as well as her beautiful face, and who was envied by the other wives because of her cooking skills, left one hundred thousand drachmas as an inheritance when she passed away, bequeathing one-third to her sister's son. Aisha, upon learning that some did not want to give such a large amount to the nephew because he was Jewish, immediately intervened:

"Fear God and give him what was bequeathed to him!"[211]

The wives of the Prophet strived to be fair, and when one of them was hurt, they immediately tried to please her and help her forget what had happened. As the wives of God's Messenger, it was impossible not to desire the simplicity and purity of their lives.

When Umm Habiba was dying, she turned to Aisha, who was with her and said:

"Since both of us were the wives of God's Messenger, it is possible that there were certain rights you had over me and vice versa. May God the Almighty forgive both you and me for this reason."

---

[210] *Abu Dawud*, Adab, 40 (4875); *Tirmidhi*, Sifatu'l Qiyama, 51 (2502).
[211] Ibn Sa'd, *Tabaqat*, 8:128.

Available sources do not indicate even a small problem between Aisha and Umm Habiba. But these blessed women were sensitive because they enjoyed the pleasure of being the wife of God's Messenger, and they were so conscious of their responsibilities that they did not want to leave anything unfinished or broken as they passed from this world to the next. In response, Aisha prayed:

"May God the Almighty forgive you for everything, pardon your imperfections and keep you away from troubles."

Umm Habiba became very happy. She looked at Aisha and said:

"You have made me happy, may God make you happy, too!"[212]

They were the best examples of virtue and their relationships with each other were also virtuous. We must indicate once more that small jealousies and envies that occasionally erupted were never permanent. The Messenger and his revelations and behavior caused them to ponder deeply and return to moderation and justice.

One day, the wives came together in Sawdah's room and discussed Aisha's status with God's Messenger. After long conversations, they concluded:

"O Umm Salama, we swear to God you see that people wait for Aisha's day to bring a gift to the Messenger of God. As Aisha wants nothing but good deeds, we also want nothing but good deeds. Why don't you visit God's Messenger and tell him to tell his people to bring gifts whenever they want and however they wish instead of having this preference."

This was the general consensus, so Umm Salama told God's Messenger. He was displeased and turned away. Returning in misery, Umm Salama explained what had happened, but they insisted she go again. His reaction was the same—God's Messenger was displeased by this suggestion. Umm Salama again returned dispirited. Still, they wanted her to return and ask again, and when Umm Salama went to God's Messenger for the third time with the same request, he became angry and said:

---

[212] Hakim, *Mustadrak*, 4:24 (6773); Ibn Sa'd, *Tabaqat*, 8:100.

"O Umm Salama, do not give me a hard time about Aisha. I swear to God I never receive a revelation when I am with any of you, but only her."

Realizing the gravity of the issue, Umm Salama immediately changed her attitude and gave up the request:

"I ask forgiveness from God since I gave you a hard time about Aisha, O Messenger of God."

The other wives, who had felt neither the atmosphere or the strength of the Prophet's reply, probably thought she had not been able to express their opinion clearly. This time, they asked Fatima to mediate:

"Go to the Messenger of God and tell him about our situation, saying, 'your wives expect justice from you about the daughter of Abu Bakr, for the sake of God'."

Probably not aware of what had happened, Fatima passed on the message from the wives to the Messenger of God. She witnessed a great change in his countenance—he suddenly became angry and asked:

"O my daughter, do you love the one I love?"

It was a rhetorical question, and she answered yes without hesitation.

It seemed God's Messenger did not like third parties to interfere with an issue between himself and his wives. His tone froze Fatima in her place, and she gave up her request; she explained the situation to his wives. They wanted her to return and explain their intention more clearly, but Fatima refused. For the Prophet's daughter, this door was closed, and all their insistence was in vain, for they were not able to change her mind.

The wives next decided to send Zaynab with the message. She had distinction among his wives, for their marriage had been revealed to God's Messenger by Gabriel, in a verse that is recited. Her kinship with God's Messenger, too, gave her maturity and standing. Zaynab came and insisted:

"Your wives ask for justice about the daughter of Abu Quhafa's son, for the sake of God."

She raised her voice a little, and Aisha heard it as well. Noticing that Aisha had overheard, God's Messenger glanced at Aisha, and was guided by her reaction. Then Aisha and Zaynab started to talk amongst themselves. Aisha was brilliant, and had a well-known talent for discussion and persuasion, and finally Zaynab gave up her argument. Watching all that unfolded, the Messenger of God looked at Aisha and praised her:

"After all, you are Abu Bakr's daughter!"[213]

## THE PROHIBITION *(TAHRIM)*

The Messenger of God got into the habit of visiting his wives after the Afternoon Prayer. He asked about their well-being and spent some time with them. He established a regular time for each of them, to just be with them. After the visits became habit, the Prophet's wives began to expect his arrival, and began to await the visit of God's Messenger after every Afternoon Prayer.

One day, as they sat and waited for God's Messenger, the time became late and they did not hear from him. Every passing minute made them anxious because they were concerned they would miss the time with the Messenger of God to which they were accustomed.

God's Messenger suddenly appeared, and they became excited and welcomed him immediately. Even though it was late, his shining face appeared, honoring their home with his presence. But a suspicion lurked in their hearts. Aisha spoke on behalf of the other wives and asked the reason for the delay. The Prophet said:

"A woman from Zaynab's tribe brought me a bowl of honey as a gift."

---

[213] *Bukhari*, Hiba, 7 (2442).

The women understood that the reason for the delay was Zaynab. They were slightly envious, but they did not reveal this to God's Messenger.

Speaking amongst themselves, they remembered that the Messenger of God was sensitive to bad smells and avoided them.[214] So they decided to ask when God's Messenger came near, "What did you drink?" and "What is this smell?" Then, when he responded, "I drank honey sherbet," each wife would reply something to the effect of, "perhaps that bee gathered pollen from malodorous flowers."

It happened as they planned. Whomever he approached, the Messenger of God got the same reaction. Each time, he said:

"No, I only drank honey sherbet near Zaynab."

Though his reply was mild, God's Messenger was offended and saddened, and he even swore that he would never drink honey sherbet again.[215]

Such a minor oath by an ordinary person would mean very little, but the Messenger of God was not ordinary. He was the sole recipient of revelation, which was ongoing. The religion was shaped under the light of revelation. Therefore, a judgment was established on every sentence that passed his lips, and would become an example for his followers.

A short time later, Gabriel came with a new revelation. The Messenger of God was sweating and seemed to be suffering under the burden of responsibility settled on his shoulders, almost as if he were crippled.

Afterward, a smile appeared on his face again. God the Almighty had addressed him:

> O Prophet! Why do you forbid (yourself) what God has made lawful to you, seeking to please your wives? And Allah is Forgiving, Merciful (at-Tahrim 66: 1).

---

[214] *Bukhari*, Hiyal, 11 (6571).
[215] *Bukhari*, Tafsiru's Sura, 386 (4628).

From the verse, the warmth of being close to God was felt, and revealed new aspects of religion to humanity on the behalf of God's Messenger. The first was that a person should never regard something that God permitted as unlawful. The second was that such a position would require forgiveness, and the knowledge that we can only be forgiven by God, through His All-Forgiving and All-Merciful attributes. The third was to clarify that those who swore an oath to give up a permissible thing could revoke it by paying its atonement. The verse continued:

"God has already decreed for you (O believers) on the breaking of your oaths (of not fulfilling what is not just and right, and the expiation thereof). God is your Guardian, and He is the Knowing, the Wise."

## AISHA AND FATIMA

Among the daughters of God's Messenger, Fatima had the closest relationship with Aisha. They lived together in the same house for a while, until Fatima married Ali. Aisha was among those who prepared Fatima for her wedding. Though their lives were very simple, their pleasure was immense. In telling us of that day, Aisha passed on the following lessons:

"The Messenger of God told us to prepare Fatima since she was going to marry Ali. We went to the home immediately and brought an amount of soft soil from Batha, which we spread on the ground. We filled two pillow sheets with fiber. Then we prepared bowls of dates and grapes and spring water to drink, and placed a stake at one edge of the house for clothes, pots, and pans to be hung. I have not seen any wedding better than Fatima's!"[216]

Only a wall separated the room where Fatima lived with Ali from Aisha's room, and that wall had a window. Sometimes, they came together and talked through this window.[217]

---

[216] *Ibn Majah*, Nikah, 24 (1911).
[217] Nadawi, *Siratu Sayyidati Aisha*, 122.

Aisha was Fatima's best friend and shared nearly everything with her. Fatima talked of her joy, her sadness, and her goals she was not able to achieve. One day, when her hands became swollen from grinding wheat into flour, Fatima asked God's Messenger for a maid. She returned without one, and Aisha was the one with whom she shared her problems.[218]

Fatima loved Aisha very much. Their love and respect was mutual, because for Aisha, Fatima held a unique place. One day Aisha was asked:

"Who was the most beloved at the side of God's Messenger?"

Without thinking, she responded, "Fatima."[219]

Aisha also said:

"After her father, I have never seen anyone more beautiful than Fatima."[220]

She never looked at Fatima with malice. She said:

"I did not see anyone, more than Fatima, who looked more like the Messenger of God in terms of the dignity and serenity of her behavior, and the elegance and politeness of her posture and manner of walking... When she entered the Messenger of God's place, he used to stand up for her, kiss her and make her sit near him. When God's Messenger came to Fatima's place, she would do the same thing."[221]

The virtue of Fatima was conveyed to Muslim society through Aisha. During the incident of *Ahl al-Bayt* (household members), taking first Fatima, then Ali, Hasan and Husayn under his wool blanket, the Messenger of God said:

"These are my *Ahl al-Bayt*."[222]

It was the days before the death of God's Messenger. His wives came together and sat in his presence. Then Fatima came, and her style

---

[218] *Bukhari*, Khums, 6 (2945).

[219] *Tirmidhi*, Manaqib, 61 (3874); Hakim, *Mustadrak*, 3:171 (4744).

[220] Tabarani, *Mujamu'l Awsat*, 3:137 (2721); Abu Ya'la, *Musnad*, 8: 153 (4700).

[221] *Abu Dawud*, Adab, 155: (5217).

[222] *Tirmidhi*, Manaqib, 61 (3871); Ahmad ibn Hanbal, *Musnad*, 6:304 (26639).

did not depart from her father's; even her steps were parallel to his. Upon seeing her, the Messenger of God said:

"Welcome, my daughter."

With great respect and concern, he bade her to sit near him. It was as if there had been something missing and her arrival allowed the scene to become complete.

Then the wives witnessed that the Messenger of God bent to Fatima's ear and whispered something to her secretly. The room was filled with a deep silence. She started to cry. Her weeping apparently touched God's Messenger, and to stop it, he came closer and again said something in her ear. Shockingly Fatima, who had been sobbing, began to smile. Aisha could not stand not knowing what made her cry first and smile later, so she went to Fatima and asked:

"The Messenger of God preferred to say something only to you, despite the presence of his wives, and you started to cry. Could you please tell me what he said?"

Fatima responded:

"I cannot reveal the secret of God's Messenger."

Fatima would not share what the Messenger of God had told her with anyone, not even Aisha. Yet, Aisha would not give up until she satisfied her curiosity.

After the Messenger of God had passed away, Aisha asked Fatima again:

"For the sake of my rights over you, what did the Messenger of God whisper to you that day?"

When Fatima responded, "I can tell you now," Aisha became very happy, as if the whole world had been given to her, because she would learn a secret only Fatima knew, information that was related to the Messenger of God's feelings for his society. Fatima said:

"The first time when he whispered in my ear, he told me that although Gabriel usually came once every Ramadan to recited the whole Qur'an, this year he came twice. He said, 'I guess my death is near!' and he advised me to 'Be patient, fear God, and to not give up piety.'"

"When he saw that I had started to cry, he leaned in again and told me the good news that I would be the first one among his family who would be reunited with him. He said, 'O Fatima! Do you want to be the first lady among believing women or the first lady of this world?' This was the reason for the smile you saw."[223]

## THE LAST DAYS WITH THE MESSENGER OF GOD

Days had passed. The day that Aisha married the Messenger of God was fresh in her memory, as if it were yesterday, though ten years had passed. She had been living a completely different life for a decade— she was the mother of believers; the open door for the weak, the needy, orphans, women, and those who sought knowledge. But signs indicated her time with the prophet was coming to an end. For the last year, there had been a sense of saying farewell.

It was the last Monday of the month of Safar. The Prophet went to the Baqi Cemetery to perform a final duty for his Companions— again making amends for all that had passed with those in their graves.

While he walked back, his head started to ache severely, and he became feverish. His temperature was so high it could be felt outside the turban he wrapped around his head.

At the same time, Aisha's head began to ache, too. To express that they were together even in difficulties, Aisha turned to the Messenger of God and said:

"Oh, how bad my headache is!"

She hoped to make the Messenger of God talk a little and forget his troubles a bit. But she got a response she did not expect:

"How bad my headache is!"[224]

Everyone looked at the Messenger of God with compassion. His was clearly a different kind of headache that they had not noticed at first, and one whose pain did not seem to ease.

---

[223] *Bukhari*, Manaqib, 22 (3426).
[224] Ibn Sa'd, *Tabaqat*, 2:206, 233.

His state did not improve for the next eleven days. But he continued to come to the mosque to lead his society in congregational Daily Prayers.

Even while dying, his good manners and sense of justice made him abide the daily schedule for his wives. Yet his wives understood that both his heart and mind were with Aisha. Everything they had experienced until that day elevated their understanding to a point where they started to consider his preference as natural. Aisha, who had an unparalleled perception and acuity, should witness his final days, to accurately record what she saw and heard. All of his wives gave up their turns, and because their voluntary preference made the Messenger of God happy, it pleased Aisha even more. The Messenger of God spent his last days with Aisha, until he would reunite with the ultimate beloved one.[225]

The Messenger of God had difficulty standing up, and most of the time, he could only walk by dragging his feet. He went to Aisha's room with the help of two people. He would stay there until his last breath.

He appeared among the people again on Thursday, and despite his pain, he wanted them to write down what he said to keep them away from taking wrong steps after his death. He told those near to himself:

"Come close to me and let me dictate something, and in this way, you will not fall into heresy after me."

It was a touching scene, but many who saw his suffering said:

"Don't you see how the Messenger's pains have increased and how he suffers! We have the Qur'an, and God's book is enough for everything."

The Companions were divided in two. Some felt this way, others thought they should do as he asked and record what he said. As the conversion continued, the Prophet looked uncomfortable, and he turned to them and said:

---

[225] *Bukhari*, Janaiz, 94 (1323).

"Keep away from me!"

He returned to Aisha's room. Despite his high fever and the severity of his pain, he continued to appear in society and perform Prayers with them. He went to the mosque for the Evening Prayer and recited the entire chapter of Al-Mursalat during the Prayer.

Then he returned home again, and the scene frightened Aisha, because his illness increased with every minute. He looked as if he did not have the strength to stand up. He turned to Aisha and asked:

"Has the congregational Prayer been performed?"

It had not been. Until that day, they had performed every congregational Prayer in the mosque following God's Messenger. Since the Messenger of God had not come yet, they had waited for him, without performing the Prayer before his arrival. Aisha said:

"No, O Messenger of God. They are waiting for you."

He forced himself to stand up and said:

"Prepare water so that I may perform ablution."

What had been said was done. He raised himself, and with difficulty, performed the ablution. As he was leaving for Prayer, he fainted. The Messenger of God was unable to go to the mosque where he had gone every day. To the house of felicity came a terrible agitation and Aisha ran around in desperation. Fortunately, he came around soon after and asked:

"Did the people perform the Prayer?"

Aisha replied:

"No, O Messenger of God. They are waiting for you."

Though it was nice they had waited for God's Messenger, he did not think he had the strength to lead them. To Aisha, he said:

"Tell Abu Bakr to lead the people in Prayer."

This was also understood to be an approval of his closest Companion to become the leader of his society after he was gone. But Aisha said:

"O Messenger of God, my father is a tenderhearted person. He cannot hold back his tears when he starts to recite the Qur'an! Why not assign someone other than him?"

Behind her answer was anxiety that no one could fulfill the leadership position of God's Messenger. She felt that people would criticize any person who attempted to fill his absence, because they would feel the Messenger of God's absence, and Aisha wanted to protect her father from criticism. But the Messenger of God insisted:

"Tell Abu Bakr to lead people in Prayer!"

Aisha asked again, but his answer did not change. Her insistence annoyed the Messenger of God, and to indicate that her persistence was irrelevant, he said:

"It's as if you are like the women who quarreled about Prophet Joseph. Tell Abu Bakr he should be the imam and lead the people in Prayer."[226]

Aisha understood. Leading the people after the death of the Messenger of God would be difficult, but God's Messenger was choosing his successor. It meant her father, Abu Bakr, would manage his duties properly. So she sent a message to Abu Bakr and he led the Prayer. But his leadership would not be restricted to only one Prayer. After that time, the Messenger of God could never again attend the mosque, and Abu Bakr would lead the Prayers from then on.[227]

On Sunday, the Prophet was distributing whatever he owned, apparently aiming to leave this world as he had entered it. He gave to such an extent that Aisha sent their empty oil lamp to a woman and asked for a few drops of oil, in order not to leave God's Messenger in the dark.[228]

---

[226] *Bukhari*, Jama'a, 11 (633), 18 (646, 647).
[227] From the Isha Prayer on Thursday until the Fajr Prayer on Monday, Abu Bakr led seventeen Prayers in total before the Prophet passed away.
[228] Ibn Sa'd, *Tabaqat*, 2:239.

In their house, no food remained. They gave the Prophet's suit of armor, worn in battle, as collateral to a Jewish neighbor for thirty units of barley.[229]

On Monday, the Messenger of God moved aside the curtain that opened into the mosque from Aisha's room and looked upon his society. He was pleased with the scene—the congregation was orderly, following its imam, and performing their duties of worship. He closed the curtain with pleasure and returned to Aisha's room.[230]

After the Messenger of God whispered to his daughter, Fatima, he called his grandsons, Hasan and Husayn, kissed them and advised them to have good manners. At this time, the other wives went to Aisha's room, to witness the final moments of God's Messenger. The wives of God's Messenger were among those in his presence; he gave them advice in his last moments.

He turned to Aisha and asked:

"O Aisha, what did you do with the gold?"

Aisha went and immediately brought the gold to which he referred.

Taking the pieces in his hand, he counted, "...five, six, seven. How can Muhammad enter the presence of God while these gold pieces are with him? Take them and give them as charity!"[231] His pains grew more severe and he turned to Aisha and said:

"O, Aisha, you should have no doubt that I still feel the suffering of the meal that I ate at Khaybar. I feel as if my veins are being torn today as a result of that poison!"[232]

He covered his face with a piece of black wool cloth. When he felt hot and drowsy, he uncovered his face. Meanwhile, he spoke of Prayer:

"Prayer, Prayer." He repeated the word many times. He told his people to be sensitive and behave humanely toward slaves and

---

[229] *Bukhari*, Jihad, 88 (2759).
[230] *Bukhari*, Sifatu's Salat, 12 (721).
[231] Ahmad ibn Hanbal, *Musnad*, 6:49 (24268).
[232] *Bukhari*, Maghazi, 78 (4165).

servants.[233] On any issue in which he was afraid for his people's possible negligence, he gave advice.

Meanwhile, Aisha sat close to him and recited An-Nas and Al-Falaq, and stroked his holy body with her hand in the way she had learned from him.[234] After each recitation, she blew her breath over him, and asked God to heal him.

The signs were clear that the Messenger of God would soon depart this world for the Hereafter. He rested his head on Aisha's bosom and fixed his eyes on the ceiling. Abu Bakr's son, Abdurrahman, entered the room with a *miswaq* in his hand. The Messenger of God's eyes followed the *miswaq*. Our perceptive mother understood that he liked using the *miswaq* and asked:

"Should I take that for you?"

He nodded. She took it from her brother to give to God's Messenger. But the miswaq was so hard that Aisha asked:

"Should I soften this for you?"

He nodded again.

She softened it and then gave it to the Messenger of God.[235]

After cleaning his teeth, he held his finger up. His eyes were directed to the ceiling and his lips were moving. To hear him, Aisha brought her ear close to his mouth:

"Please forgive and embrace me with Your mercy together with the Prophets, the martyrs, and the true believers upon whom You bestowed blessings. Accept me to Your highest abode."[236]

Aisha had a gnawing suspicion, because once when he was healthy, she had heard him say:

---

[233] Hakim, *Mustadrak*, 3:59 (4388); Ahmad ibn Hanbal, *Musnad*, 6:311 (26699).

[234] *Bukhari*, Maghazi, 78 (4175), Tib, 31 (5403).

[235] *Bukhari*, Khums, 4 (2933).

[236] *Bukhari*, Tafsir, 69 (4310).

"No Prophet's soul is ever captured unless he is shown his place in Paradise. After that point, he either continues to live or is given the option to die."

As soon as she heard that he was asking for the highest abode, Aisha remembered his statement and told herself, "he will not be with us anymore."[237]

This was a time when there were no words. Asking God from the heart was the most vital action for the believer. Aisha implored God while holding the hand of the Prophet. She did not expect it, but just then he pulled his hand away. It was time to depart, and it was not proper to hold on to the world.

When he gave his last breath, his blessed head was on her bosom.[238]

It was Aisha's saddest day. Covering her face with her hands, she sobbed. She tried to stay strong, and placed a pillow under the head of God's Messenger. Then she called people to give them the sad news.

For the Companions who had waited for the time when he would return among them, it was a catastrophe. Medina was filled with mourning. Some, like Umar, who considered it impossible to live in a world without the Prophet, did not know what to do. But death was God's order. It had come and taken the Messenger of God to the other side of the thin curtain that separates this world from the Hereafter.

It was time to perform the final duty for the Messenger of God. The Companions, who did not know what to do in their suffering, were indecisive about where to bury his pure body. Then Aisha's father, Abu Bakr, recalled something in a flash:

"I remembered something that I had heard from the Messenger of God but had forgotten; the Messenger of God said, 'No doubt, God the Almighty takes the soul of a Prophet in the place where he would love to be buried!' So, we must bury him where his bed is."[239]

---

[237] *Bukhari*, Maghazi, 79 (4194).
[238] *Bukhari*, Janaiz, 94 (1323).
[239] *Tirmidhi*, Janaiz, 33 (1018).

God's Messenger would thus be laid to rest in Aisha's room. Touched by the scene, Abu Bakr said to Aisha:

"See, this is the first and most auspicious of your moons, O Aisha."

It was the statement that only Aisha could understand.

Years before, Aisha had had a dream in which three moons, in succession, rose over her room. When she had told Abu Bakr of her dream, he said:

"If this was a truthful dream, the most auspicious three people on earth will be buried in your room."[240]

Now, the most auspicious moon was rising over her room, as the Prophet was being buried there.

The Messenger of God would stay near her. The place was filled with so much warmth that she left only when she came to Mecca for a pilgrimage, or for short visits. This practice would continue until the end of her life.

---

[240] Hakim, *Mustadrak*, 3:62 (4400); Malik, *Muwatta*, Janaiz, 1:232 (548).

# Chapter 4

## After the Prophet

## THE ERA OF THE FOUR RIGHTLY GUIDED CALIPHS AND MUAWIYA

Though they suffered, life continued. Though the Messenger of God was absent, Aisha, who had spent the most time with him, and who had carefully observed him in a variety of situations, remained.

In her presence was a two-sided communication—people came and asked Aisha questions, or Aisha intervened when something wrong happened. Conveying the message continued, with Aisha as the teacher. She shared the knowledge that she had acquired from the Messenger of God, and was reassured that future generations would have healthy information about the religion.

One day, there was a land dispute between one of the Companions, Abu Salam, and others. The two sides could not agree to whom the land belonged. Abu Salam shared his troubles with Aisha, probably expecting her support. But after she had listened to him, Aisha told Abu Salam to keep away from that land since she had heard from the Messenger of God that whoever behaves unjustly, even for one unit of land, will be tormented after death.[241]

Another day, someone came to her and said that a number of people recited the whole Qur'an in one night, in one or two sessions, and wanted to know whether that was proper. She said:

"They recite, but in reality, they do not understand! The Messenger of God and I used to get up and perform Prayer nearly the whole

---

[241] *Bukhari*, Mazalim 14 (2321).

night. He recited Al-Baqara, Al Imran and An-Nisa. When he came to a verse that had a threatening expression in it, he immediately sought refuge in God from that punishment. When he recited a verse that included good news, he turned to God and asked for that reward."[242]

As before, people continued to bring their newborn children to the house of felicity to ask for prayers and blessings, and Aisha prayed and asked for God's blessings. One such day, while she was putting the baby back on his pillow, she noticed an amulet used for fortune telling on the pillow. She looked at it carefully and put it aside, and asked:

"What is this?"

They said:

"It will protect the baby from an evil spirit."

Aisha became angry. It was a deviation, and such a deviation so early after the death of God's Messenger meant an open invitation to many mistakes in the future. She threw away the amulet and said:

"There is no doubt that the Messenger of God banned fortunetelling, and was very angry with those who practiced his, too."[243]

After the conquest of new lands, people wondered about the permissibility of beverages that they had recently encountered, and so they asked Aisha. She approached each issue carefully, and reminded them of the statements of God's Messenger about intoxicants, and advised them to avoid drinking beverages of an unknown nature.[244]

During the season of *Hajj*, when all roads led to Mecca, women gathered around Aisha to ask any questions on their minds. It happened so frequently, that she would walk with a group of women who gathered around her. She considered their talks as a time to convey the message and advise them.[245]

---

[242] Ahmad ibn Hanbal, *Musnad*, 6:92 (24653).
[243] *Bukhari*, Adabu'l Mufrad, 1:314 (912).
[244] *Bukhari*, Ashriba, 7 (5273).
[245] Ahmad ibn Hanbal, *Musnad*, 6:225 (25923).

When she was in Mina, Aisha witnessed some teenagers laughing together amongst themselves. Pointing to them, she asked those around her what made them laugh.

They said:

"Someone was tangled up in the tent's rope and fell down, and he was about to break his neck and lose his eye."

She warned them:

"Beware, do not laugh. I once heard the Messenger of God saying, 'a Muslim is given a (higher spiritual) rank because of the thorn that pierced his foot or any suffering worse than this, and one of his sins is forgiven'."[246]

Aisha always had the goal of representing justice without considering who addressed her. People knew she was a treasure trove of knowledge, and continued to visit her often to receive the maximum benefit.

## THE CALIPHATE OF ABU BAKR

After the passing of God's Messenger, Abu Bakr became the Caliph (leader of the Muslim community). Although he was a sensitive and tenderhearted person, Abu Bakr regarded the consent of God above everything else. Uthman came to him during the early days of his Caliphate and mentioned that some of the Messenger's wives had requested their inheritance. But the Messenger of God had really left no wealth behind. Abu Bakr decided to ask his daughter, Aisha, whether she had any additional knowledge about the issue, because he knew that she was not among those asking for an inheritance.

Hearing this, Aisha shuddered and said:

"Glory be to God! There cannot be an inheritance when the Messenger of God said, 'We Prophets do not leave inheritance; we leave alms.'"

---

[246] *Muslim*, Birr, 46 (2572).

The other wives and the Caliph then understood; no new judgment was needed on an issue that already had a clear judgment. The wives of God's Messenger gave up their request and returned to their plain lives.[247]

From then on, Aisha was a significant source of information for Caliph Abu Bakr. When impure people tried to confuse or muddle issues, he often consulted Aisha. In those days, Abu Bakr had many troubles, some of which were large enough to crush mountains into dust. Aisha's knowledge had been invaluable. Nearly two and a half years had passed quickly. There were apostates and false prophets. Abu Bakr became tired, but had the serenity of fulfilling the trust of the Messenger of God.

But Abu Bakr fell ill. He continued to show the same sensitivity during his sickness. He kept his daughter nearby and shared his confidential thoughts. His general demeanor seemed to indicate that he had received an invitation from heaven—it was understood that his time on earth was ending. Abu Bakr had been able to endure the loss of God's Messenger for only for two years, three months and ten days.

Aisha, who had witnessed the last days of God's Messenger, also took care of her father during his sickness.

Abu Bakr was as sensitive in his dying as in his life. He called Uthman to his side to write a pact. Then he asked Aisha to give his remaining wages to the state's treasury upon his death. He said:

"Umar asked me and I was obliged to take six thousand drachmas from the treasury. All of them are hidden under the wall in a certain place. Please find them and return them to Umar.[248]

His words conveyed his perception and intelligence, and indicated whom he chose as his successor, as well.

He had something else to tell Aisha, and told her to come closer as he advised:

---

[247] *Bukhari*, Khums, 1 (2926, 2927).
[248] Ibn Sa'd, *Tabaqat*, 3:193

"I have spent neither a drachma or a dinar of the Muslim people's money since I have taken on the responsibility of caring for them. On the contrary, I stayed hungry and dressed in the oldest clothes."

Abu Bakr's excitement and the beating of his heart increased with each passing minute, and he made haste to give up the burden on his shoulders. He looked at his daughter with compassion. He treated her like his own mother, since she had married God's Messenger. The warmth of his looks showed how much he loved her. His love did not stop him from sharing the difficult problem that he had held back, and he said:

"My precious daughter, you know that I love you and admire you most among people. Do you remember that I gave land to you, but could you give it back to me since I am not fully satisfied with how I allocated it? I want the division of wealth among my children to be aligned with God's Book. In the presence of God, I do not want to be in the position of he who has preferred some of his children over others."

Without hesitation, she answered that she would fulfill his wish at once.[249]

Abu Bakr asked his daughter:

"On which day did the Messenger of God die?"

"A Monday."

By his posture she understood he was thinking. He asked:

"What is the day today?"

"Monday."

He took a deep breath, and the following wish poured from his lips:

"I ask and beg of God that there will not be one more night after this!"

Then he asked:

"How many shrouds were wrapped around the Messenger of God?"

---

[249] Ibn Sa'd, *Tabaqat*, 3:195.

Aisha replied:

"We shrouded his body with three new white clothes, which are called *sahuliyya*. His turban and shirt were not among them."

Indicating the cloth he wore, he said:

"Wash this cloth of mine, because there is a saffron stain on it. Add two more clothes to it and shroud me with them."

The gravity of the situation had become apparent. Her father and the Caliph of the Muslim people was about to die. Aisha felt confused and had forgotten her own grief because she was so busy with the requests, coming one after the other. She generally showed great sensitivity in fulfilling her father's dying requests, but she did not approve of this one. He was not just anyone; he was the Caliph and leader of the believers, the trusted successor to the Messenger of God. She objected:

"But that one is old."

But Abu Bakr was determined and said:

"That is okay. Living people have more need for new clothes than dead ones. Either way, the shroud of death will decay."[250]

He had another request. He wanted to continue the togetherness with God's Messenger that had started with revelation and lasted twenty-three years. He wanted to be buried near the Messenger of God, away from display and ostentation. He wanted his wife, Asma bint Umays, to wash his body and his son, Abdurrahman, to help her. Aisha's eyes filled with tears.

As he had hoped, he was reunited with God's Messenger that night, and was buried near him. The second moon, which Aisha had dreamt of and which Abu Bakr had interpreted, rose over her room. Aisha's house of felicity hosted the moon of the first Caliph next to the moon of the Prophet.

---

[250] *Bukhari*, Janaiz, 92 (1321).

# THE CALIPHATE OF UMAR

During the Caliphate of Umar, Aisha remained an important authority to consult on issues that arose. Though he bestowed respect on all the widows of God's Messenger, Aisha's knowledge made her unique. He addressed her as "the beloved of God's Messenger."

Umar first considered the Prophet's widows when he was allocating the wealth gained in territorial expansions, giving each of them ten or twelve thousand drachma annually. He gave two thousand more than this to Aisha, because of her position at the side of God's Messenger.[251]

Umar carried a heavy responsibility. He intervened immediately when he saw someone incorrectly deducing religious rulings, and he did not allow religious matters to be discussed randomly. Surely, he wanted to avoid mixing the Qur'an and the Sunnah with other matters. In light of his era, it was a wise decision. In Medina, during the time of Umar, when people did not lightly or capriciously discuss religion, Aisha was a leader issuing *fatwas* (rulings) when issues were uncertain.

Umar was a regular visitor of Aisha's; he asked her about anything of which he had no knowledge, and made decisions based on Aisha's responses. His attitude toward her was equally true for the other widows; he attended to them and always gave priority to them. He asked if they needed anything, and preferred for them to benefit first from any opportunities or wealth he gained. When he received some out-of-season fruits, he put them in separate baskets and sent them to the wives of the Prophet.[252] When he slaughtered a sacrificial animal, he first remembered them. Aisha said:

"Umar thought of every detail, without discriminating, and never neglected to send each of us our share from a sacrificed animal."

When the land of Mesopotamia (modern-day Iraq) was conquered, it was time to divide the gains of war. The leading Compan-

---

[251] Hakim, *Mustadrak*, 4:9 (6723).
[252] Malik, *Muwatta*, 1:279 (618).

ions came together in a gathering to discuss the allocation. After some brainstorming, Umar said:

"In my opinion, their spoils belong to those who worked hardest in the conquest, and must be shared among them."

Everyone replied in agreement. So Umar asked:

"Then with whom should we start?"

They replied:

"Who may deserve this more than you? Surely, you should start with yourself first."

As the Caliph, it probably seemed to the others he was most deserving because of his status. Yet, he had never witnessed the Messenger of God behave in this way. God's Messenger preferred being last when wages were allocated, even though he was at the frontline when there was service to be done. Thus he replied:

"No, I will start with the people of God's Messenger's home."[253]

Again, after the same conquest, a small cloth bag full of jewelry was brought to the Caliph. He asked the people around him:

"Do you know the value of this?"

They did not know. Since no one was sure of its value, Umar (may God be pleased with him) could not allocate it fairly. So he asked:

"Would you allow me to send it to the most beloved of God's Messenger?"

The Messenger of God's beloved was loved by everyone and without hesitation, they replied in the affirmative.

With emissaries, Umar sent the small cloth bag to Aisha. In a self-possessed way, she opened the bag carefully. When she saw the jewelry, she shuddered and pondered. Most likely, she was contemplating the austere life of the Messenger of God. She muttered:

"Why does Umar do this to me after the death of God's Messenger?"

---

[253] Imam Shafii, *Musnad*, 1:326 (1519).

With her palms turned up, she prayed: "My God, do not give me even one more chance to experience his benevolence; please take my soul before I see another such gift!"[254]

Umar displayed the same sensitivity when allocating the gains after the conquest of Khaybar. He did not forget the Prophet's wives, giving them the chance to choose between lands or a monthly wage.[255]

Aisha was shy in front of Umar because she had seen that God's Messenger behaved differently with Umar, and God's Messenger had said that even the devil was frightened by Umar. Mutual respect was preeminent between them. When knowledge of religion was under consideration, Aisha's status was indisputable for Umar. He also continued Abu Bakr's tradition of visiting Aisha or sending an emissary to consult her about problems he faced. It was not only this way for the Caliphs; this consideration reflected the general attitude of the Companions and the following generation of Muslim scholars, particularly when an issue related to knowledge of hadiths arose.[256]

One day, Umar heard that Amr ibn Umayya had given a roll of cloth to prostitutes, who were excluded from society because of their morals, and he became very angry. Umar told Amr that such charity would not be accepted as charity by God. But Amr insisted, saying that the Messenger of God had said, of prostitutes:

"The things that you give to them are considered as alms for you, too."

His defense increased Umar's anger, and Umar said he was slandering the Messenger of God. As their quarrel grew, they agreed to come to Aisha for the solution. Amr said:

"For the sake of God, I want you to tell us: didn't you hear the Messenger of God saying 'the things that you give to them are considered as alms for you, too'?"

---

[254] Hakim, *Mustadrak*, 4:9 (6725); Ahmad ibn Hanbal, *Fadailu's Sahaba*, 2:875 (1642).

[255] *Bukhari*, Muzaraa, 7 (2203).

[256] Ibn Sa'd, *Tabaqat*, 2:375.

Aisha's reply was clear:

"As God is my witness, yes, I heard."

Her response made Umar step back in shock, because his judgment was notable. He started to question himself and thought, "Who knows how much I missed hearing from God's Messenger while I was busy in my business?"[257]

Days followed days, and then ten years had passed. It was time for the predestined journey of Umar—the Caliph was assassinated, and he lay down in his blood. A short curved dagger had been poisoned, and the Caliph was about to say goodbye to this world. He was agitated because he had lacked the courage to tell Aisha he wanted to be buried near God's Messenger, at his feet. Aisha's permission was necessary. But time was working against Umar and he was about to lose his chance. He called his son, Abdullah, near to him and said:

"Go to the mother of the believers, Aisha, and be careful not to say that the Caliph sent you. From now on, I am not the leader of believers. Say 'Umar ibn al-Khattab sent me' and then say, 'he is asking permission to be buried near his two former friends.'"

It was a very delicate message. The good manners of the community addressed by God's Messenger were beyond comparison. Though Umar's heart was in favor of his request, he did not want to put pressure on Aisha by using his title. He wanted it to be received as the request of an ordinary person. Abdullah went to Aisha immediately. Aisha had heard the poignant news, and was crying for what had happened to Umar. Greeting her first, Abdullah asked for permission to speak, and said:

"Umar sends his greetings to you. He wants to be buried near his two friends."

Who did not want to be buried near the Messenger of God and his loyal friend? It was what Aisha wanted too. But she knew she must prefer her Muslim brothers and sisters to her own self. She turned to Abdullah ibn Umar and said:

---

[257] Zarkashi, *al-Ijaba*, 20.

"I was planning that for myself, but today I prefer Umar to myself."

On learning about the answer, Umar took a deep breath. The worry he had felt was gone, and his eyes were smiling. It was time to leave. Then, a final anxiety appeared in his mind. Perhaps permission had been granted under the influence of his authority as Caliph. He decided to confirm it once more, and called his son to him and said:

"O Abdullah, when I die lay me down over my cedar, and take me to Aisha's door and say, 'Khattab's son Umar asks permission from you.' If she gives her permission again, bury me there. If you realize that she changed her mind, beware and do not insist. Instead, bury me in the public cemetery like everyone else. I am worried that she felt pressured by the authority of the Caliphate when she gave her permission."

Umar showed thoughtfulness, even while he struggled against death. With his last breath, Umar had set off for his eternal journey. Medina felt a painful grief; it was almost as if the city had never experienced disaster until that day. It was time to fulfill his last request.

Abdullah ibn Umar came to Aisha and said what his father had asked. Aisha paused for a moment with wondering admiration—what a lesson in courtesy he had given while leaving this world. Surely, Umar showed greatness, courtesy and delicacy, but it was not unique to him.

But she had already given her word, and she considered it unnecessary to grant permission again. She repeated herself to be clear and make the people feel better. And so Umar began his eternal rest in the place that Aisha had chosen for herself.[258] As a result, Aisha's dream became complete, and the third moon rose over her room.

Umar's burial meant the beginning of a new era for Aisha, for she no longer felt the same comfort visiting the Messenger of God and her father. After Umar was buried, she covered her face as she had not on her previous visits. Although Umar was dead, she remained veiled in

---

[258] *Bukhari*, Fadailu's Sahaba, 8 (3497).

the place where Umar was buried. Because her room was not large enough for a fourth person, Aisha moved to a place nearby.[259]

## THE CALIPHATE OF UTHMAN

The status afforded Aisha during the previous two Caliphs continued during the era of Uthman. People from the outlying areas of the Caliphate's expanding borders came to Aisha for information that would enlighten them. Though Uthman was their leader, his attitude was no different than Umar regarding the wives of God's Messenger, especially Aisha. He tried to fulfill their wishes and make them comfortable when they worshiped, and tried to improve their conditions.

Aisha's attitude toward Uthman attracted notice, for she was shy in front of Uthman, because the Messenger of God had felt shy around him, as well. About Uthman, the Messenger of God had said:

"How could I not feel shy around the person whom the angels feel shy?"[260]

The Messenger of God had married two of his daughters with him, and had prayed for him many times.[261]

There was safety, serenity and tranquility in the first six years of his Caliphate, which lasted twelve years. But in the seventh year, signs of trouble arose, and some groups of people started to voice their objections. The door into *fitnah* (discord) was broken and some people began to think differently of the Caliph. Some began talking offhandedly and tactlessly about him, and as a result, the Caliph became a target. Some, such as Ibn Saba, wanted to defame Islam through the Caliph.

Aisha was saddened by this internal strife, and warned those who were behind the discord:

---

[259] Nadawi, *Siratu Sayyidatu Aisha*, 154, 155.
[260] *Bukhari*, Adabu'l Mufrad, 1:211 (603).
[261] Ahmad ibn Hanbal, *Musnad*, 6:261 (26290).

"People who curse Uthman are not aware that they will be the target of every kind of curse. Surely God will curse them, too. One day, I saw the Messenger of God sitting with his knees touching Uthman's. He was receiving a revelation and I was wiping the sweat from his brow. Moreover, God's Messenger married two of his own daughters to him. He affectionately called Uthman, 'my little Uthman.' Do not forget that the man who was so worthy to God's Messenger was also a valuable servant of God."[262]

She also narrated that the Messenger of God told Uthman three times:

"O Uthman, when the day comes, God will make you wear an important shirt by making you leader; if the Hypocrites want to take that shirt off you, beware and do not take it off!"

Even during the Messenger of God's sickness, he turned to Aisha and said:

"I want some people from my society to come to me."

Aisha asked:

"O Messenger of God, should I call Abu Bakr?"

He stayed silent. Aisha asked:

"Should I call Umar?"

His silence continued. It was clear that there was someone he wanted to see but would not say it. Aisha asked:

"Should I call Uthman?"

A smile appeared on his holy face immediately and he said yes.

Uthman was called to the presence of God's Messenger and they talked at great length. God's Messenger apparently reminded him of the significance of the responsibility that would be on his shoulders when discord appeared. By slightly opening the curtain to the unknown future, he advised him to bear the discord with patience. Many years later, after everything had come to pass, Uthman said:

---

[262] Ahmad ibn Hanbal, *Musnad*, 6:250 (26173).

"The Messenger of God promised me I should bear it by being patient!"[263]

Aisha was surely the one who had best understood Uthman's position at the side of God's Messenger. However, she did not refrain from pointing out any mistakes she saw. She was not embarrassed to express these mistakes, particularly in political decisions, and did not abstain from warning the friend of God and His Messenger.

During these times, when the borders had expanded and internal problems arose, some notable tribes appeared at the opposition's forefront, which increased the desire of others to oppose the Caliphate. It was the perfect environment for those who thrived on discord, such as Abdullah ibn Saba. He started a rumor that God's Messenger had left the position of Caliphate to Ali. The territories controlled by Muslims had expanded, from the Byzantine Empire to Africa, and he gathered and provoked people and invited them to rebel. These rebels chose Egypt as their home.

The turmoil spread to other areas and caused sincere people to turn indecisive. Muharik ibn Thumama, a leader in Basra, hesitated in response to what he had heard. He sent his sister, Umm Kulthum bint Thumama, to Aisha to ask a question:

"Go to Aisha and ask her opinion about Uthman ibn Man, because people here say many things about him."

He also sent a letter detailing what he had heard, asking Aisha's opinion of Uthman. Umm Kulthum delivered the letter and said:

"O my dear mother, some of your children sent me to you. They give their greetings and their respect and ask your opinion of Uthman ibn Affan."

Aisha started by saying:

"God curses the one who curses Uthman."

---

[263] *Tirmidhi*, Manaqib, 19 (3711).

Detail by detail, Aisha explained Uthman's honorable place in the sight of God's Messenger. Then she said that those who said offhand or tactless things about him would be cursed.[264]

One day, Uthman heard the news that thousands of people from a different region were gathering and starting to move toward the Hejaz, "to perform the pilgrimage." Though it looked innocent, their real aim was the Caliphate. Interpreting the matter correctly, Uthman assigned Ali to turn them back. Ali went and talked with them in great detail.

These were people who had transgressed all limits and they praised Ali to the skies. Yet Ali's sermon clearly indicated that they were wrong. Aiming to control the situation, they pretended to calm down at first, though they would later return to take the Caliphate. Aisha's own brother, Muhammad ibn Abu Bakr, was among them. His choice made Aisha very sad. She told him that he was on the wrong path, but was not able to make him listen. She even asked him to perform pilgrimage with her, to take him away from the rebellious people, but he did not agree to go with her. The Caliph of God's Messenger was forced to surrender; the rebels did not let even allow one sip of water reach him. Even an attempt by Umm Habiba failed that day—she was about to be killed for bringing water to the Caliph, and was only able to escape in a large crowd.[265] The situation continued like this for three weeks.

When Medina's atmosphere was as dark as it could be, pilgrimage season came. Aisha went to Mecca to perform the pilgrimage. Even when people told her it was better to stay in Medina in peace, Aisha remembered what had happened to Umm Habiba and said:

"If I had been there, I would have spoken against them and I would be subjected to what happened to Umm Habiba."[266]

[264] *Bukhari*, Adabu'l Mufrad, 1:288 (828).
[265] Tabari, *Tarikh*, 2:672.
[266] Ibn Kathir, *al-Bidaya*, 7:187.

After *Hajj*, she was returning to Medina when the sad news was conveyed to her that the third Caliph of God's Messenger had been martyred. Her first response was to those who had criticized Uthman:

"The reason for this was your criticizing all that the Caliphate had done!"

Their criticisms of Uthman, who had tried to bring some of the leaders who had caused discord to his own side, had gone too far. Uthman had wanted to decrease the tensions within his society by bringing opponents to his side and assigning them notable roles. But people did not understand his attempts for peace. They continued to open say that the Caliph was doing wrong.

When Aisha met Talha and Zubayr, she asked them:

"What news do you have?"

They had escaped from the poisonous atmosphere of Medina to the peaceful city of Mecca. The people who filled the streets were far from righteousness or just, and what they might do next was not clear. Aisha recited a part of the chapter al-Hujurat:

> If two parties of believers fall to fighting, make peace between them (and act promptly). But if one of them aggressively encroaches the rights of the other, then fight you all against the aggressive side until they comply with God's decree (concerning the matter). If they comply, then make peace between them with justice and be scrupulously equitable. Surely God loves the scrupulously equitable. The believers are but brothers, so make peace between your brothers and keep from disobedience to God in reverence for Him and piety, so that you may be shown mercy. (al-Hujurat 49:9-10)

She then added:

"How people need to hold fast to this verse at this moment."[267]

Aisha started to think; her mouth was sealed in grief. Instead of returning to the disorder in Medina, she stayed in Mecca, and went to the Ka'ba. She said nothing, and did not want to hear anything from

---

[267] Malik, *Muwatta*, Siyar, 1002; Hakim, *Mustadrak*, 1: 168 (2664).

anyone. She came to the door of the Ka'ba and then to Hijr Ismail, where she prostrated, weeping for what had happened to Muslim society.

When people heard she was there, they came and gathered around her in a large crowd. They waited for Aisha to speak:

"O people!"

She summarized what had happened and advised them to act perceptively.

"They put so much pressure on Uthman that even if the defamatory claims about him were true, he would be as pure as the gold gathered from dust, or as pure as clothes soaked in water, and would go to the presence of God thus purified."[268]

Though there was no benefit in realizing yesterday's mistakes, she hoped to impart a lesson from the past to help them avoid the same mistakes in the future.

Aisha's feelings were deeply wounded and she had difficulty accepting reality. Ashtar al-Nahai came during the early days when the shock of the incident had not yet passed, and asked:

"What is your opinion on the martyrdom of the Caliph?"

She replied:

"God forbid! How can I consent to the bloodshed of Muslims' leader? How can my heart accept it?"[269]

But past troubles stayed in the past, and it was time to take a new step forward. Being able to control the streets depended on a new Caliph. Aisha's candidate for Caliphate was Ali, and she said so to whomever came to her.

Building the Muslim state after Uthman was significant in its own right, and careful plans needed to be made. But the discordant environment was an obstacle to sound thinking and good planning; the purity of the Messenger of God's time fell further into the past with every passing day, leaving everything murky and muddled. It was a

---

[268] Tabari, *Tarikh*, 3:6.

[269] Ibn Sa'd, *Tabaqat*, 8:485.

precursor of more troubles. The *fitnah* that had turned life upside-down continued and no one could guess when it would end. Under such clouded circumstances, secret hands intervened, hoping to misguide even the most sincere believers. As the Messenger of God had indicated years before, they were stepping into a new era. Aisha wanted to postpone her return to Medina until the discord had settled.

This turmoil resulted in the murder of the Caliph Uthman. They had shed blood forbidden to be shed, in the city where bloodshed was forbidden, and tried to take wealth that was forbidden to them during the holy months. Aisha said that even if the rebels were numerous enough to fill the whole world, she did not consider all of them equal to even one finger of Uthman, because of the malice of their actions.[270]

## THE CALIPHATE OF ALI

In order to stop the turmoil and re-establish safety, Ali started by replacing the provincial governors who had been involved in the *fitnah*. But this would create endless new problems for Ali.

Aisha was becoming more anxious about Medina; bad news arrived constantly. People gathered around her, including provincial governors from the Uthman era. Although they had acknowledged the Caliphate of Ali, leaders such as Talha and Zubayr came to Aisha in Mecca, unable to endure their grief alone, which attracted the notice of others.

Mecca became the meeting place for those who were anxious about recent events. The city became a central location for those who wanted to avenge Uthman, whose assassins had not been brought to justice. The idle crowds seemed anxious about the destruction of many years' work; those who were sincere stayed together to find peace again. Though the pilgrimage season was over and people were expected to leave Mecca, they did not. The voices rising up from the crowd said:

---

[270] Tabarani, *Musnadu'sh Shamiyyin*, 2:75.

"We will not leave here until Uthman's murderer is found."

The leaders gathered to share their thoughts. While some proposed to stay in Mecca, some of them thought they should go back to Medina. The majority believed their target should be Basra, because it was thought that the people who had murdered Uthman were from Basra. Thus, Basra became their goal. Their intention was to avenge Uthman's murder and re-establish the system that had fallen apart.

An army that would punish ibn Saba and his rebellious supporters was established at a headquarters in Abtah; some donated hundreds of horses and camels, while others procured war supplies, and others still donated silver and gold.

Aisha and the other wives of God's Messenger were together. But they stayed behind when the crowd went to Basra, and with tears, wished them a safe journey.

Ali set out on a military expedition toward Mesopotamia (Iraq) in order to re-establish his authority. But when he received the news about Aisha and the crowd moving toward Basra, he returned. Ali wanted to pacify the crowd, which included leading Companions, primarily Aisha. One Companion, Imran ibn Husayn, the leader of Abu al-Aswad ad-Duali, went to Aisha. Basra's governor, Uthman ibn Hunayf, had sent a party to learn the intentions of the group coming toward them. They said:

"Our leader sent us to you in order to learn your intentions." They awaited Aisha's reply.

Aisha said:

"I swear to God, a person like me does not act secretly or by not telling the truth to her children." She explained at length her worry over the chain of mistakes, and how she had begun on this journey to enjoin good and forbid evil.[271]

Talha and Zubayr had a similar response. Everyone wanted to find the murderers of Uthman and put an end to the turmoil.

---

[271] Tabari, *Tarikh*, 3: 14.

They held fast to re-establishing peace. Aisha's sermons had a profound effect on those who listened. The crowd divided into two, and a large group of them stopped opposing her.[272]

To those who followed her, Aisha advised them never to draw their swords unless they were forced to do so. Despite the tension, she explained that no one had permission to fight or hurt another person, except in self-defense. Aisha wanted for Uthman ibn Hunayf, who had been captured at the riot that broke out during the turmoil, to be set free. She said he should be given the choice to go wherever he wanted.[273]

Aisha had sent similar letters to the people of Kufa, asking them to assist in creating a peaceful environment. Many leaders received her letters; she directly asked them to show sensitivity.[274]

To Muhammad ibn Abu Bakr and Muhammad ibn Talha, who asked Aisha how to act in situations where Muslims fought their Muslim brothers, she reminded them of the sad story of the two sons of Adam. Though Cain intended to kill him, Abel promised not to raise a hand against him. Aisha said:

"O my dear son! If you are able to do what the most auspicious son of Adam did, do it!"[275]

## MUSLIMS' TEST WITH THEIR BROTHERS: THE BATTLE OF THE CAMEL

While just seven hundred people were with Ali when he left Medina, this number swelled to seven thousand by the time he arrived in Kufa. When the people from Basra joined, the total number was around

---

[272] Tabari, *Tarikh*, 3:15. In spite of everything, the two sides opposed the next day and swords were drawn. However, even some of the people who opposed her opinion did not tolerate any insults against Aisha, by other people in their own ranks (Nadawi, *Siratu's Sayyida Aisha*, 180).

[273] Tabari, *Tarikh*, 3:15

[274] *Ibid*, 3:20, 21.

[275] Ibn Abi Shayba, *Musannaf*, 7:544 (37823).

twenty thousand. On the other hand, those who were with Aisha numbered thirty thousand. It was as if they were going down a path with no exit - only a dead end. It was possible that the swords which had been drawn to fight unbelievers and bring justice were to be drawn against beloved brothers who prayed beside each other. It was a sad day for both groups. The Battle of the Camel would be the hardest test that the Muslim community had yet faced.

The two crowds met at Zakar. First, the envoy of Ali, Qaqa ibn Amr, came to Aisha and said:

"O my dear mother, could you please tell me the reason why you came to this city, and what drove you to take such a step?"

Aisha replied with the same politeness:

"Assuring peace among our people."

They had used the same language and had the same aim. Ali asked Talha and Zubayr to come and mediate. When they came, he asked the same question and added Aisha's words. Their own replies were no different. Perhaps the matter could be solved before it really began. The envoy Qaqa addressed them:

"Could you please tell me how this peace will be?"

They said:

"Avenging the murder of Uthman by punishing his murderers, because not doing this means not following the order of the Qur'an!"

They were right, but there were other truths to consider. The envoy Qaqa said:

"Let's say you kill the murderers from Basra who assassinated Uthman. But wouldn't your situation before you kill them be better than your situation after you kill them? You would be killing six hundred people, and as a result six thousand people would rush into the streets against you. The man you want is Hurqus ibn Zuhayr, who killed Uthman, but six thousand men have agreed not to give him to you. If you leave them to their own devices, isn't that going to be a step against peace? If you kill them, isn't it a bigger problem than it is now? If you take steps to punish Hurqus ibn Zuhayr, you will find six thousand people who do not want to deliver the real murderer to you. This matter cannot be solved so easily. Should you not excuse Ali? He certainly wants to find and punish the murderer of Uthman, but he is waiting for the turmoil to calm down, in order to not shed more blood. He is waiting for the right time to exercise the punishment."

Aisha interrupted him:

"Then what do you think, O Qaqa?"

"It is true there is an unsolved matter, which is only possible to solve under serene conditions. When the turmoil lessons, everything will be made right. I advise you to choose peace without acting hastily, to renew your acknowledgement of Ali as Caliph, and by being the leader in good deeds as you have been before, and not to inadvertently help those who seek to create discord."

Aisha said:

"You are right. You have spoken well. Go back, and if Ali shares your opinion, know that the matter is over and that peace is essential to us."

As the turmoil decreased, Qaqa went back to Ali and explained everything. His words pleased Caliph Ali, who expected that the problems would die down. It seemed the matter would be settled without unnecessary bloodshed. Ali was very pleased and wanted to share his pleasure with his army. He stood before them and shared his happiness about the truce.[276]

It was a time of serenity, as Ali and his people, and Aisha and her people, met in peace and agreed to delay the solution for the right time. Since the Caliph did not think differently about punishing the murderers of Uthman, the responsibility was left to him. Aisha and her people prepared to return.

Talking with Talha and Zubayr, Ali addressed them, "O my brothers," and said:

"I am not someone who is ignorant of what you know. But how could I do this to the community that dominated the streets and over whom we do not have authority? Here, look at them—our slaves

---

[276] Tabari, *Tarikh*, 3:29; Ibn Kathir, *al-Bidaya*, 7:238.

go with them, and even some Arabs we never expected, accompany them. You see them walking among you as they like. Tell me, is it possible for me to fulfill your request immediately under these conditions?"

It was time to return with a satisfied soul. As the preparations continued, suddenly every eye was turned to Aisha. Something had happened to her, and it was clear that she felt regret; her every movement indicated remorse.

When some time had passed, she asked those nearby:

"Where are we?"

They responded, "Haw'ab."

With sadness, she said:

"Haw'ab?"

"Surely, we belong to God and to Him we are bound to return!" (as Muslims are supposed to say when a disaster befalls them).

She grew even more dejected. Her anxiety became agitation and then she was frantic with sorrow. People gathered around her and could not understand her behavior. With curiosity and impatience, they watched the change in Aisha.

Then words of misery and regret poured out from her lips:

"I swear to God, it has turned out that I am of the one mentioned about the dogs of Haw'ab. We should return immediately."

The people still understood nothing. Her behavior became even more elusive and their curiosity increased. With their looks, they indicated they would not take one more step unless they were told what was going on. Desperately, Aisha said:

"I heard the Messenger of God say to us, 'One among you will come to her senses when she hears the barking of Haw'ab dogs.' That day, I smiled on hearing this, and he warned me by saying, 'Beware O Humayra, you might be that person!'"[277]

---

[277] Hakim, *Mustadrak*, 3: 129 (4610). After having said this, the Prophet turned to Ali and told him to treat her kindly if he overtakes an issue about her in the future.

As the dogs' voices echoed in her ears, she wanted to scream:

"O Messenger of God, you spoke the truth!"[278]

That day, Zubayr told Aisha:

"While God would bring peace through you, are you going to give up and go back?"

Others revealed similar thoughts:

"On the contrary, you should continue on your path so that God Almighty grants peace among people."[279]

The desire for peace and serenity was a common feeling among Aisha's people.

Once more, they felt the rightness of the decision not to fight. They planned to rest during the night and return to Medina with the first light of dawn.

But there were other plans, too. The Hypocrite Abdullah ibn Saba and his friends, who enjoyed creating discord, were not pleased with peace. During the night, they concocted a wretched plan to make the two groups fight each other. During the darkest hour of the night, they attacked both sides at the same time. Those who attacked Aisha and her people pretended to be Ali's soldiers, while those who assaulted Ali and his army used Aisha's name.

A great panic started. As armed people attacked them unexpectedly, people awakening from their sleep hastily found their weapons and naturally tried to protect themselves. At the same time, there were cries of help from actors according to the planned scenario, saying that they had been betrayed. It was a battle and it was difficult to understand what was going on.[280]

Both groups began to think that the other side had betrayed them. In a situation where feelings were so heightened, thinking and reasoning were impossible. They were unable to see who attacked them or who asked for help. If they had been more careful and inquiring,

[278] Ahmad ibn Hanbal, *Musnad,* 6:52 (24299).
[279] Ahmad ibn Hanbal, *Musnad,* 6:92 (24299).
[280] Tabari, *Tarikh,* 3:39, 40; Ibn Kathir, *al-Bidaya,* 7:240.

they would have realized that their attackers were those who took to the streets, saying, "We killed Uthman." If only they had realized.

It was a matter of life and death. It was unknown who killed whom. But they drew their swords on each other, and many were killed.

Neither the advice of Caliph Ali or the efforts of Aisha, Talha, and Zubayr were helpful. Hope vanished with every drop of blood and hearts broke with every injured limb. If they had not used the sword to protect themselves, they would have been beheaded. Acting in self-defense, they had their brother's blood on their hands. It was a difficult and terrible test.

Ibn Saba and his men even turned toward Aisha, and made her palanquin the target of their arrows. Aisha said:

"O God! O God! Be afraid of God! Remember the Day of Judgment."

But no one heard her. Ali's heart skipped a beat. To rescue Aisha, an open target on the standing camel, it was necessary to make the camel sit down. Every second was important. In order to save Aisha, they hit the camel's feet with swords to make it sit down. Aisha was saved, for there was a fleshy castle around her. Her palanquin began to look like a hedgehog, with the many arrows sticking out of it.

In the riot, seventy people became martyrs to protect Aisha. At the end, Ammar ibn Yasir and her brother, Muhammad ibn Abu Bakr, took her out of the palanquin. At that time, her brother's hand touched her back. She turned immediately, and despite being close to warfare and death, she scolded:

"Whose hand is this? Take it off my body. No one else's hand other than the Messenger of God's has touched me until today."[281]

Even when she realized it was only her brother's hand, she was still offended and said:

"You rascal you!"[282]

---

[281] Tabari, *Tarikh*, 3:55.
[282] *Ibid*.

Ali, who became greatly upset when he heard what had happened, went to Aisha and asked:

"How are you, O my dear mother?"

He ordered his men to construct a tent in a safe region for Aisha. Aisha replied:

"Thanks be to God, I am fine." Then Ali prayed for her:

"May God the Almighty grant you His forgiveness."

Aisha replied:

"For you as well."

Ali took a great risk, because Aisha was the target of ibn Saba and his men. It seemed that there was no possible way to solve this crisis. It could not be solved by the sword, and the power of diplomacy became necessary. Ali tried to stop the turmoil by addressing those who were open-minded. He talked to Talha and Zubayr, with whom Ali had fought side by side since the first days of revelation. They were brave like Ali, and it was impossible not to respond to the Caliph. Both of them went to the front lines. Ali said:

"O Talha, how could you consent to fight with the family of God's Messenger while your own family was safe at home?"

Ali spoke as an intimate friend who was hurt, and the statements of an intimate friend may sting sometimes. But who could have a response to this true, sincere question?

Then he said:

"You, O Zubayr! Do you remember the day you saw me entering the presence of God's Messenger and smiled at my arrival? Thereupon, meaning me, the Messenger of God asked you, 'Do you love him?' And you replied, 'yes.' Then he said: 'But one day you will behave unjustly to him and fight against him, on the opposite side.'"

The statements were exactly as Zubayr remembered. Ali's words were like skillful weapons, and made people put their own swords back in their sheaths. Zubayr's world was upside down, and there was only one thing that he could say:

"You are right! You made me remember what I forgot."

It was the decision of a just person. He put down his sword and left the battlefield. Talha, too, left the battle.

Coming to battle was straightforward, but leaving did not come easily. Destiny would make the decision for both of them. Some people targeted Zubayr, who was returning with great regret. They lay in ambush for him, and killed him on the spot.[283] Talha's destiny was not different. Soon, an arrow hit him and he, too, left this world. Their sense of justice and leaving the field of battle displeased those who set their hopes on chaos, and Zubayr and Talha paid with their lives.

The efforts of Aisha, who had watched what had happened with confusion and grief, were useless, for Talha and Zubayr were no more. Many people gathered around Aisha's palanquin in mourning. They were looking for guidance for the future, and had good intentions, but their gathering also indicated a different danger.

Then Ali called Aisha's brother, Muhammad. He had prepared a safe place for her and invited her there by sending a message through her brother. Both were deeply hurt. Ali assured Aisha that she could go in safety to Mecca, and that no one would be able to harm her.

Ali prepared for Aisha's journey to Mecca and assigned forty female leaders of Basra to accompany her, so she would not feel alone.

Despite the sorrow they had experienced, both sides were careful to be just. Though the times were emotional, which made reasonable behavior almost impossible, both Aisha and Ali demonstrated that it was not necessary to give into chaos. On the day when Aisha was leaving, she said to those around her:

"O my sons, unfortunately we hurt each other, experienced painful incidents, and became very tired. After this moment, no one should look at each other with malice or fight about what happened or the wrong statements others made. Surely, there is no problem between Ali and I that is greater than any normal matter between a woman and

---

[283] Tabari, *Tarikh*, 3:55.

her brother-in-law. Although I experienced some troubles, he is the most auspicious man for whom I wish goodness and well-being."[284]

Aisha was grave, knowing that Ali had a special place at the side of God's Messenger. Years before, she had not allowed anything to be said against Hassan ibn Thabit, who had been trapped during the slander campaign, and she still considered him as a "defender of God's Messenger." Aisha would treat Ali as she always had, and thus destroyed the hopes of those who wanted to exaggerate the incident. Ali was touched, because the speaker had been taught by God's Messenger. But he was hurt, too, because many of his relatives were killed in order to assure peace. Responding to the statement that had mollified the injuries in his heart, Ali said:

"She is telling the truth and I swear to God, how beautiful she expressed it."

It was the most eloquent way to heal the wound. It was necessary to calm both sides, in order not to be attacked a second time in the same place. Aisha could not be left unsupported, so Ali turned to those nearby and said:

"There is only this small distance between her and me. Surely, she is the most benevolent wife of God's Messenger, both in this world and the Hereafter."[285]

Their journey started again. Ali led the people who walked with Aisha to wish her a safe journey. His sons accompanied her as well, and Ali told them to walk with her for a while.

Aisha aimed to go to Mecca, to stay until the *Hajj* (pilgrimage) season. She felt as if she had lived many years and grown old in a very short time; she had experienced so much sorrow that she regretted saying yes to the requests of the crowd. She expressed her regret in the following words: "If only I had not been created and had no body;

---

[284] Tabari, *Tarikh*, 3:60-61.

[285] Tabari, *Tarikh*, 3:61. Years later, when Aisha met someone who had been there in the ranks of Ali, she asked some questions about that day, and she could not help crying on hearing the answers she received (see: Tabari, *Tarikh*, 3:47-48).

if only I had been a tree, a rock or a sun-dried brick that glorifies God in its language! If only I had died twenty years before!"[286]

Aisha became ashamed to even visit the Messenger of God. Until recently, she had been planning to be buried near God's Messenger, but now she said: "After the death of God's Messenger, I have been involved in many sad incidents," and she wished to be buried in the Baqi Cemetery, like the other wives.[287]

When praying or reciting the Qur'an, when she came to the verse meaning *"remain in your homes..."* (al-Ahzab 33: 32), which particularly addressed the wives of the Prophet, she stopped and cried until her clothing became soaked with tears.[288]

One day, Uqba ibn Sahban visited her and asked what was meant by the verse:

> ... among them are those who wrong their own selves, and among them are those who follow a moderate way, and among them are those who, by God's leave, are foremost in doing good deeds. That is the great favor. (Fatir 35:32)

He hoped to hear Aisha's interpretation. She said:

"O my dear son, all of them are the people of heaven. The ones who outstrip each other through good deeds were the people that lived together with God's Messenger during his era; the moderate ones were the people who followed them; and the ones who wrong themselves are the people like you and me."[289]

They had survived a poignant experience. Aisha grew sad, as all believers were. It would not be enough to restore the past. There is no doubt that they did not judge their world through past events; they continued their relationship on the grounds that they should live

---

[286] These remarks of Aisha were probably made in different times and places. (Ibn Abi Shayba, *Musannaf*, 7:544 (37818); Ibn Sa'd, *Tabaqat*, 8:73-74.)

[287] *Bukhari*, Janaiz, 94 (1327).

[288] Ibn Sa'd, *Tabaqat*, 8:80; Abu Nuaym, *Hilyatu'l Awliya*, 2:49.

[289] Hakim, *Mustadrak*, 2:462 (3593); Haythami, *Majmuatu'z Zawaid*, 7:96.

together. From this perspective, we see that Ali came to Aisha on every matter he had not been able to solve, while Aisha consulted Ali when she was indecisive on an issue.

However, the gates of discord and sedition had been broken in their era and slanderous news had circulated, destroying the peace and serenity of the people. Some said the Messenger of God had made Ali Caliph before he died. When Aisha heard this rumor, she reacted to it like a door slamming in the face of one who expects it to be opened:

"When did this happen? The Messenger of God rested his head on my bosom or lap when he was passing away. Then he wanted a rock from me, and took his last breath in the same position. I was with him during his last minutes. So when did he give this testimony for Ali?"[290]

## THE CALIPHATE OF MUAWIYA

After Ali had been murdered, Muawiya became Caliph.

It was a time when many sorrowful incidents occurred, and although Aisha felt deeply grieved about what had happened, she could not do anything. What had happened during the Incident of the Camel became an important lesson for her; she did not want to be bitten in the same wound. She tried to pacify those who came and asked for her help, and advised them to behave carefully and thoughtfully. She was plunged into a deep, silent contemplation, as if she had closed her door to the world and the people in it, and she started to live entirely focused on the Hereafter. She took no break from worship, and spent all the rest of her time pursuing knowledge.

Aisha was like a sun, enlightening everyone who consulted her. She was like a safe harbor, a peaceful cove for those uncomfortable in the grief and anger of modern society. The sad news continued. God's Messenger's grandson, Hassan, whose head he had patted and who had been brought up carefully, was murdered. His greatest wish had

---

[290] *Bukhari*, Wasaya, 1 (2590).

been to be buried near God's Messenger. One day he had asked his brother to ask Aisha:

"If I die, you go to her and ask for her permission to bury me near the Messenger of God. If she allows it, bury me there in her house. But perhaps people will not consent to what you ask. If they reject the idea, do not insist; otherwise, it might cause sedition. In that case, take me to the Muslim cemetery and entrust me there!"

When Husayn attempted to fulfill his brother's final wish, he was met with hostility from Medina's governor, Marwan ibn al-Hakam, even though Aisha had replied yes to his request. People were gathered around Husayn, and the governor and his men, and it seemed like a riot was about to break out. Then the leader, Abu Hurayra, spoke up and reminded them of Hasan's own words about sedition, and so they decided to bury him in the Baqi Cemetery. Hasan would lie next to his mother, Fatima, instead.[291]

One day a man from Mesopotamia, Abdullah ibn Shaddad, visited Aisha to ask some questions and to ask her to pray for him. But Aisha wanted to ask him about something as well:

"O Abdullah, do you promise to tell only the truth in response to what I ask? For the sake of God, why and how did they kill Ali?"

Abdullah ibn Shaddad said:

"Why wouldn't I tell the truth?"

"Then tell us!"

Abdullah ibn Shaddad started to explain. Ali had tried to convince those who had opposed him and they had refused to listen to him. They had mounted a campaign against the Caliphate's authority by calling an arbitrator. Ali recited the Qur'anic verse that requires two arbitrators from each side's family in order to solve the problem between a husband and a wife. Then he asked, "Isn't the problem of Muhammad's society more important than the problem between a couple?" Then Ali reminded them of the treaty signed with Suhayl ibn

---

[291] Ibn Abdilbarr, *Istiab*, 1:392; Suyuti, *Tarikhu'l Khulafa*, 1:170; Ibnu'l Athir, *al-Kamil fi't-Tarikh*, 3/460

Amr at Hudaybiya. But no one listened. Abdullah ibn Abbas had tried to pacify the situation; and though this affected some people, generally the group would not back down. Ali did not change his firm stance on the path of the Qur'an and the Sunnah, and said, "God and his Messenger tell the truth!"

Aisha asked:

"For God's sake, are you sure he did not say anything more? Didn't he say anything else?"

"In God's Name, no, he did not say anything other than that."

"How beautifully he spoke. God and His Messenger tell the truth. May God Almighty bestow his mercy upon Ali. Surely, God and His Messenger tell the truth. The people of Mesopotamia (Iraq) went too far, saying many things about him that made me sad."[292]

It was an era when people were split into sects. The people of Egypt and Mesopotamia opposed Uthman, while the people of Damascus were unanimous against Ali. Both groups decried the Caliphs. The Kharijites rebelled against both Caliphs and spoke openly against them. Aisha, deeply upset, said:

"They are ordered to repent for the friends of God's Messenger, and yet, they make vulgar statements about them!"[293]

Though it was a difficult time, like the previous Caliphs, Muawiya was sensitive to Aisha. He showed great respect, always inquired about her well-being, and asked Aisha about the problems he had been unable to solve. He frequently sent gifts, too, but Aisha, who preferred to live humbly, always gave away the gifts, no matter who had sent them.

One day, Caliph Muawiya's men visited her and brought clothing, silver and other beautiful things. When Aisha saw them, she started to cry. She murmured something in a low voice that the envoys were not able to hear, but the people nearby heard her say:

---

[292] Ahmad ibn Hanbal, *Musnad*, 1:86, 87 (656); Hakim, *Mustadrak*, 2: 165 (2657).

[293] *Muslim*, Tafsir, 15 (3022).

"The Messenger of God never touched any of this, nor owned anything like it."

Aisha turned to the people around her and asked them to give all of the gifts to needy people. How could anything Aisha wanted not be fulfilled? By that night, nothing remained, not even one drachma.

One day, the Caliph sent a letter to her asking for advice. In her response, Aisha wrote:

"May God's peace be upon you! To put it briefly, I heard the Messenger of God say, whoever is after the consent of God despite people's opposition, God the Almighty will protect him against the troubles caused by people. Whoever is only after the consent of people without taking God's wrath into consideration, God Almighty will manifest His wrath and leave that person to his people, and to their anger.' Peace be upon you, too."[294]

Aisha did not abstain from criticizing Muawiya, despite his generous gifts and his respect toward her. She felt ashamed to express his wrong actions, but did so in the hopes that he would give them up. She criticized the murders of Hujr ibn 'Adiy and his seven friends who, like Ali, were killed after various periods of unrest. In a letter she sent with Abdurrahman ibn Harith, Aisha requested the following from Muawiya:

"If your promise has value and we are able to change the progress of affairs, we want to prevent the assassination of Hujr. This is a hard test for us."

But her efforts were not enough to save Hujr and his friends. She was shaken by the news of their martyrdom while Abdurrahman was on the way to Muawiya. It was already too late; Aisha, upset because she had been late, acquitted Hujr and talked about him with gratitude.

When Aisha came into the presence of the Caliph, she said:

"Where is the gentleness and good temper of Abu Sufyan? Where are you?"

---

[294] *Tirmidhi*, Zuhd, 64 (2414).

She tried to indicate the difference between Muawiya and his father.

Later Muawiya came to Mecca to perform the pilgrimage. He visited Aisha. Aisha, always the one to speak frankly, immediately brought the conversation around to Hujr and asked:

"O Muawiya, did you never fear God when you killed Hujr and his friends? Why didn't you have mercy on Hujr; why did you withhold it from him?"

Muawiya was embarrassed and said:

"I did not kill Hujr and his friends."

It did not tranquilize Aisha. He was Caliph, and this murder had happened on soil under his control. Truthfully, Muawiya felt his responsibility and was depressed under its burden:

"We cannot judge this matter here, in this world. Please leave the matter between them and me until the day we will reunite with our God!"

# Chapter 5

## Aisha and Knowledge

## AISHA WAS THE SOURCE OF
## KNOWLEDGE FOR EVERYONE

It was not only Caliphs who came to Aisha for information and insight; a great number of people visited her often, considering her advice as the safest way to learn. Those who were not able to visit either sent messages through someone else or sent her a letter.

Ziyad ibn Abu Sufyan, the governor of Basra and Kufa during Muawiya's Caliphate, wrote one day to ask whether a statement made by Abdullah ibn Abbas was true. Abdullah ibn Abbas asserted that until an animal was sacrificed, the prohibitions of pilgrimage were applicable even to the person who did not go to pilgrimage himself, but sent his sacrificial animal there.

Aisha wrote:

"This is not true. I prepared the ropes for sacrificial animals of God's Messenger and he tied them up with his own hands, and then sent them to Mina with my father. Until the time that the animals were slaughtered, nothing that God permitted was forbidden to the Messenger of God!"[295]

Some Companions had thought wearing perfume was forbidden while doing the *Hajj* rites, after cutting their hair, and during the stoning in Mina. But Aisha did not consider perfume a problem based on the behavior during the era of God's Messenger.[296] When they heard

---

[295] *Muslim*, Hajj, 39 (1190).
[296] *Bukhari*, Ghusl, 12, 13 (264, 267).

from Aisha, Abdullah ibn Abbas and the others left behind their preference and did as Aisha said.

Another day, ibn Abbas was incorrect about when to take off the pilgrimage garb, and when it reached her, she again revealed the truth through examples from God's Messenger's life.

The exchange of knowledge between them was so natural that Abdullah ibn Abbas, who had problems with his eyes toward the end of his life, asked Aisha whether to apply the treatment that doctors had recommended, and did not start using it until he became unable to perform ablution and Daily Prayers.

One day Abu Hurayra said:

"There is no fasting for someone who wakes up with the necessity of making *ghusl* in the morning."

He had probably not been informed of the new judgment or depended upon incomplete information. When Abu Bakr ibn Abdurrahman heard this, he said it to Abdullah ibn Harith. The questioning continued, because the people of that era considered nothing they heard as fact, until they heard its confirmation. This sensitivity was especially observed on issues that appeared to go against general knowledge. Abdullah ibn Harith told his father, who also found the information strange. Finally, they went to Aisha to clarify the confusion.

Umm Salama was with Aisha, and both were asked. They responded:

"On the mornings when the Messenger of God woke up like that, he still fasted those days."

The matter was clarified. The two went to the governor of Medina, Marwan ibn al-Hakam to tell him. Because incorrect information was circulating that needed correction, Marwan said:

"It is your duty to go and tell Abu Hurayra what you told me; I demand it."

Leaving Marwan, the two went directly to Abu Hurayra, who asked:

"Is this really true?"

They responded in the affirmative.

"Our two mothers know better."

From then on, he began to fast as he had learned from the wives of the Prophet.[297]

On another day, Imam Shurayh visited Aisha and expressed his discomfort over something that had been said:

"O mother of the believers, I heard Abu Hurayra narrating a hadith from God's Messenger that, if it is true, means all of us will perish."

"Whoever perished has already perished, but tell me, what is the real reason for your worry?" asked Aisha.

"The Messenger of God said, 'Whoever desires to reunite with God and likes this idea, God wants to reunite with him; but whoever considers reuniting with God undesirable, God considers him undesirable, too.' But who among us does not fear death and see it as undesirable?"

Aisha then understood the reason for the transformation in Shurayh and asked him to recite the following to relieve all believers:

"Yes, the Messenger of God said this, but it is not how you think. May God bestow mercy on Abu Hurayra, for he narrated you the ending of the hadith but not the beginning. The Messenger of God said, 'When God the Almighty wishes to reward one of His servants, He sends him an angel in the year that he is going to die and gives good news by supporting him for the Hereafter. In this way, when the angel of death comes to him, and says, 'O soul at rest (*nafs al-mutmainna*), let you set forth toward the mercy and good pleasure of God,' and stays near him. Then the servant feels the excitement to leave as soon as possible, and this means God loves to reunite with that servant. When God the Almighty wills to punish one of His servants, He sends him a devil in the year that he is going to die and the devil misleads him. When the angel of death comes to him, and says, 'O evil-commanding soul (*nafs al ammara*), come on prepare for the wrath and

---

[297] *Muwatta*, Siyam, 4 (639); Bayhaqi, *Sunan*, 4:214 (7785); Nasa'i, *Sunanu'l Kubra*, 2:180.

displeasure of God.' At that moment, the servant shakes like a leaf and starts to gulp. He never wants to reunite with God and God does not wish to reunite with him, either. When death is faced and it stares without blinking, the soil starts to part and moves from the chest; the fingers become paralyzed, and the hair on the skin stings like a prick. Whoever wants to meet with God, God wants to reunite with him; whoever doesn't want to meet with God, God doesn't want to reunite with him."[298]

When an important Companion, Abu Said al-Khudri was on his deathbed, he made his final preparations to go into the presence of God. He changed his old clothes for new ones, remembering the following statement from the Messenger of God:

"No doubt that the dead person will be reborn with the clothes he was wearing at the time of death."[299]

He thought the hadith meant the burial shroud, the last clothing one wears after dying. But the opinions of others, including Aisha's, were different, and she said:

"May God bestow mercy upon Abu Said."

The duty of revealing the truth again fell on her shoulders. Aisha had interpreted the hadith differently, because she had analyzed it generally and combined it with what she already knew. The clothing of this world did not have any value in the Hereafter, and being reborn was like one's first birth into the world. She explained:

"In this hadith, the Messenger of God meant the *deeds* of a person when he died, because God's Messenger also said, 'On that day (the day of Resurrection), people will be reborn without clothes, naked like they were when they were born of their mothers.'"[300]

---

[298] *Muslim*, Dhikr, 17 (2685); *Nasa'i*, Janaiz, 10 (1834); Ahmad ibn Hanbal, *Musnad*, 2:346 (8537). The information from two different narrations are combined.

[299] *Abu Davud*, Janaiz, 18 (3114); Hakim, *Mustadrak*, 1:490 (1260).

[300] Bayhaqi, *Shuabu'l Iman*, 1:318 (359). See also: *Bukhari*, Riqaq, 45 (6162); *Muslim*, Janna, 56 (2859).

It is also true that Aisha's brilliance did not only benefit those who lived during her time, but her legacy continued to illuminate the world after her death. This will continue until the Last Day. She was sought by those who know the value of correct knowledge. Umar ibn Abdulaziz sometimes sent letters to Muhammad ibn Amr ibn Hazm and in these letters, he wrote:

"Explore and search around yourself closely. If you find a hadith of God's Messenger, a tradition that remained after him, or a statement belonging to Amra, tell me about it. During the times when the people of knowledge are leaving us, one by one, I am afraid that some knowledge may be lost."[301]

Amra was a special student of Aisha's, and the aunt of Medina's governor, Abu Bakr ibn Muhammad.

## AISHA AND TRANSMISSION OF KNOWLEDGE

There is no doubt that among the Companions, Aisha was a leader in knowledge. From the beginning, she analyzed everything that happened, assimilated new information, clarified obscure issues by asking questions, and learnt intimate details that others could not witness by directly asking the Messenger of God. God's Messenger was at the centre of her life, and she dedicated her life to his cause. Her conditions supported her work, for she shared his room. Day and night, Aisha went to his well of fresh water and filled her bucket until it overflowed. She asked about everything, even intimate things that other people could not ask out of modesty, and received answers directly from the Messenger of God. She used the advantage of having a room which was adjacent to the Prophet's Mosque, and was able to follow the Messenger of God's sermons. Whenever something stuck in her mind and bothered her, she resolved it by asking God's Messenger when he

---

[301] Ibn Sa'd, *Tabaqat*, 8:480; Ibn Abdilbarr, *Tamhid*, 17:251; Ibn Hajar, *Tahzibu't Tahzib*, 12:466 (2850).

returned to the house of felicity She never quit asking until she frilly understood.[302]

Aisha's inner nature enjoyed questioning and contemplation. She was uncomfortable, and never believed anything she saw or heard until she learnt the reality behind it.

Describing her, Ibn Abu Malayka made the following statement:

"When she was faced with something that she did not know, she was not able to stand it without learning more."[303]

Perceptive scholars, such as Hakim, have said that one-fourth of the body of religious knowledge was transferred to us through Aisha.[304] In her time, people came to her for guidance about their problems; today, she is still the source of much authentic information.

Expressing her superiority, Abu Musa al-Ashari said:

"As the Companions of God's Messenger, whenever we came across a complicated issue, we took it to Aisha, because she always had the information that could solve a difficult question."[305]

Ata Abu Rabah confirmed this assessment, saying:

"Aisha was the most intelligent, scholarly person, and the one who had the best thoughts and opinions."[306]

Elders, such as Hisham ibn Urwa, confessed:

"I did not see anyone more well-informed than Aisha about the medical sciences, *fiqh* (classical jurisprudence), or poetry."[307]

Imam Masruq expressed:

"I saw the leading Companions of God's Messenger asking questions to Aisha about obligatory duties related to division of inheritance."[308]

Another leading imam, Muhammad ibn Shihab al-Zuhri, said:

---

[302]  Ahmad ibn Hanbal, *Musnad*, 6:75 (24507, 24511, 24514).
[303]  *Tafsiri Baghawi*,1:374; Ayni, *Umdatu'lQari*, 2:136.
[304]  Tahmaz, *Sayyidatu Aisha*, 174.
[305]  *Tirmidhi*, Manaqib, 63 (3883).
[306]  Hakim, *Mustadrak*, 4:15 (6748), Dhahabi, *Siyar*, 2:185, 200.
[307]  Hakim, *Mustadrak*, 4:12 (6733).
[308]  Hakim, *Mustadrak*, 4:12 (6736); Darimi, *Sunan*, 2:442 (2859).

"She was the most knowledgeable of people. For this reason, the most important Companions of God's Messenger learnt things by asking her[309] ... if the knowledge of Aisha was put on the right scale, and the knowledge of all the women, including the other wives of God Messenger was put on the left scale, Aisha's knowledge would be vastly superior."[310]

Abu Salama, the son of Abdurrahman ibn Awf, said:

"I did not see anyone who knew the Sunnah better than Aisha. No one possessed more knowledge about *fiqh* or was better acquainted with where each verse or declaration was revealed."[311]

Her nephew and special student, Qasim ibn Muhammad, underlined the depth of her knowledge about Islamic theology (*kalam*) and eloquence:

"I did not meet anyone as eloquent as Aisha, or anyone who was as cognizant of Islamic theology as her, either among men or women, or before and after her."[312]

Her unique knowledge did not only attract the attention of scholars; almost everyone agreed on her merits. One day, Caliph Muawiya called Ziyad, a key name of the era, to his presence and asked:

"Who is the most knowledgeable among the people?"

"Certainly you, O leader of believers."

But Muawiya, who was aware that this response reflected flattery more than truth, insisted:

"For the sake of God, tell the truth."

"For God's sake, it is Aisha."[313]

Whole books, such as *Al-Ijaba* by Zarkashi, were written about just the superiority of her knowledge. Her intellectual curiosity was unequaled. When God's Messenger told Fatima a secret before his

---

[309] Ibn Sa'd, *Tabaqat*, 2:374.
[310] Hakim, *Mustadrak*, 2:12 (6734); Ibn Hajar, *Isaba*, 4:349.
[311] Ibn Sa'd, *Tabaqat*
[312] Isbahani, *Aghani*, 20:331.
[313] Hakim, *Mustadrak*, 4:15 (6747).

death, Aisha learned what it was after his passing. If she had not insisted on learning it, no one would ever have learnt what the secret was.

Her inquisitive personality had not changed since the day she had entered the house of felicity; she recognized early on that the door of knowledge would be opened by asking questions, and thus asked the Messenger of God about every matter that occurred to her. It was her defining characteristic. She judged what she had heard or seen, and was discriminating about adding to her knowledge. She compared and contrasted new information to what she knew, and asked God's Messenger about any inconsistencies.

A living witness of revelation, Aisha had arranged her copy of the Qur'an, placing chapters and verses according to Gabriel's recitation of the whole. This copy would become the standard in the times to come, and people from outlying parts of Islam's expanding borders wanted to learn the ordering of the Qur'an from her.

## INTERPRETATION *(TAFSIR)*

The major interpreter of the Qur'an was the Messenger of God. He was the only one who knew the divine purpose and recognized when to give this information to the people. Aisha closely followed the explanations of God's Messenger related to the Qur'an and learned the obscure points directly. She acquired the ability to understand the purpose of the Quran, and to interpret general principles within the framework of Islam. She was not only a narrator who conveyed what she had heard and seen, but also an interpreter of meaning. Narrations related to understanding the Quran generally passed through Abdullah ibn Abbas and Aisha, which proved Aisha's importance as an interpreter.

One day, Aisha's nephew Urwa, asked her about the verse:

> If you fear that you will not be able to observe their rights with exact fairness when you marry the orphan girls (in your custody), you can marry, from among other women who seem good to you, two, or three, or four. However, if you fear that (in your marital

obligations) you will not be able to observe justice among them, then content yourselves with only one, or the captives that your right hands possess. Doing so is more likely that you will not act rebelliously. (an-Nisa 4:3)

She answered:

"O my nephew! The orphans mentioned in the verse are those under the care of their guardian and after some time, when they grow up and attract attention because of their beauty, the guardians may start to desire them and want to keep them without giving a bridal due, or by giving a very small one. In this verse, the guardians were forbidden from their former behavior, and directed to marry other women."

After the explanation of the above verse, people questioned God's Messenger further. Then another verse came:

> They ask you to pronounce laws concerning women. Answer them: "God pronounces to you the laws concerning them, and it is recited to you in this Book concerning female orphans, to whom you do not give what has been ordained for them (as bridal-due or for their maintenance), and yet desire to marry them (out of greed to get their charms or wealth for yourselves, or by refusing to let them marry to continue benefiting from their wealth); and also concerning the weak, helpless children (whose rights should be protected), and you must be assiduous in observing the rights of orphans." Whatever good you do — surely God has full knowledge of it. (an-Nisa 4:127).

In those days, a female orphan would be desired if she was beautiful and wealthy. She was engaged according to her bridal due and genealogy. But problems arose if there were some deception about her beauty or wealth. In these circumstances, men had nothing to do with orphans and married other women. It was therefore ordered to give the exact amount of bridal due that orphans deserved, whether they were desired or abandoned.[314]

---

[314] *Bukhari*, Nikah, 1, 38 (4777, 4838).

Aisha's Qur'anic knowledge was beyond the comprehension of other Companions, although they were also leaders in knowledge. Abdullah ibn Abbas said the verse:

*"If the guardian is rich (enough to support himself and his family), let him abstain (from his ward's property); but if he is poor, let him consume thereof in a just and reasonable manner"* (an-Nisa 4:6) was abrogated by revelation of the verse: *"Surely those who consume the proper-ty of orphans wrongfully, certainly they consume a fire in their bellies; and soon they will be roasting in a Blaze"* (an-Nisa 4:10).

In response, Aisha indicated that whoever abused the wealth of orphans would be punished, but not those poor guardians who need-ed the orphan's wealth to care for them. She said there was no contra-diction between the two verses. The punishment is reserved for those who take the wealth of orphans although they do not need or deserve it.[315]

Aisha's uniqueness in interpreting the Qur'an was her closeness to God's Messenger. Some Companions concluded that the middle Prayer expressed in the verse, *"Be ever mindful and protective of the pre-scribed Prayers, and the middle Prayer, and stand in the presence of God in utmost devotion and obedience"* (al-Baqarah 2:238), was the Morning Prayer, while other Companions, such as Zayd ibn Thabit and Usama, asserted it to be the Noon Prayer. But Aisha said the *Asr* (Afternoon) Prayer was intended, based on what the Messenger of God himself had said. In the copy of the Qur'an she kept, near the mentioned verse, she noted it as the *Asr* Prayer.[316]

Her approach reflected the majority of the Companions' opinion, primarily Ali, Abdullah ibn Mas'ud, and Samurah ibn Jundub.[317]

Something similar happened about the verse: *"Whether you repeal what is within yourselves (of intentions, plans) or keep it secret, God will call you to account for it"* (al-Baqara 2:284). Leading imams, such

---

[315] *Bukhari*, Buyu, 95 (2098), Wasaya, 23 (2614), Tafsir, 81 (4299).

[316] *Muslim*, Masajid, 207 (629).

[317] *Abu Dawud*, Salat, 5 (409), Ahmad ibn Hanbal, *Musnad*, 5:205 (21840); *Tirmidhi*, Tafsir, 3 (2984, 2985).

as Abdullah ibn Umar, Abdullah ibn Abbas and Ali, asserted that this verse was abrogated by the verse, "God burdens no soul except within its capacity," which was revealed after the earlier verse. But Aisha said this wasn't true:

"No one has ever asked me about the verse since I asked the Messenger of God. He said, 'It is for those who have a high fever or illness, or any kind of disaster or wealth that he was afraid to lose after possessing it, which is bestowed on a servant by God. By the cause of those things, a servant can be purified of his sins like gold is purified from dust and rust.'"[318]

## HADITH

Surely the house of felicity was the primary school of knowledge about the hadiths. A broad range of people - masters and servants, children and women, young and old, Arabs and non-Arabs - frequently visited this school. And Aisha was the most frequently addressed teacher. Her room was adjacent to the Prophet's Mosque, so she knew what took place in the mosque, even when she was in her room. She frequently went to the mosque and regularly attended the Prophet's congregational Prayers, and never missed his sermons. She followed all religious principles (*ahkam*) and new revelations. Before nearly anyone else, Aisha knew of the most up-to-date information on Islam.

In hadith science, some Companions, such as Abu Hurayra, Abdullah ibn Umar, and Anas ibn Malik, narrated so many hadiths from the Messenger of God that they were called "Mukthirun" (those who reported many hadiths). Even so, Aisha's position among the Mukthirun was special, because in most of those she narrated, she was the only one to do so. This was the natural result of her being with God's Messenger in places where it was impossible for others to be. Such hadiths are termed *fard* (individual) or *munfarid* (individually). And it was not only her intimacy that allowed this: Aisha is the resource for information about the family life of God's Messenger, his

---

[318] *Tirmidhi*, Tafsir, 3 (2990-2992).

private state, his Night Prayers, and how he spent his time alone. From this perspective, it can be said that if Aisha had not been there, much knowledge about the private life of God's Messenger would have been lost and the *Ummah* (community) would have been deprived of a treasure trove of information.

If she had attended every gathering where the Messenger of God was present, like the other *mukthirun*, and had attended many journeys, and if she had not spent most of her time at her home, she would have narrated even more hadiths. As it is, she narrated more than two thousand hadiths from the Messenger of God.

When making a healthy decision, the true reason should be known. Aisha always learnt the reason behind the judgment, by witnessing what happened or directly asking the person. The Messenger of God recommended performing *ghusl* (full body ablution) on Fridays. While other Companions who narrated this hadith said it in a general way, Aisha's narration includes details that explain the reasoning. The Messenger wanted believers who were soaked with sweat from the morning's work to cleanse themselves of their dirt and wear perfume when they came to the congregational Prayer that purified them spiritually. Aisha's narration stated:

"On Fridays, people, particularly those who came from far away, were covered in dust and dirt, and were sweating heavily. When I was near the Prophet, such a man came to the mosque, and the Prophet asked the man: 'Why don't you clean yourself for this day?'"

Another hadith that Aisha narrated stated:

"People were working at their businesses and came to the Friday Prayer in the same condition that they were in while working. At that time, I said to them, 'I wish you came after you performed whole-body ablutions'."[319]

During a Feast of Sacrifice (*Eid al-Adha*), the Messenger of God said:

---

[319] *Bukhari*, Jumu'a, 13, 14 (860, 861).

"No one among you should eat the meat of a sacrificed animal for more than three days."

While leading Companions, such as Abdullah ibn Umar and Abu Said al-Khudri, thought of this as an absolute judgment that meant storing meat more than three days wasn't permitted,[320] Aisha had a different opinion. Since, storing the meat of a sacrificed animal by salting it was a common practice in that day, she believed the Prophet's statement was an encouragement to instead give more meat to needy people. As it was possible to preserve the meat for more than three days, the meaning of the hadith needed to be clarified. To Rabia, who asked:

"Is it true that the Messenger of God banned the meat of a sacrificed animal?"

Aisha replied:

"No. In those days, the number of people in society who sacrificed animals was very few and they were asked to give some of the meat as charity to those who were not able to sacrifice an animal. We ate the front leg of a lamb even ten days after *Eid al-Adha*."[321]

While some people thought that the Messenger of God liked the shoulder meat of lamb, Aisha attracted attention to this detail:

"The lamb's shoulder was not the portion that God's Messenger enjoyed most. In those days, meat was so scarce that when they had it, they rushed to offer it to the Messenger of God. The shoulder meat was simply the part that could be cooked easily and quickly."

Each year, the Messenger of God sent a civil servant to collect alms from Khaybar. Narrations indicate that the civil servant was guessing the amount of fruit produced there without offering a reason why. But Aisha's narration offers a reason:

"God's Messenger ordered the civil servant responsible for collecting alms to estimate the amount of possible alms based on the amount of fruit some had eaten."

---

[320] *Muslim*, Adahi, 26 (1970).
[321] *Tirmidhi*, Adahi, 14 (1511); *Ibn Majah*, At'ima, 30 (3313).

The completeness of Aisha's narrations is attributable to multiple factors, including witnessing similar incidents many times, and asking about the matters that she did not witness or that contradicted her previous knowledge. Aisha was very sensitive and was always searching. She followed up on any information that she had heard, attempting to get confirmation from its original source.

One day, two visitors told her of a hadith:

"There is bad luck in three things: woman, mount, and house." And they asked her, "What do you think of that?" The words made Aisha angry, and her wrath was apparent in her behavior. Looking around, she said:

"I swear to the One who revealed the Qur'an to Abu Qasim that this matter is not like what Abu Hurayra said. While the Messenger of God was talking, Abu Hurayra entered. At that moment, God's Messenger was stating: 'During the Age of Ignorance, people used to say, "There is bad luck in three things: woman, mount and house"!'"

Abu Hurayra had heard the end of the hadith, but not the beginning. After explaining it, Aisha recited the verse (al-Hadid 57:22) meaning, "No affliction occurs on the earth, or in your own persons, but it is recorded in a Book before We bring it into existence..."

With the verse, Aisha explained that there cannot be such misunderstandings in the presence of Absolute Will and drew attention to the domain of human will.

During the Age of Ignorance, family structure had changed; many different forms of marriage were practiced. The practice of mut'a, temporary marriage, was very common.

Islam's final judgment of mut'a was revealed in the seventh year of Hijra, during the conquest of Khaybar. The Messenger of God firmly told his society that mut'a was forbidden. There were some who had not heard this yet and who favored mut'a. When some people witnessed this and told Aisha, she flew into a towering rage: *"They guard their private parts, except for their wipes or those (bondmaids) whom their right hands possess..."* (al-Muminun 23:5-6).

Once, Aisha heard a ruling that women should undo their hair braiding when they performed the ritual full-body ablution. Abdullah ibn Amr ibn As asserted this, and she immediately said:

"I am surprised with Abdullah ibn Amr ibn As' statement. He orders women to undo their hair braiding while they are performing the ritual full-body ablution! Why doesn't he order them to shave their heads, too? Nonetheless, the Messenger of God and I used to perform ritual full-body ablution in the same place, and I used to pour water onto my head only three times."[322]

Another day, Aisha heard the *fatwa* of Abdullah ibn Umar, who asserted that kissing one's spouse invalidated ablution. He was making a judgment according to general principles in a field in which he was not well-informed. But Aisha felt she must correct his statement. She explained how God's Messenger himself had behaved:

"The Messenger of God used to kiss some of his wives and go for the Daily Prayer without performing ablution again."[323]

She also taught others about the Prophet's manner of speaking and how a hadith should be reported. Someone had asked about the speaking style of God's Messenger, and Aisha answered:

"He used to speak so slowly and distinctly that whoever wanted to count his words could do so easily."[324] At another time, while Aisha was performing Prayer, she heard someone outside narrating hadith. He passed on the statements of God's Messenger, but was speaking very quickly and almost none of his sayings were understood.

Aisha, naturally, was bothered by the narration of the hadith in this manner. She said:

"A man came and narrated hadith from God's Messenger in front of my room in a way that I could hear, and then disappeared instantly. I was busy reciting my invocations, and he finished the hadith before

---

[322] *Muslim*, Hayd, 59 (331); *Ibn Majah*, Tahara, 108 (604).

[323] When the person who reported the hadith asked Aisha whether it was her, she smiled and replied in the affirmative. See *Abu Dawud*, Tahara, 69 (178, 179); *Tirmidhi*, Tahara, 63 (86).

[324] *Bukhari*, Manaqib, 20 (3374).

I finished my invocations. If I had been able to catch him, I would have told him, 'God's Messenger would have never put forward a hadith like you did!'"[325]

## FIQH: MUSLIM CANONICAL JURISPRUDENCE

Aisha was one of the few who could make novel rulings based on her previous knowledge of the Qur'an and the Sunnah. *Fiqh* depends on comprehending the reasoning and justification for judgments. Called *illa* (real cause) in jurisprudence, it explains the principal aim in religious judgments. When there is no clear statement, a tilling could only be made by reasoning, and Aisha's knowledge was advanced compared to her peers.

As explained before, Aisha asked the Messenger of God for the reasoning behind many issues when she was unable to comprehend their lawful cause; she received the answers directly from him. She corrected misunderstandings with examples from the Prophet's own life.

Aisha, who expressed that a divorced or widowed pregnant woman could marry someone else when she gave birth, concluded that the waiting period of the woman ended with the birth of the baby. She based this on an incident she had witnessed, when the Messenger of God allowed Subaya al-Aslamiyya, who gave birth after the death of her husband, to marry someone else.[326]

Explaining why the obligatory part of the Sunset Prayer is three cycles, Aisha said, "Because it is the *witr* of day!" She knew why the Morning Prayer is two units, and considered it akin to reciting the Qur'an —expressing that the quality, not the quantity, was essential.[327] Aisha, who warned people not to get stuck on the physical aspects of. pilgrimage, stated that actions such as the circling of the Ka'ba, the going back-and-forth between Safa and Marwa, and the

---

[325] *Bukhari*, Manaqib, 20 (3375).
[326] *Muslim*, Talaq, 36 (1480); *Tirmidhi*, Nikah, 37 (1195).
[327] Ahmad ibn Hanbal, *Musnad*, 6:241 (26084).

stoning of the devil were causes to remember God.[328] She also explained that visiting Muhassab Valley, which was called Abtah, was not required in pilgrimage, and expressed that since the aforementioned valley was on the closest route during that time, it was the preferred road.[329]

Aisha questioned the Messenger of God whether the Hatim, a crescent-shaped place adjacent to the Ka'ba, would be considered part of the Ka'ba and asked, "Why isn't it included in the Ka'ba?"

God's Messenger replied:

"During those days, your people were struggling financially. Thinking of their own means of survival did not let them do that."

She asked:

"Why is the door of the Ka'ba so high"

He said:

"Your people did so in order to allow those people they wanted to enter, and to prevent those people they did not want."[330]

She asked:

"O Messenger of God, don't you think you should reconstruct it on the foundation of Prophet Abraham?"

God's Messenger said:

"If your people had not recently been saved from paganism, I would have done it."[331]

Such a brilliant mind as hers would conclude many results from these expressions. She learned not to insist obstinately on a matter that people would not be able to accept before the right time and place, and that it was sensible to postpone some issues for later days or years, or even centuries. Aisha was one of the few who understood the essential point that judgments may change according to time and conditions. For example, she believed that the ruling encouraging women to

---

[328] *Abu Dawud*, Manasiq, 51 (1888); *Tirmidhi*, Sawm, 64 (902).

[329] *Bukhari*, Hajj, 146 (1676).

[330] *Muslim*, Hajj, 405 (1333); *Bukhari*, Ilm, 48 (126).

[331] *Bukhari*, Ilm, 48 (126).

attend congregational Prayers at the mosque had changed in later years. She said the conditions had changed, and the purity of the Prophet's time had not been maintained. Thus, the judgment should be rethought according to current conditions and a fresh conclusion should be reached.[332]

Aisha's knowledge of *fiqh* originated directly from the Qur'an and the Sunnah, as did her knowledge about tafsir and hadith. She drew conclusions by reshaping information from those resources, and expressed her opinion when it was time. When a matter was brought before her, she first resorted to the Qur'an and the Sunnah and searched for a similar or comparable judgment. On matters where she could not find any support, Aisha would interpret it according to logic. When she was asked whether the meat of animals that fire worshippers slaughtered could be eaten, Aisha reminded them of the Qur'anic prohibition on eating the meat of an animal that was not slaughtered in God's Name. She indicated that since the Persians slaughtered animals without the Name of God, their meat was forbidden.[333]

Aisha differed from others too, by differently interpreting the length of the obligatory waiting period for divorced women as stated in the Qur'an. If the divorced woman wants to marry another man, she must wait to make sure she is not pregnant. Aisha interpreted this length as the end of three menstrual cycles, not their beginning, and told others to act accordingly. Abu Bakr ibn Abdurrahman said, "I did not see any *fiqh* scholar other than her, who interpreted and explained this issue like that."[334]

While some Companions considered a separation as a divorce, Aisha asserted there had been no divorce. Her support for the assertion came from her own experience. To those who wondered about her reasoning, she said:

---

[332] *Bukhari*, Sifatu's Salat, 79, (831).
[333] Al-Baqarah 2:173; Qurtubi, *al-Jami*, 2:224.
[334] Malik, Muwatta, Talaq, 1198.

"God's Messenger gave us the choice to leave or stay and we preferred to stay with him. He never considered this a divorce."[335]

One day, Sad ibn Hisham asked:

"I wanted to ask you about celibacy. What do you say about leading a celibate life?"

Aisha, without hesitation, replied:

"Do not do it! Did not you hear God the Almighty say, '... *We sent Messengers before you, and (like every other man) appointed wives and children for them*' (ar-Ra'd 13:38). Keep away from celibacy."[336]

Many appreciated her knowledge of *fiqh* as well. Scholars like Abu Salama ibn Abdurrahman[337] expressed that they never saw someone more knowledgeable than Aisha. While people like Abu Umar ibn Abdul Barr thought Aisha was a unique product of her era,[338] others, like Qasim ibn Muhammad, said she had become like a self-governing *fatwa* (legal pronouncement) office during the Caliphates of Abu Bakr, Umar, and Uthman.[339] In those days, people from Basra to Damascus, from Kufa to Egypt, were surging in large crowds to Medina to ask Aisha questions about religion. Those unable to attend sent letters and gifts. Aisha's special student, Aisha bint Talha, wrote replies to their letters and gifts.[340]

## ISLAMIC THEOLOGY *(KALAM)*

Aisha was very sensitive to information that contradicted the Qur'an. After the Ascension (*Miraj*), some Companions, such as Abdullah ibn Abbas, had the opinion that the Messenger of God had seen God. They asserted some proofs and claimed that the following verses

---

[335] *Bukhari*, Talaq, 4 (4962, 4963).

[336] *Tirmidhi*, Nikah, 2 (1082); Ahmad ibn Hanbal, *Musnad*, 6:97 (24702).

[337] Ibn Sa'd, *Tabaqat*, 2:375.

[338] Zarkashi, *al-Ijaha*, 9.

[339] Ibn Sa'd, *Tabaqat*, 2:375.

[340] Ahmad ibn Hanbal, *Musnad*, 6:93 (24667), 95 (24685); *Bukhari*, Adabu'l Mufrad, 1:382 (1118).

proved this: *"Indeed, he saw him on the clear horizon"* (at-Takwir 81:23), *"Assuredly he saw him during a second descent, by the lote-tree of the utmost boundary,"* (an Najm 53:13-14), *"Indeed, he saw one among the greater revelations of his Lord?"* (an-Najm 53:18). The famous scholar Abdullah ibn Abbas said:

"God Almighty, who raised Prophet Ibrahim to the rank of *Khalilullah* (friend of God) by making His relationship to him unique, and who elevated Prophet Moses to the rank of *Kalimullah* (one to whom God talked) by honoring him with His speech, surely exalted Prophet Muhammad, peace and blessings be upon him, with the blessing of seeing Him."[341]

Not everyone agreed with him, namely leaders such as Aisha, Abu Dharr, Abdullah ibn Mas'ud and Ubayy ibn Ka'b, who said the one who God's Messenger had seen was Gabriel, and said that the hadith about the Ascension should be considered from this perspective. Hearing this, Abdullah ibn Abbas found himself at Aisha's door, and he asked:

"O my dear mother, did the Messenger of God see his Lord?"

Aisha answered:

"When I heard your words, I felt as if my blood froze. There are three points. First, whoever tells you 'Muhammad saw his Lord,' does not tell the truth: *'Eyes comprehend Him not, but He comprehends all eyes. He is the Subtle (Latif), the Aware'* (al-An'am 6: 103) and, *'And it is not for any mortal that God should speak to him unless it be by revelation or from behind a veil...'* (ash-Shura 42:51). Second, whoever tells you 'the Messenger of God knows what will happen tomorrow' is lying,[342] because God the Almighty says, *'No soul knows what it will reap tomorrow'* (Luqman 31:34). Third, whoever says, 'Muhammad concealed some parts of revelation,' you should know this person is lying, because God the Almighty clearly orders His Messenger: *'Convey and*

---

[341] See the *Tafsirs* of Ibn Kathir and Tabari (an-Najm 13-15).

[342] If God Almighty wills, He may let His Messengers know about events to happen in the future. Otherwise, they have no ability to know anything about the future as they wish.

*make known in the clearest way all that has sent down to you from your Lord...'* (al-Maedah 5:67). However, he saw Gabriel in his true form twice."[343]

## AISHA'S LITERARY SKILLS

Aisha was a master of the Arabic language. She knew what to say and how to say it. When she spoke, she commanded the attention of others. Her power of description was strong, and she showed sensitivity in choosing words. For example, while she described the first revelation of God's Messenger, she used the expression meaning, "He never had a dream, but it came up like the morning light."[344] When Aisha expressed the troubles the Messenger of God had when he received verses, she said, "Then the conditions that appeared during revelation were seen as he received the Divine word. He was sweating because of the burden of the revealed Word. Though it was winter, beads of sweat, like pearls, poured down his face."

When she learnt that she was being slandered by the Hypocrites, she expressed her troubles:

"That day, I mourned so much that no tears remained in my eyes, as if my tear ducts dried up. I did not sleep, nor close my eyes long enough to put on kohl."[345]

Aisha was poetic, not satisfied to use everyday expressions, but choosing words that conveyed a depth of meaning and the ability to persuade.

Aisha learnt the sciences of genealogy and history from her father, Abu Bakr. Her sense of poetry, eloquence, and aesthetics came from the same source.[346] Abu Bakr was a resource of knowledge for even the

---

[343] Concerning this "seeing," see *Bukhari*, Badu'l Khalq, 7 (3062); Tabarani, *Mujamu'l Kabir*, 12:90 (12565). Ahmad ibn Hanbal, *Musnad*, 6:241 (26082).

[344] *Bukhari*, Badu'l Wahy, 1 (3).

[345] *Bukhari*, Shahadat, 15 (2661), *Maghazi*, 34 (4141).

[346] Ahmad ibn Hanbal, *Musnad*, 6:67 (24425).

most distinguished scholars of the time.[347] Once, the Messenger of God directed the famous poet, Hassan ibn Thabit, to Abu Bakr, saying:

"Go to Abu Bakr; since he knows genealogy of other tribes more than you do."

From the knowledge that Hassan acquired from Abu Bakr, he was able to make statements to answer the pagans. Witnessing that he recited poems of depth and knowledge, the Quraysh expressed their confusion and approved the superiority of Abu Bakr:

"Only ibn Abu Quhafa (Abu Bakr) can know the contents of these poems to such an extent. There is no doubt that these are ibn Abu Quhafa's poems."[348]

Classical and modern scholars say that Aisha was the most fluent and eloquent of her time.[349] The tutelage and guidance of God's Messenger, who would leave an indelible mark on the future with his statements, and growing up under the protection of a master of language such as Abu Bakr, made her a child of destiny.

Musa ibn Talha, an important scholar and student of Aisha's, said:

"I saw no one better than Aisha in eloquence or clarity of speech."[350] Another leading scholar, Ahnaf ibn Qays, said:

"I heard the sermons of Abu Bakr, Umar ibn al-Khattab, Uthman ibn Affan and Ali ibn Abi Talib and all other Caliphs who have been Caliphs up until today. Yet from them, I did not hear such fluent and beautiful utterances as I heard from Aisha!"[351]

While visiting Aisha, Muawiya leaned over to Zakwan, who was with him, and said:

"I swear to God, except for the Messenger of God, I have never seen anyone more eloquent than Aisha!"[352]

---

[347] *Muslim*, Fadailu's Sahaba, 157 (2490).
[348] Ibn Abdilbarr, *Istiab*, 1:342.
[349] Zarkashi, *al-Ijaba*, 57; Buti, *Aisha: Ummu'l Muminin*, 79.
[350] *Tirmidhi*, Manaqib, 62 (3884).
[351] Hakim, *Mustadrak*, 4:12 (6732).
[352] Dhahabi, *Siyar*, 2:183.

Besides the superior literacy of her father Abu Bakr, the reasons for Aisha's outstanding expressiveness were her knowledge of the Qur'an, attending the sermons of God's Messenger, a willingness and aptitude for understanding and memorizing the statements of God's Messenger, and the emphasis on oral tradition, poetry, and storytelling of the Bedouin culture of seventh-century Arabia. She also witnessed Muslim poets who traveled to Medina from other places.

She chose words carefully, and recommended others to use the phrases of the Qur'an. When Yazid ibn Babnus and his friend visited her, he addressed her from the other side of the curtain. He asked her about a husband's relations with his wife while she was menstruating.

In his explanation of the situation, Aisha realized there were expressions that the Qur'an did not use, so she warned him:

"Use the words that God prefers."[353]

She always warned those who broke off their relationship with the Qur'an, and never approved of being busy with something other than God's Book. Her words invited others to regain their conscience when she witnessed them using disliked phrases.

One day, ibn Abu Saib came to her. When she saw him, Aisha said:

"There are three things on which you must submit to me, or I will struggle against you until the end."

"O mother of believers, if you tell me what they are, surely I will submit to you!"

"While you are praying, do not have an attitude and behavior that would infringe on the seriousness of being in God's presence, because I never witnessed the Messenger of God or his Companions doing that. Instead of doing it every day, advise people only once, on Fridays, or if you want to do so more frequently, perhaps twice, or at most, three times. Do not cause people to lose their enthusiasm for this book, the Qur'an. I hope I won't see you interrupting when people are talking in a gathering. When you come across such a situation, leave

---

[353] Ahmad ibn Hanbal, *Musnad*, 6:219.

them alone. If they show respect and ask you to advise them, then talk to them."[354]

Aisha spoke distinctly and clearly, as she had witnessed in God's Messenger. Her manner of speaking carried significance, particularly when she addressed crowds. When minds are confused or muddled by conflicting information, one must speak with authority, and perhaps even repeat some phrases to convey what needs to be understood. Aisha objected to those who spoke hurriedly. She said words should be pronounced carefully, and used God's Messenger as an example. Aisha insisted that words should be chosen to affect hearts.

Aisha described God's Messenger's generosity as an uninterrupted wind that took everything with it.[355]

Her words answered the deepest troubles existing in her society:

"Certainly, engagement is like service to God. You should be careful with whom you engage your daughter."[356]

## POETRY AND ORATORY

Poetry was the gift of the Arabs; they expressed themselves in its language. Aisha was born in an era when her father, Abu Bakr, was able to recite poetry for days without stopping. During that time, the most valued commodity in the market was poetry; they noted history in poetry, explained themselves through poetry, and livened up their gatherings with poetry. According to Aisha, poetry came in two forms: good and beautiful poetry, and bad and ugly poetry. She recommended: "Leave the bad and ugly and be in search of goodness and beauty." She had heard this directly from the Messenger of God.[357]

One day the Shurayh asked Aisha:

"Has the Messenger of God ever recited a poem?"

---

[354] Zarkashi, *Ijaba*, 176.
[355] *Bukhari*, Badu'l Wahy, 1 (6).
[356] Said ibn Mansur, *Sunan*, 1: 191; Ibnu'l Jawzi, *Zadu'l Maad*, 5:189.
[357] *Bukhari*, Adabu'l Mufrad, 1:299 (865).

She answered that God's Messenger had recited a poem written by Abdullah ibn Rawaha and did not neglect to give examples from the poem.[358]

Aisha had a photographic memory. She never forgot what she had heard, and could always recall it at the right time, in the right place.

Years later, she passed on what she had heard from the Meccans about the rout they had experienced in the Battle of Badr; she told believers about the hatred and rancor that the Meccans felt against Islam.[359] Aisha had the sincere feelings of an old woman who, years later, was saved from the darkness of the pagan world, and entrusted herself to the warm climate of the Prophet's Mosque.[360] Aisha presented some of them to the Messenger of God. And it was Aisha, again, who passed on the poems frill of nostalgia that had belonged to Abu Bakr, Bilal, and Fuhayra, whom she had visited after the Emigration.[361]

One day, when she was near the Messenger of God, Aisha recited two couplets from a poet of the Time of Ignorance, Abu Kabir al-Huzali. In the poem, Abu Kabir al-Huzali wrote of his son and his legendary bravery. Then Aisha said:

"If Abu Kabir al-Huzali had seen you, he would have surely deemed you worthy of being the subject for his poems."

At Aisha's words, the Messenger of God stood up and kissed her forehead, and said:

"May God Almighty reward you with the most beautiful and beneficial prize, O Aisha. May God please you as you have pleased me!"[362]

Aisha related how Sa'd in Muadh had recited a poem on the day of the Battle of the Trench. In response to unbelievers who maligned Islam and the Muslims, the Messenger of God asked Abdullah ibn Rawaha, Ka'b ibn Malik, and Hassan ibn Thabit to defend Islam.

---

[358] *Bukhari*, Adabu 'l Mufrad, 1:300 (867).
[359] *Bukhari*, Manaqibu'l Ansar, 45 (3921).
[360] *Bukhari*, Salat, 57 (439); Manaqibu 'l Ansar, 26 (3835).
[361] *Bukhari*, Fadailu'l Medina, 12 (1889); Manaqibu 'l Ansar, 46 (3926); Marda, 8, 22 (5654, 5677).
[362] Bayhaqi, *Sunan*, 7:422 (15204).

Aisha was the one who passed along these poems.[363] She also shared poems that the Muslim women of Medina recited during weddings.[364]

Surely, Aisha's poems were not restricted to these. She was a woman with a treasure trove of poetry stored in her memory, sharing them when it was time, and able to use the beauty of poetry to declare the values she believed in.[365]

She said:

"Feed your children poetry so that their tongues shall be sweet."

She thought it was vital to teach poetry to children to help them speak more fluently, and express themselves well.[366]

It is a fact that poetry has both a beautiful and an ugly face. The important thing for believers is to use language in good and beneficial ways. Aisha explained that language could be used to hurt people, like a biting snake:

"The most sinful person is he who ridicules a tribe or a group of people in his poetry without any distinction."[367]

This was also the advice of the Prophet, because Abdullah ibn Umar narrated from the Prophet that, "poetry resides in speech; the beauty of it is like the beauty of speech; the ugliness of it is like the ugliness of speech, too."[368]

When Abu Bakr passed away, Aisha heard that some people were lobbying against her father and she became even more upset. Evidently, it was a deliberate effort by the Hypocrites. The truth needed to be told, to warn people before they believed the lies. She called together a group of people who would listen to her advice. She made a speech

---

[363] *Muslim*, Fadailu's-Sahaba 156 (2489, 2490).

[364] Bayhaqi, *Sunan*, 7:289 (14466).

[365] For more detailed examples about the poems Aisha recited, see: Bayhaqi, *Sunan*,7:289 (14466); Tabari, *Tarikh*, 3:7, 47; 10:3; Ibn Kathir, *al-Bidaya*, 7, 244; Tabarani, *al-Mujamu's Saghir*, 1:214 (343); *al-Mujamu'l Awsat*, 3:360 (3401).

[366] Ibni Abdirabbih, *al-Ikdu'l Farid* ,5:239.

[367] *Bukhari*, Adabu'l Mufrad, 1:302 (874).

[368] *Bukhari*, Adabu'l Mufrad, 1:299 (865).

to make clear the position of the late Caliph, with the details that some may have overlooked.

She had finished her remarks and awaited the people's opinion. She asked:

"For the sake of God, please tell me: is there anything that you found odd or untrue in what I have told you?"

The reply arose from the fair people gathered there:

"No, we swear to God that everything you said was true!"[369]

When Aisha received the news that Uthman had been assassinated, she asked whether it was true. Then she said:

"May God the Almighty bestow His mercy upon him and forgive him. Nevertheless, he was saved from the troubles of this world. Since in the past you raised no objection to those who opposed and resisted him and you submitted to them, today you should support justice once more, and you should work to augment Islam's strength by exalting it. In return for so much benevolence from God, who bestowed on you blessings upon blessings in your religion, you still greedily desire this world and left behind the idea of helping His religion. You know very well that destroying something is much easier than constructing it. Do not forget that when you expect thanks for your ingratitude, the blessings that you earned will vanish."[370]

On another day, Uthman ibn Hunayf asked her:

"O my dear mother, what is the reason for your visit here? Is it a duty that the Messenger of God promised to you or is it your own interpretation?"

She replied:

"On the contrary, I came here out of my own volition when I heard that Uthman was murdered. By killing Uthman, you violated three prohibitions and conducted three forbidden acts at the same time. You ignored the sacredness of this area, violated the honor of the

---

[369] Ibn Abdirabbih, *al-Ikdu'l Farid*, 2:206; Kalkashandi, *Subhu'l Asha*, 1:248; Nuwayri, *Nihayatu'l Arab*, 7:230.

[370] Abu Hayyan, *Imta*, 511; Ibn Tayfur, *Balaghatu'n Nisa*, 5; Buti, *Aisha*, 81.

Caliphate, and defied the holy months. Although he had fulfilled your wishes, you caused him problem after problem, and killed him, thus purifying him like a white cloth made spotless. Your tyranny made him suffer, and I am angry with you because of what you did to him. Do you think that this is too much, that I became angry with you for wielding a sword against Uthman?"[371]

Although Aisha was a small woman, she had a resonant voice. She lessened the tension in a crowd by increasing her volume. During the Incident of the Camel, Aisha often used her considerable powers of expression to achieve peace. In one of her sermons, which was marvelous in its language, she said:

"As surely as I have the rights of motherhood over you, I have the right to advise you."

She explained that her intention was peace—she spoke of the blessings that God Almighty had bestowed on her because of God's Messenger, and her father's efforts to ensure justice during his Caliphate. She addressed them with gratitude:

"As you know, only the ones who rebel against God accuse me. The Messenger of God passed away while he was on my bosom. I am one of his wives in heaven. My Lord prepared me especially for him by protecting and securing me from negativity. You know that I really believed, and the Hypocrites tried to cause discord among you. Because of me, God Almighty bestowed on you the ease of taking ablution with clean dust. You know that my father was one of the two people, whose third was God. He was the fourth Muslim. He received the title of The Loyal. The Messenger of God was content with him while he was passing away, and he surely gave strength to the Caliphate. When the unity of Islam was shaken, it was he who gathered the two sides together and strengthened them. But the *fitnah* (discord) fire had been set, and some became unbelievers after having believed."

These sermons left a deep impression on the listeners. The people of Basra were split into two, and a significant number of them gave up

---

[371] Ibn Kathir, *al-Bidaya*, 7:232.

their opposition to her. Those who had listened to the sermon later said they had never before heard such clear and eloquent speech, and gave up obeying Uthman ibn Hunayf, who had been leading them.[372]

## MEDICINE

Aisha also had expertise in medicine. Comparing the science and medicine in modern and premodern times is, of course, impossible. Cures were mostly obtained by using different mixtures from herbs, plants, and animals. Usually, a master-apprentice relationship was necessary for the transfer of this knowledge to future generations. Those who had knowledge of this science handed over knowledge and expertise to the next generation, and so on.

But Aisha was unusual in that she neither took studied medicine or was an apprentice. The most well-known doctor of Aisha's era was Harith ibn Kalda, called "the doctor of the Arab people."[373] Women were known for being able to cure young children. Looking at the general state of society, we see that there was a sharing of duties between men and women. While men fought on the battleground, women undertook the duty of treating the wounded. Because Aisha was present at many battles, it is not difficult to guess how the experiences affected a keen intellect like hers.

As mentioned before, Aisha never forgot what she heard or saw, and was not at ease until her questions were answered. Aisha investigated everything that happened around her.

The home of the Prophet was a multipurpose school. Not only did she follow knowledge, but knowledge came to her. This was how she learnt about medicine.

Her information attracted notice, and people came to ask her about many things. Of course, there were some, even among her relatives, who found her knowledge of medicine strange, and asked how

---

[372] Ibni Asakir, *Tarikh Dimashq*, 30;390; Muttaqi, *Kanzu'l Ummal*, 12:224, 225 (35638).

[373] *Bukhari*, Wasaya, 2; Faraiz, 6.

she had obtained it. Urwa ibn Zubayr, the son of her older sister Asma, came to Aisha one day and asked:

"O my dear mother, I am never amazed about your intelligence, depth of knowledge, comprehension or memory; because I said to myself, 'She is the wife of God's Messenger and also the daughter of Abu Bakr,' and considered it normal. I never found your knowledge of poetry or history strange, and accepted it by saying, 'She is the daughter of Abu Bakr, the most learned of all people and the scholar of the Quraysh.' But I do not understand your knowledge of medicine at all. Please tell me, how did you learn it and where did you get the education for it?"

Aisha rested her hand on his shoulders and said:

"O my Urwa, during the very last days of God's Messenger, he became sick so often and there were groups of doctors all around, both Arab and Persian, who came to him to provide different kinds of treatments. Applying the treatments was my duty and I practiced them on God's Messenger. This is the source of my knowledge."[374]

From her own statements, Aisha learnt treatment methods from a range of sources and applied them. Many wanted to benefit from her experience, and referred to her as the authority on healing. But it is also possible to say that this issue remained secondary, because during this period of social unrest, the necessity of seeking and applying Aisha's religious knowledge was primary. On one occasion, Urwa lamented the fact that Aisha was questioned so often about the religious sciences that there was no time for medical science, and untold volumes of information on medicine had been lost with her death.[375]

## HER STUDENTS

Aisha had a special talent for passing her information to others. With no child of her own to raise and educate, she was the mother of all. She

---

[374] Ahmad ibn Hanbal, *Musnad*, 6:67 (24425); Hakim, *Mustadrak*, 4:218 (7426).
[375] Dhahabi, *Siyar*, 2: 183.

found orphans and needy people, and fought to educate useful members of society. She not only provided their material needs, but aimed to turn them into stores of knowledge.

During those days, Medina was the heart of the Muslim world in terms of knowledge. And Aisha was the city's foremost scholar. She was visited frequently by one and all who sought information. When she came to Mecca to perform the pilgrimage, a tent was set up between the Hira and Sabir mountains, and people visited her there and returned to their homes with enlightenment.[376]

Aisha, who used all her days on earth to learn and teach, taught many students in various areas, primarily in the field of hadith. Because of her, thousands of authentic hadiths are available to every single Muslim.

Her door was open to everyone, whether free men or slaves, from intimate to distant relatives. There was only one condition: that each must observe the essentials of religion. They came into her presence and listened to her lessons with great attention, and left with the intention to pass their knowledge to others.

About religious matters, Aisha followed a path that anyone could pursue, and answered questions in a way that was easy to understand. When she saw that someone was shy to ask a question, she encouraged them and made it easier to ask and learn about the thing they were hiding inside.[377]

Aisha started a wave of knowledge that would reach more people and would become more valuable in future generations.

The environment of the Messenger of God was felt within her teachings. To her regular visitors, Aisha passed on the matters that she had witnessed in the conversations between God's Messenger and his Companions, using the Messenger's own style. She avoided hastiness, and adopted a specific attitude to those who thought they could

---

[376] Ahmad ibn Hanbal, *Musnad*, 6:40 (24170); Ibn Sa'd, *Tabaqat*, 5:595; 8:68.
[377] *Ibn Majah*, Tahara, 111 (610); Ahmad ibn Hanbal, *Musnad*, 6:97, 265 (24699, 26332).

acquire everything immediately in the first lesson. She told them that God's Messenger had not behaved that way.[378]

Aisha's school of knowledge was frequented by Umar and his son, Abdullah ibn Umar, Abu Hurayra, Abu Musa al-Ashari, Abdullah ibn Abbas, Abdullah ibn Zubayr and by other well-known Companions, such as Amr ibn As, Zayd ibn Khalid al Juhani, Rabia ibn Amr alJurayshi, Saib ibn Yazid, and Harith ibn Abdullah.

The scholars of the next generation competed with each other to benefit from this spring of knowledge. It is said that around one-hundred and fifty scholars attended her lectures and listened to her teachings. Urwa ibn Zubayr, Qasim ibn Muhammad, Abdullah ibn Yazid, Alqama ibn Qays, Mujahid, Iqrima, Shabi, Zirr ibn Hubaysh, Masruq ibn al-Ajda, Ubayd ibn Umayr, Said ibn al-Musayyib, Aswad ibn Yazid, Tawus ibn Kaysan, Muhammad ibn Sirin, Abdurrahman ibn Harith ibn Hisham, Ata ibn Abi Rabah, Sulayman ibn Yasar, Ali ibn Husayn, Yahya ibn Ya'mar and ibn Abi Malaika were among the scholars. These are the distinguished names that enlightened not only their own times, but also the eras after them.

Abu Amr, Zakwan, Nafi, Abu Yunus, ibn Farruh, Abu Mudilla, Abu Lubaba Marwan, Abu Yahya and Abu Yusuf were freed slaves (called *mawali*) and were also among Aisha's students.[379]

Not only men benefitted from her school of knowledge. In the gatherings, there were important women, such as her sister Umm Kulthum bint Abu Bakr, Amra bint Abdurrahman, Amra bint Aisha bint Talha, Asma bint Abdurrahman, and Muaza al-Adawiya, Aisha bint Talha, Jasra bint Dajaja, Hafsah bint Abdurrahman ibn Abu Bakr, Safiyya bint Shayba, Barira, Sayiba, Marjana and Hasan al-Basri's mother, Hayra. Around fifty women total attended her lectures.

---

[378] *Bukhari*, Manaqib, 20 (3375).
[379] Ahmad ibn Hanbal, *Musnad*, 6:32 (24845), 258; *Tirmidhi*, Da'awat, 129(3598).

Being a student of Aisha's was a special virtue. The people closest to her were envied, but without malice. Her nephew Urwa's position attracted the notice of almost everyone.[380]

## URWA IBN ZUBAYR

Urwa ibn Zubayr was young, born in the twenty-third year of the Islamic calendar, during the last year of Umar's Caliphate. He sought knowledge since the earliest days of his childhood. We see in him the desire to become a store of knowledge which could benefit other people.

We see evidence of this when he and three friends he met on the Hijr, adjacent to the Ka'ba, were talking about the future. Although Musab ibn Zubayr, Abdullah ibn Zubayr, and Abdullah ibn Umar each had different wishes, Urwa asked:

"O my Lord, bestow on me knowledge that people will benefit from after my death."[381]

Perhaps as a result of his Prayer, a short time later he became one of Medina's scholars, respected by the elderly in spite of his youth. He stayed close to Aisha, hardly ever leaving her alone, trying to get more information from her. Kabisa ibn Zuayb said:

"Surely Urwa was the one among us who best knew Aisha's hadith knowledge, because he was the only one among us who entered the presence of Aisha without any difficulty."[382]

Ibn Shihab al-Zuhri, himself a leader in hadith science, expressed Urwa's knowledge as an ocean whose bottom was unreachable.[383]

Urwa himself said:

---

[380] Ibn Hajar, *Tahzibu't Tahzib*, 12:463.

[381] Abu Nuaym, *Hilyatu'l Awliya*, 1:309; 2:176; Ibn Asakir, *Tarikh Dimashq*, 40:267.

[382] Ibn Hajar, *Tahzibu't Tahzib*, 7:165; 12:463.

[383] Ibn Sa'd, *Tabaqat*, 5:181.

"During Aisha's last four or five years, I thought to myself, 'If our mother Aisha passes away, there is no hadith in her knowledge treasure trove that I do not know.'"[384]

One day, Urwa ibn Zubayr and his son Muhammad went to visit Walid ibn Abdul Malik in their barn. While they were in the barn, the startled horses got out of control. Muhammad died in the turmoil. Urwa himself received a serious blow to his leg, which later had to be removed because the injury turned into gangrene. The fortitude that he showed while his leg was amputated before his eyes, without anesthetic, was impressive. When the surgery was complete, he read the verse meaning, "We had some difficulties in this journey of us." There was no one holding him, and finally, he fainted.

When he came to his senses, he wiped the sweat from his brow and asked those who were there to give him the amputated leg. Holding it in his hand, he said:

"I swear to God, who exalted me by walking with you, I neither gave in to a sin with you nor stepped into it."[385]

Then the people around him heard him pray:

"O my Lord! I had four limbs, two hands and two legs. You took one of them and left the other three to me; surely, as always, praise be upon you! I had four sons. You took one of them and left the other three to me; surely, as always, praise be upon you! Aren't the ones that become everlasting the ones you take?"[386]

Urwa had inherited the perfect manners of Aisha in worship, generosity, and benevolence. It was he who transferred her habits about worship to future generations. He spent his nights reciting the Qur'an, finishing one-quarter of it in one night, and kept long vigils at Prayer. Even after his leg was amputated, Urwa never shortened his worship. Only one night was he not able to spend his night in Prayer and recitation—the night his leg was removed—but he performed the worship

---

[384] Ibn Hajar, *Tahzibu't Tahzib*, 7:165.

[385] Ibn Asakir, *Tarikh Dimashq*, 61:410.

[386] Abu Nuaym, *Hilyatu'l Awliya*, 2:179.

the following night. He never wanted to lose his place in his spiritual life. He advised his family to pray all the time.

"When any of you see something worldly that you like, you should go home and advise the family to perform Prayers; you should incline towards worshipping because God Almighty advises his Prophet: *Do not strain your eyes toward what We have given some groups among them to enjoy, the splendor of the present, worldly life, so that We may test them thereby. The provision of your Lord is better and more lasting!*" (Ta Ha 20:131).

Of Urwa, his son Hisham said:

"My father fasted his whole life and he was fasting on the day that he died."[387]

Urwa inherited Aisha's generosity, too. In the season when the dates were ripening, he picked them from trees, spread them on his wall, and invited people to his garden to take some. People came from all around to visit his house and none left empty-handed. Whenever he entered his garden, he said *Mashallah* (how beautifully God made!) and recited the verse (al-Kahf 18:39) meaning, *"What Allah wills (will come to pass)! There is no strength save in Allah!"*[388]

The following statements express his depth and are very meaningful:

"When you see someone doing a good deed, know that there are brothers of the good deed near that person too. Similarly, if you witness someone doing a bad deed, know that there are brothers of the bad deed near that person as well. Thus, a good deed is the forerunner of other good deeds; a bad deed is a sign of more bad deeds."

Urwa died in the ninety-fourth year of the Muslim calendar. Since there were many other scholars who started their eternal journey in the same year, this year started to be called "the year of *Fiqh* scholars (*sanatul fuqaha*)."[389]

---

[387] Ibn Sa'd, *Tabaqat*, 5:180.
[388] Abu Nuaym, *Hilyatu'l Awliya*, 2:180.
[389] Ibn Sa'd, *Tabaqat*, 5:181.

## QASIM IBN MUHAMMAD

Since his father had become a martyr, Qasim ibn Muhammad grew up near Aisha and acquired all his knowledge from her presence. She took care of him, placed him under her own protection, and concerned herself with his education. Aisha even cut his hair and dressed him up for festivals herself.

But surely the most important inheritance that Aisha left to him was knowledge. It is said that Qasim, together with Urwa and Amra, was one of the three people who had learnt Aisha's extensive knowledge of the hadiths.[390] At the same time, he was humble. He disliked being regarded as important, and did not think himself superior than others.

One day, someone from Badiya asked him whether he was more knowledgeable than the famous scholar Salim.

Qasim ibn Muhammad thought neither of exalting Salim with false modesty, or of stroking his own ego by bragging. In response to the man's insistence, Qasim told the man to ask this question to Salim.[391]

Like Urwa, Qasim lived without asking for anything from other people and never inclined, even slightly, toward any behavior that might damage his morality and gravity. One day, Umar ibn Ubaydullah sent him one thousand drachmas, but he returned them all. Some people insisted that he should keep just one hundred of them, but his attitude did not change. Qasim would not eat one bite of the benevolence that was offered to him.

The Caliph of the time, Umar ibn Abdul Aziz, treated Qasim with great respect and regard throughout his life. He even recommends Qasim as a Caliph candidate after himself, and did not hesitate to say this openly.[392]

---

[390] Ibn Hajar, *Tahzibu't Tahzib*, 8:300.
[391] *Ibid.*
[392] Dhahabi, *Tazkiratu'lHuffaz*, 1:97.

When Qasim saw people speculating about different interpretations of destiny, he warned them:

"You too should behave carefully on the points that God avoided expounding on."

He interpreted the conflicts of the people who had lived before him, primarily the Companions, as God's great mercy for the following generations.[393] When he lost his vision at the age of seventy, he called his son near him when his death was close and told him his will:

"Use the clothes that I performed Prayer in, including my shirt, *izar* and *rida*[394] as my burial shroud."

His son asked:

"Oh my dear father, why don't we prepare a two-piece shroud for you?"

His answer was like Abu Bakr's, whom he considered an example:

"O my dear son, Abu Bakr left this world with three pieces of cloth. Do not forget that those who live need new clothes more."[395]

## AMRA BINT ABDURRAHMAN

Amra bint Abdurrahman was sister of As'ad ibn Zurara of the Banu Najjar, one of the leaders of *Ansar*, and the granddaughter of Sad ibn Zurara. She was a relative of God's Messenger on his mother's side.

Aisha, who took Amra and her siblings under her protection, turned this family into distinguished scholars. She felt responsible for spreading the knowledge that she had accumulated during the era of God's Messenger among the children whose talents she had noticed.

Like her siblings, Amra appreciated Aisha's consideration and took her place in history as the leading scholar of her time. The wellknown ibn al-Madini said, "Amra was among the most reliable

---

[393] Ibn Sa'd, *Tabaqat*, 5:188, 189.
[394] An *izar* is a wrapper covering the body below the waist and a rida is a cloak covering the upper body.
[395] Ibn Sa'd, *Tabaqat*, 3:204.

scholars who were cognizant of Aisha's hadith knowledge,"[396] and "Amra bint Abdurrahman understood this matter and had the incredible vision to comprehend the knowledge of Aisha."

Ibn Hibban said: "She was the most knowledgeable of people about Aisha's hadith knowledge."

Sufyan Sarwi called her, "the most well-informed person who comprehended Aisha's hadith knowledge."[397]

The people of Amra's time liked her very much. Everyone who was interested in Aisha's knowledge was likewise interested in Amra's, and showed their love with gifts. But she sent the gifts to the needy, just as she had learned from Aisha. And she never sent gift-senders home empty-handed, either.[398]

After Aisha, the duty of correcting interpretation errors fell to Amra. She corrected judgments and tried to explain the truth, together with its reasoning.[399]

One day, Qasim ibn Muhammad asked Imam Zuhri:

"I see you are very desirous for learning. Do you want me to show you a bowl frill of knowledge?"

"Yes."

"You should go directly to Amra bint Abdurrahman because she was educated by Aisha."

Zuhri, who went to Amra bint Abdurrahman following Qasim ibn Muhammad's recommendation, later said:

"I realized that she was like an ocean where it was impossible to reach the bottom."[400]

Though people sought knowledge in those days, Amra went well beyond what was usual. When she opened her eyes to the world, Aisha was next to her; from early childhood, she was surrounded by Aisha's

---

[396]   Ibn Hajar, *Tahzibu't Tahzib*, 12:466.

[397]   Ibn Hibban, *Siqat*, 5:288 (4881).

[398]   *Bukhari*, Adabu'l Mufrad, 1:382 (1118).

[399]   Malik, *Muwatta*, Hudud, 11 (1531).

[400]   Dhahabi, *Tazkiratu'l Huffaz*, 1:112; *A'lam*, 4:508; 5:347.

treasure trove of information. Amra was one of the few who followed the path of Aisha, in searching for knowledge and applying it to her life, primarily in the *hadith* and *fiqh* sciences. She narrated hadiths from Rafi ibn Hadij, Ubayd ibn Rifa'a, Marwan ibn al-Hakam, Habiba bint Sahl, Hamna bint Jahsh, Umm Hisham bint Haritha, and Umm Salama, as well as Aisha.

During an age when the well-informed continually sought information, people visited her often. She turned her home into a *madrasa*, a place of teaching and learning, and educated many students. Among the students she taught were: Haritha ibn Abi Rijal, Ruzayq ibn Hakim, Sa'd ibn Said, Sulayman ibn Yasar, Abdullah ibn Abu Bakr ibn Muhammad ibn Amr, Abdirabbih Ibni Said, Urwa ibn Zubayr, Amr ibn Dinar, Malik ibn Abi Rijal, Muhammad ibn Abu Bakr ibn Muhammad ibn Amr, Muhammad ibn Abdurrahman, Muhammad ibn Muslim,, ibn Shihab al-Zuhri, Yahya ibn Said, Yahya ibn Abdullah, Abu Bakr ibn Muhammad, Raita al-Muzani, Fatima bint Munzir.

She passed away in the ninety-eighth year of the Muslim calendar. Her death caused great sadness among scholars and people looked for the information she had left behind. The Caliph of Umayyad, Umar ibn Abdulaziz, who had showed a special deference to Amra while she lived, and consulted her on matters that confused him, said:

"No one who knows Aisha's hadith knowledge remained among us after Amra's death."

He assigned a team of people to search for any information, hadith, or application that she had passed to future generations.[401]

## MUAZA AL-ADAWIYAH

Muaza al-Adawiyah, known by her nickname Umm Sahba, was the widow of Sila ibn Ashyam, who had been murdered on a battleground near Qabil with his son, Sahba. Muaza, who had inherited the good manners and knowledge of Aisha, had such strength of character that

---

[401] Ibn Sa'd, *Tabaqat*, 8:480; Dhahabi, *Siyar*, 4:507, 508.

upon hearing the death of her husband and son, she told the women who came to offer their condolences:

"If you are coming to congratulate me, you are welcome. But if you have some other intention, it would be better not to come."

This great woman, who promised to spend her life in worship, kept vigil every night, particularly after the martyrdom of her husband. She was known as one of the most pious people of that time. Muaza, who attracted notice because of her depth of faith and worship, one day told those around her:

"I swear to God that my love for this world is not about making myself prosperous or about enjoyment or happiness. I swear to God, I love this world only because I want to get closer to my God while here. In this way, I hope that God Almighty will let me meet with my son and Abu Sahba in heaven."[402]

She performed Prayers from night until morning, and when she felt sleepy or lazy, she walked around a little to restore her vigor, and said to herself:

"O my *nafs* (soul)! Here sleep is, right in front of you; if you submit to it, you should know that you will sleep in your grave at great length. But there is one difference—this sleep will bring you either yearning in regret or happiness in mercy."[403]

When her time approached and the signs of death started to be seen, those nearby witnessed that she wept in great sorrow, and then smiled. They asked:

"Why did you cry and why are you smiling?"

"I thought that my illness would draw me away from fasting, Prayers and remembrance of God, so I became sad and cried. But then Abu Sahba, in a two-piece green cloth, together with a group of people, appeared in the garden. I swear to God, I never saw beauty like their's in this world, so I smiled. I do not think that I will be here for even one more Prayer."

---

[402] Ibnu'l Jawzi, *Sifatu's Safwa*, 4:23.
[403] *Ibid*, 4:22.

As she had foretold, Muaza al-Adawiyah died that day, in the eighty-third year of the Muslim calendar, before it was time for another Prayer.[404]

## AT WHAT AGE DID AISHA MARRY THE PROPHET?

When covering the life of the Prophet, one of the most debatable topics is that of the age of his wife, Aisha, when the two married. Her alleged young age has been used in smear campaigns against the Prophet.

Reports showing that Aisha bint Abu Bakr was 6 or 7 years old when she became engaged, and 10 when she married,[405] have been the generally accepted assumptions regarding her age of marriage. It should not be forgotten that such practices were extremely widespread at the time, and children developed earlier in those times. For these reasons, this subject was not made into a contentious issue until recently.

Orientalists, who do not consider the context of the time period in which an action occurred and who examine Islam from the "outside," have made this a current issue. The Muslim world's reaction to this different stance has been mixed. While some have insisted that Aisha's afore-mentioned age at marriage is correct[406] others are of the opinion that Aisha was older.[407] In this situation, where it is not always possible to maintain a balanced view, various approaches have

---

[404] *Ibid.*

[405] *Bukhari*, Manaqibu'l Ansar, 20, 44; *Muslim*, Nikah, 71; Fadailu's Sahaba, 74; *Abu Dawud*, Adab, 55; *Ibn Majah*, Nikah, 13; *Nasa'i*, Nikah, 78; *Darimi*, Nikah, 56.

[406] Azimli, Mehmet, "Hz. Aişe'nin Evlilik Yaşı Tartışmalarında Savunmacı Tarihçiliğin Çıkmazı," *İslami Araştırmalar*, Vol. 16, Issue 1, 2003.

[407] See Doğrul, Ömer Rıza. *Asr-ı Saadet*, Istanbul: Eser Kitabevi, 1974, 2/141; Nadwi, Sayyid Sulayman. *Hazreti Aişe*, (trans. Ahmet Karataş), Timaş, Istanbul: 2004, p. 21; Savaş, Rıza. "Hz. Aişe'nin Evlenme Yaşı ile ilgili Farkll Bir Yaklaşım", *D. E. Ü. İlahiyat F. Dergisi*. Issue 4, Izmir: 1995, pp. 139-144; Yüce, Abdülhakim, *Efendimiz'in Bir Günü*, Istanbul: Işık Yayınları, pp. 82-83, 2007.

developed to answer the Orientalists' claims, including those that choose to deny the reports or ignore the existence of other alternatives.

First of all, it should be known that everyone is a child according to the standards and norms of their time; therefore, any questions about cultural norms must be evaluated within these specific contexts. There are certain values that form a society's customs, and when a society is evaluated, these values have to be taken into consideration. Otherwise, if we were to attempt to evaluate historical events within today's conditions, we should remember that we are bound to make mistakes in judgment.

It is known that during the time of the Prophet, young girls were married at an early age[408] and that age difference was not important in marriage.[409] Especially in regard to young girls, it should not be forgotten that there was social pressure for this - that they matured earlier due to climatic and geographical conditions, and that they were seen as goods that needed to grow in their husband's house. Moreover, this is not a matter just related to girls; boys were also married at ages 8, 9 and 10, and they became heads of a family at an age that is perceived as very young today.[410] It should be remembered that during this time, many people did everything they could to slander the Prophet, be it questioning his marriage with Zaynab bint Jahsh or slandering Aisha after the Murayso expedition. If Aisha's age was not questioned by these people, it's a sign that, within the context of historical circumstances, it was a common practice.

---

[408] Abdul Muttalib, the grandfather of the Prophet, married Hala bint Uhayb, who was young then. Since he married off his son, Abdullah, to Amina at an early age at around the san1e time of his own marriage with Hala, the Prophet was almost of the same age as his uncle, Hamza.

[409] In order to have family relationship with the Prophet and thus further his close relation with God's Messenger, Umar ibn al-Khattab married Ali's daughter, Umm Kulthun1, and this marriage was not found strange, at that time.

[410] Amr ibnu'l As, for instance, was 12 years older than his son, Abdullah. This means that he was around 10 when he got married. For further information see Ibn Athir, *Usudu'l Ghaba*, 3:240.

In the verses of the Qur'an that came at the same time, the age for marriage was mentioned and it was emphasized that children should be married when they come of age.[411] Opposing a divine suggestion was not an option. Using the mentality of Umar, if intervention had been a matter of consideration here, the Prophet would surely have been warned in a coming revelation and a step would have been taken to resolve the issue. At any rate, the Prophet's wedding to Aisha took place in accordance with direction from divine will.[412]

Putting the extremes aside and using moderate criteria, the sources related to Aisha's age at marriage are examined as follows:

1. While listing the names of Muslims during the first days of Islam, Aisha's name, together with her older sister, Asma, are listed immediately after the names of the Sabiqun al-Awwalun (the first and foremost representatives) like Uthman ibn Man, Zubayr ibn Awwam, Abdurrahman ibn Awf, Sa'd ibn Abi Waqqas, Talha ibn Ubaydullah, Abu Ubayda ibn Jarrah, Arqam ibn Abi'l Arqam, and Uthman ibn Mad'un. Being the 18th person to accept Islam, Aisha's name precedes the names of Umayr ibn Abi Waqqas, Abdullah ibn Mas'ud, Salit ibn Amr, Ja'far ibn Abi Talib, Abdullah ibn Jahsh, Abu Hudayfa, Suhayb ibn Sinan, Ammar ibn Yasir, Umar ibn Khattab, Hamza ibn Abdilmuttalib, Habbab ibn Arat, Said ibn Zayd, and Fatima bint Khattab.[413]

This means she was living then and was mature enough to make such a choice and exercise her will. In addition, the information in the reports that indicates "she was a small girl then" shows that her name was mentioned in a conscious way.[414]

This date refers to the early days of Islam. For it is known that Aisha's sister, Asma, who was born in 595, was 15 when she became a Muslim.[415] This indicates the year 610, when the Prophet started to

---

[411] Nisa 4:6.
[412] *Bukhari*, Ta'bir, 21, Manaqibu'l Ansar, 44, Nikah, 9; *Muslim*, Fadailu's Sahaba, 79; Ibn Hanbal, *Musnad*, 6:41, 128.
[413] Ibn Hisham, *Sira*, 1:271; Ibn Ishaq, *Sira*, Konya, 1981, 124.
[414] Ibn Hisham, *Sira*, 1:271; 124.
[415] Nawawi, *Tahzibu'l Asma*, 2:597; Hakim, *Mustadrak*, 3:635.

receive the revelation, and this shows that Aisha was at least 5, 6, or 7 that day, and that she was at least 17 or 18 when she married the Prophet in Medina.

2. In regard to the days in Mecca, Aisha said, "I was a girl playing games when the verse, 'Indeed, the Last Hour is their appointed time (for their complete recompense), and the Last Hour will be more grievous and more bitter'[416] was revealed to God's Messenger."[417] This information opens other doors regarding her age.

The verse under consideration is the 46th verse of Surah Qamar, the 54th chapter of the Qur'an, which explains the miracle of the split moon [the splitting of the moon is one of the miracles performed by the Prophet]. Revealed as a whole, this surah came while the Prophet was in Ibn Arqam's home in the fourth (614),[418] eighth (618), or ninth (619)[419] year of his mission, according to differing reports. Looking especially at necessity, some scholars focused on the date being 614; if this date is taken, Aisha either had not been born or had just been born. Thus, if 614 is the accepted date, it appears that she must have been born at least eight or nine years earlier.

The situation does not change much when 618 or 619 are taken as the date. On either date, she would have only been 4 or 5 years old, neither of which is an age at which she would have been able understand this event and relate it years later.

According to this second possibility, she was probably born when Muhammad's Prophethood had just begun.[420]

---

[416] AI-Qamar 54:46.

[417] *Bukhari*, Fadailu'l Qur'an, 6; Tafsiru's Sura, (54) 6; Ayni, Badruddin Abu Muhammad Mahmud ibn Ahmad, *Umdatu'l Qari Sharh Sahib Bukhari*, 20:21; Asqalani, *Fathu'l Bari*, 11:291.

[418] Suyuti, *Itqan*, Beirut, 1987, 1:29, 50; Dogrul, *Asr-i Saadet*, 2: 148.

[419] The month difference stems from the lunar calendar.

[420] Taking this information into account, some people calculate Aisha's age at marriage as at least 14 or 22, even up to 28. We have not focused on these as they are not supported by the sources.

Another matter worth mentioning here is that while describing that day, Aisha stated, "I was a girl playing games." The word she used to describe herself, *jariya*, is used to describe the passage into puberty.

If we look at the issue, using 614 as the year that Surah Qamar was revealed, Aisha would have been born at least eight years before the Prophetic mission - or in 606. If we accept 618, then her year of birth would have been 610; this event alone makes it impossible for her to have been 9 when she married.

When this information is combined with her name being on the list of the first Muslims, we can conclude that Aisha's date of birth was probably 606. Consequently, she would have been at least 17 when she married.

3. Of course, Aisha's memories of Mecca are not limited to this one event. In addition to this, the following memories confirm the matter:

a) She talked about having seen two people begging who had remained from the Year of the Elephant (the year in which Yemeni King Abraha sent an army of elephants to Mecca in order to destroy the KaCba; the elephants were pelted with pebbles dropped on them by birds), which occurred 40 years before the Prophetic mission and is accepted as a milestone for determining historical dates. Her sister, Asma, was the only person Aisha handed this information down to.[421]

b) She described, in detail, that during difficult times in Mecca, God's Messenger had come to Abu Bakr's house, morning and evening, and that her father, who could not endure this hardship, attempted to migrate to Abyssinia.[422]

c) She stated that first it was mandatory to offer two cycles of obligatory Prayer and that later it was changed to four cycles

---

[421] Ibn Hisham, *Sira*, 1:176; Haythami, *Majmatuz Zawaid*, 3:285; Ibn Kathir, Taftir, 4:553; *Bidaya*, 2:214; Qurtubi, Taftir, 20:195.

[422] *Bukhari*, Salat, 70, Kafala, 5, Manaqibu'l Ansar, 45, Adab, 64; Ibn Hanbal, *Musnad*, 6:198.

for residents, but that during military campaigns two cycles were performed.[423]

d) In reports about the early days, she made statements like, "We heard that Isaf and Naila had committed a crime at the Ka'ba and for this reason God turned them into stone, as a man and woman from the Jurhum tribe."[424]

4. Being betrothed before the engagement: Another factor that supports Aisha being older is that at the time when the Prophet's marriage was a topic of discussion, Aisha was engaged to Mut'im ibn Adiyy's son, Jubayr. The suggestion for the Prophet to marry Aisha came from Hawla bint Hakim, the wife of Uthman ibn Mad'un, someone not from the family. Both situations show that she had come to the age of marriage and was known within the community as being ready for marriage.

As is known, this betrothal was broken by the Ibn Adiyy family due to the possible religious conversion of their son to Islam, and it was only after this that Aisha's engagement to Muhammad, peace and blessings be upon him, took place.[425] Consequently, the marriage agreement was either made before the Prophetic mission or when the call to Islam was being made openly (three years after the Prophet began receiving revelation). If it was made before the mission, it implies that Aisha was born even earlier than has been thought. For this reason, some say that she was a 13- or 14-year-old girl by then.[426]

It should not be overlooked that this decision was made during the period when the call to Islam had begun to be made openly. In regard to time, this means 613-614. If it is assumed that Aisha was born four years after the mission, it has to be accepted that she had not yet been born; had she not been born, it would've been impossible to

[423] *Muslim*, 3:463; *Mujamu'l Kabir*, 2:285, 286; *Mujamu'l Awsat*, 12:145; Ibn Hisham, *Sira*, 1:243.

[424] Ibn Hisham, *Sira*, 1:83.

[425] *Bukhari*, Nikah, 11; Ibn Hanbal, *Musnad*, 6:210; Haythami, *Majmuatu'z Zaivaid*, 9:225; Bayhaqi, *Sunan*, 7:129; Tabari, *Tarikh*, 3: 161- 163.

[426] Savaş, Riza, *D. E. Ü. İlahiyat F. Dergisi*, Issue 4, Izmir, pp. 139-144, 1995.

talk about an engagement. In this case, it has to be accepted that she was at least 7 or 8 when her engagement was broken, so the year of her birth would probably be 605.[427]

Here, another possibility can be mentioned: namely, an agreement of arranged future marriage similar to "cradle tallying," an agreement between parents in the early years after the birth of a baby. However, there are no details in any texts to confirm this.

5. The age difference of Aisha's siblings should be taken into account. As is known, Abu Bakr had six children. Asma and Abdullah were born from Qutayla bint Umays, Aisha and Abdurrahman from Umm Ruman, Muhammad from Asma bint Umays, and Umm Kulthum from Habiba bint Harija. Asma and Abdullah have the same mother, as do Aisha and Abdurrahman. The age difference between children from the same mother can enlighten our subject matter.

a) Abu Bakr's first daughter, Asma, was born in 595, 27 years before Hijra, the Prophet's emigration to Medina.[428] At the time of Hijra, she was married to Zubayr ibn Awwam and was six-months pregnant.[429] Her son, Abdullah, was born three months later, in Quba, while she was migrating to Medina. She died in the 73rd year of Hijra at the age of 100; her teeth had not even fallen out.

Here there is another critical piece of information. The age difference between Aisha and her sister Asma was 10 years.[430] According to this, Aisha's year of birth was 605 (595 + 10 = 605) and her age at the time of Hijra was 17 (27—10=17). Since her marriage took place six,

---

[427] Berki, Ali Hikmet, Osman Eskioglu, *Hatemü'l Enbiya Hz. Muhammed ve Hayatı*, 210.

[428] Nawawi, *Tahzib al-Asma*, 2:597.

[429] *Ibid.*

[430] Bayhaqi, *Sunan*, 6:204; Ibn Manda, *Marifatu's Sahaba*, Köprülü Kütüphanesi, No: 242, p. 195; Ibn Asakir, *Tarikh Dimashq, Tarajimu'n Nisa*, Damascus, pp. 9, 10, 28, 1982; Mas'udi, *Muruju'z Zahab*, 2, 39; Ibn Sa'd, *Tabaqatu'l Kubra*, Beirut, 8:59, 1968.

seven or eight months after Hijra, or just after Badr,[431] this means Aisha was 17-18 years old at that time.

b) The age difference between Aisha and her brother Abdurrahman is also striking. Abdurrahman became Muslim after the Treaty of Hudaybiya was signed, six years after Hijra. He was careful not to encounter his father at the Battle of Badr, in the second year after Hijra, and that day, Abdurrahman was 20 years old.[432] In other words, he must have been born in 604. Taking into consideration the conditions of that time, the probability is low that the sister of a child born in 604 would be born 10 years later in 614. Put another way, at a time when the age difference between brothers and sisters was usually one or two years, a large difference, such as 10 years, between Aisha and her brother is highly unlikely.

6. Reports regarding Aisha's death can also help to illuminate the issue. The year in which she died is listed as the 55th 56th 57th 58th or 59th year after Hijra[433] and her age at that time as 65, 66, 67 or 74.[434] Just as there is no agreement regarding her date of birth, there is no agreement regarding her date of death.

Reports to the effect that she died in the 58th year after Hijra and that she was 74 when she died give the impression that they are sounder than others because they give detailed information - such as the day she died being Wednesday, that it corresponded to the 17th day of Ramadan, that upon her request she was buried at night after the *Witr* Prayer in the Jannat al-Baqi Cemetery, that again upon her last request the Funeral Prayer was lead by Abu Hurayra, and that she was lowered into the grave by persons like her sister Asma's two sons, Abdullah and Urwa, her brother Muhammad's two sons, Qasim and Abdullah, and

---

[431] Ibn Sa'd, *Tabaqat*, 8:58; Ibn Abdilbarr, *Istiab*, 4:1881; Nadwi, *Siratu's Sayyidati Aisha*, Edition critique by Muhammad Rahmarullah Hafiz al-Nadwi, Daru'I Kalam, Damascus, 40, 49, 2003.

[432] Ibn Athir, *Usudu'l Ghaba*, 3:467.

[433] Ibn Abdilbarr, *Istiab*, 2:108; *Tahzibu'l Kamal*, 16:560.

[434] Ibn Sa'd, *Tabaqat*, 8:75; Nadw i, *Siratu's Sayyidati Aisha*, 202.

her brother Abdurrahman's son, Abdullah.[435] Therefore, when calculations are made according to this date, we see she lived 48 years after the Prophet's death $(48+10=58+13=71+3=74)$. This means she was born three years before his Prophethood and, in view of this information, she was 17 when she married $(74-48=26-9=17)$.

There are other issues that support this conclusion: She was at the battle front at Uhud, in the third year after Hijra; this was a battle where even boys were turned away. Her scholarly knowledge was incredible, as was her mature response to claims of slander. The age difference between her and the Prophet's daughter, Fatima, suggests she was around 17; so, too, does her knowledge and awareness of Hijra and later developments. After arriving in Medina, her marriage was consummated at her father's suggestion and after the mahr had been paid.[436] There were many differing reports about the date of marriage;[437] also, dates of birth and death were not clearly determined in that society, as they are today.

All this information strengthens the probability that she was born before the commencement of Islam, was engaged at 14 or 15 years of age, and was married to the Prophet at the age of 17 or 18.

In this situation, it is up to us to attribute the meaning "I appeared to be" to the report "I was 6 or 7 when I was engaged and 9 when I married" and to reconcile the two.[438] The fact that Aisha was physically thin strengthens this interpretation. She was affected by physical events faster and had a smaller body than her peers. Her small stature is supported by events: she became ill during the migration to

---

[435] Ibn Abdilbarr, *Istiab*, 2:108; Doğrul, *Asr-ı Saadet*, 2:142.

[436] Tabarani, *Kabir*, 23:25; Ibn Abdilbarr, *Istiab*, 4:1937; Ibn Sa'd, *Tabaqat*, 8:63.

[437] For such clifferences in narrations see, "one and a half or two years before Hijra,""when she was 6 or 7 years old," "when Khaclija passed away or three years after Khaclija passed away," "seven or eight months after the Emigration or the first year of Hijra," "Right after the Battle of Badr," see *Bukhari*, Manakibu'l-Ansar, 20, 44; 36.

[438] There are even those who attribute this information to a mistake of the narrator, claiming that it should be, "I was 6 or 7 when the first revelation came."

Medina;[439] her mother showed her special attention;[440] and when she lost her necklace after the Muraysi expedition, she was so light that when her palanquin was placed on the camel, her guards thought she was in it.[441]

In short, regardless of whether Aisha's age at marriage was 9 or 17 or 18, there was nothing strange about it in those times. It is necessary to evaluate every society according to its own rules. When we look at examples, it was quite a widespread custom to marry both boys and girls at a young age. However, when we look at information passed down to us, it should not be forgotten that the information suggesting that Aisha, may God be pleased with her, was born in 605, engaged at the age of 14 or 15, and married at the age of 17 or 18, is too strong to be ignored or discarded.

## ALI AND AISHA

Another falsehood produced against Aisha is that she was offended by Ali, and even became angry with him. Supposedly, Aisha was aloof toward Ali until the end of her life as a result of the slander incident (because of what he had said that day); it is also claimed that the Incident of the Camel was a consequence of this offense.

The only proof of this was Aisha's use of the expression, "the other man"[442] to refer to Ali, as one of the two people who helped God's Messenger walk when he came to the mosque during his final illness. They claimed that Aisha could not bear to have the name of Ali on her lips because of her anger towards him.

---

[439] *Bukhari*, Manaqibu'l Ansar, 43, 44; *Muslim*, Nikah, 69; *Ibn Majah*, Nikah, 13.

[440] *Bukhari*, Manaqibu'I Ansar, 44; *Muslim*, Nikah, 69; *Abu Dawud*, Adab, 55; *Ibn Majah*, Nikah, 13; *Darimi*, Nikah, 56; Tabarani, *Kabir*, 23:25; Ibn Abdilbarr, *Istiab*, 4: 1938; Ibn Sa'd, *Tabaqat*, 8:63; Ibn Ishaq, *Sira*, Konya, 239, 1981.

[441] *Bukhari*, Shahada, 15; Maghazi, 34; Tafsir, (24) 6; *Muslim*, Tawba, 56; *Tirmidhi*, Tafsir, (63) 4; Ibn Sa'd, *Tabaqat*, 2:65; Ibn Hisham, *Sira*, 3:310.

[442] *Bukhari*, Wudu, 44 (195); *Muslim*, Salat, 91-91 (418).

What is the real extent of the incident? Is it true that Aisha was really angry with Ali and offended by him? Is there any other information or evidence here, as there was about Aisha's age? What was the Aisha's general approach regarding anger and offense? How did she react when faced with such incidents?

First of all, other than this event, there is not the slightest indication that there was a dispute between Aisha and Ali.

Second, the authenticity of the expressions allegedly said by Ali during the slander incident is doubtful. The narrations were weak[443] and it is unscholarly to base such an important matter on a weak narration, especially while there exists stronger evidence.

Third, while it is still possible that Aisha meant Ali with the words "the other man," hadith scholars say that the person indicated could have been Usama or Fadl ibn Abbas.[444] Other scholars mention the possibility of two others, named as Burayra and Nuba. It is also suggested that "the other man" was a slave whose name was unknown.[445]

There are two possibilities—either this incident happened more than once, or the second person who took the arms of God's Messenger changed. The only one who did not change was Abbas, the uncle of God's Messenger; since he was close to the Prophet, he stayed near him constantly and held his arm at all times. If the person taking the other arm of God's Messenger rotated, it could have been Usama, Ali, Fadl, Burayra, Nuba, or another slave whose name was not known.[446]

Perhaps, instead of saying the names of all five people who rotated positions, Aisha described those who took turns as "the other man." Then, Ali was not the only one whose name was not mentioned—there were also Usama, Fadl, Burayra, Nuba and an unknown slave. It is unlikely that Aisha had a negative attitude toward all five of those people, which makes her description of Ali not pointed or intentional.

---

[443] Ibn Hibban, *Sahih*, 10:13; 16:13; Abu Ya'la, *Musnad*, 8:322, 339
[444] Ayni, *Umdatu'l Qari*, 3:92; 5:188; Ibn Hajar, *Fathu'lBari*, 1:263; 8:141.
[445] Ibn Hajar, *Fathu'l Bari*, 8:141; Ayni, *Umdatu'l Qari*, 3:92; 5:188.
[446] Nawawi, *Sharhu Muslim*, 4: 137, 138; Ibn Hajar, *Fathu'l Bari*, 8: 141; *Umdatu'l Qari*, 3:92, 5:188.

Fourth, during the slander incident, Ali said, "O Messenger of God, why are you giving yourself a hard time? May God Almighty protect you from experiencing more difficulties! There are so many women other than her! Why don't you ask this servant girl? I am sure that she will tell you something that makes you feel better."[447]

His words were clearly aimed at saving the Messenger of God from his troubles, and ought to be interpreted as, "I am worried only about you; on the occasion when you are hurt, every other matter is secondary to me."

Perhaps Ali, directing the matter to Barira, also hoped to have

Aisha acquitted by someone who knew her extremely well. Moreover, Ali knew Islam very well. A month after the slander of Aisha began to circulate, the verse (an-Nur 24: 11) was revealed: *When you heard of it, why did the believing men and women not think well of one another and declare: "This is obviously a slander!"?* These words demonstrate how believers must react to baseless slanders and lies. History shows us that many Companions exhibited the correct attitude that day, and there is no evidence that Ali was not one of them.

Fifth, that day, Ali used clear expressions to defend the innocence of Aisha. Umar, Uthman, and Ali, who entered the house of felicity while the Messenger of God was talking over the matter with his Companions, each acquitted Aisha and said there was no doubt that these words were slanders. Ali approached the matter with steadiness and precision, and acquitted Aisha in the following way:

"O Messenger of God, I understand that she is pure and innocent from an incident. Do you remember, one day you were leading us in Prayer in your shoes and at one point you took off one of your shoes. It was a puzzling point for all of us and so we asked you if that was the Sunnah. You answered no and explained that Gabriel came to you and told you that one of your sandals had dirt on it that would invalidate your Prayer. O Messenger of God, if God Almighty protects

---

[447] *Bukhari*, Shahadat, 15 (2518), *Maghazi*, 32 (3910, 3911); Itisam, 28 (6935); *Muslim*, Tawba, 56 (2770).

you on such minor matters, is it even possible that he leaves you alone about your own family?"[448]

Here, the real character and attitude of Ali is shown, and like the words of Umar and Uthman, he also said that Aisha was innocent. While his position pleased God's Messenger, it was also the attitude that the Qur'an applauded.

Sixth, we are otherwise forced to accept that Ali believed the slander about Aisha, even though historical incidents clearly deny this. The Messenger of God punished Hassan ibn Thabit, Mistah ibn Usasa and Hamnah bint Jahsh, who each repeated the slander at some point, after the verses about Aisha's chastity were revealed. If it were possible to interpret the words of Ali as believing in the slander, he would have been punished as well. The Messenger of God clearly stated that he would punish anyone who really deserves it, no matter who the person was.[449] It is impossible to imagine that he bestowed a privilege upon Ali by excluding him from punishment.[450]

Furthermore, there was no place for old hatreds or grudges in Aisha's life. It would have been impossible for her to carry such anger in her heart when she was the closest person to the Prophet, whose mission included ending the vendettas of *Jahiliyya* by ripping out the seeds of revenge in Bedouin society. Aisha was the one who told us that the Messenger of God never thought of revenge.[451] Aisha, arguably the most important conveyer of the religion in which responding to hate with hate was consistently criticized,[452] and the most special student of the Prophet, was surely free of this kind of personal flaw. There are many examples of this. For instance, when the truth of her purity appeared in the verses about the slander, Aisha never took a

---

[448] That day, Umar ibni Khattab and Uthman ibn Affan made similar remarks. See: Halabi, *Sira*, 2:624; Bursevi, *Ruhu'l Beyan*, 6:89.

[449] He clearly stated this about a noble woman who had committed theft. See: *Bukhari*, Anbiya, 52 (3288).

[450] Buri, *Aisha Ummu'l Mu'minin*, 60.

[451] *Bukhari*, Manaqib, 20 (3367).

[452] See al-Furqan 25:72.

negative stance against Hassan ibn Thabit, who was actually punished for accompanying the Hypocrites in their slander and being deceived by them. Instead, she became his leading defender. When Aisha heard someone speaking badly about Hassan, she intervened swiftly for the Companion who had defended God's Messenger in his poetry.[453]

Examples of Aisha's forgiveness are not limited to this; the attitude she took against those who had killed her brother was also striking.[454] When he visited her, Aisha asked questions of Abdurrahman ibn Shumasa. When she realized they were pleased with Muawiya as Caliph, she told him, "What he did to my brother Muhammad ibn Abu Bakr is not an obstruction for me to tell you what I heard from God's Messenger." She then imparted those narrations of God's Messenger in which he praised the governor under whom his people were pleased.

It becomes impossible to think that Aisha despised a person like Ali, who was always at the side of God and His Messenger, while she defended and behaved so gently toward the ones who killed her brother, and who took a part in the most sorrowful time of her life. It's improbable to think that she maintained such hatred until the end of her life.

Seventh, Aisha wrote a letter to Muawiya about Hujr ibn 'Adiy, who was murdered together with his seven friends because of his closeness to Ali. In the sectarian violence that occurred after the Jamal incident, she used every opportunity to end these murders. She expressed the sorrow and anxiety that she felt with reproachful words to Muawiya, "Did you never fear from God while you killed Hujr and his friends? Why did not you have mercy on Hujr; why did you withhold this from him?"[455]

---

[453] *Bukhari*, Maghazi, 32 (3914); Adab, 91(5798).

[454] Aisha's brother Muhammad ibni Abi Bakr sided with Ali at Jamal and Siffin.

[455] We preferred to combine different narrations here: Ahmad ibn Hanbal, *Musnad*, 4:92 (16878). For the details of the event, see Tabari, *Tarikh*, 3:220, 232; Ibn Abdilbarr, *Istiab*, 1:332.

Eight, we witnessed that Aisha put Ali forward at the most critical points.[456] After Uthman, she said that he should be the one to shoulder the Caliphate and directed others to believe in him, too.[457] Aisha also directed people to Ali when they had questions which he was better suited to answer.[458]

Even on the day when her grief at Jamal was at its peak, Aisha turned to those around her and said:

"O my sons, unfortunately, we have hurt each other. We experienced upsetting incidents and became very tired. No one should look at each other maliciously or fight because of what has happened or believe the lies others will say after this day. Surely, there is no problem between Ali and I that is greater than any matter between a woman and her brother-in-law. Although I experienced some troubles, he is the most auspicious person, upon whom I wish goodness and excellence."

The above statements prove Aisha's generosity of spirit. She knew that Ali had a special place at the side of God's Messenger, and she disappointed those who wanted to exploit the issue. Ali himself even walked together with Aisha to see her off to Medina, and advised his sons to accompany her during the trip, showing the same familial sensitivity.[459]

They were both excellent people in every sense. Despite what had happened the day before, they protected each other's rights and did not allow anything to be said against the another. One day, a man came to Aisha and began to complain about Ali and Ammar. She intervened immediately and did not let him speak more, and did not neglect

---

[456] *Tirmidhi*, Manaqib, 61 (3874); *Nasa'i*, Hasais, 35 (8496); Hakim, *Mustadrak*, 3: 167 (4731).

[457] Ibn Abi Shayba, *Musannaf*, 7:545 (37831); Ibn Hajar, *Fathu'l Bari*, 13:57.

[458] *Muslim*, Tahara, 85 (276); *Nasa'i*, Tahara, 99 (129); *Ibn Majah*, Tahara, 86 (552); Ahmad ibn Hanbal, *Musnad*, 1:96 (748); Abdurrazzaq, *Musannaf*, 3:128 (5029).

[459] Tabari, *Tarikh*, 3:61.

to express the virtues of both Ali and Ammar, one after the other.[460] Though she knew what the Messenger of God had said of Ammar, Aisha was also aware that Ammar was fighting with the supporters of Ali. Ammar, who had been informed by God's Messenger that he would be killed by an ebullient and ferocious community, was murdered at Ali's side.

On the other hand, people like Dhu as-Sudayya, known to have gone astray with cruelty, took their last breath on the opposite side. Aisha closely examined current events and knew that the incidents justified Ali. Seeing his troubles, she often expressed what a good person he was and prayed for him in his absence. She stood against the Kharijites who acted against Ali, even after what they had done to Uthman and said, "While they were ordered to ask for the forgiveness of God's Messenger's friends, now they make even more malicious statements about them."[461]

Aisha, who was deeply grieved by Ali's murder, asked Abdullah ibn Shaddad about his last days. After she had listened to the accounts of zeal and effort that Ali had shown for Islam, she prayed for him and made it clear that his murderers were transgressors.[462] Aisha even described the city of Harura, where they resided, as the center of evil. It is known that in later days, whenever she witnessed someone's negative attitude, she asked, "I wonder if you are from Harura, too?"[463]

Nine, Ali's attitude was no different than Aisha's. He never allowed anything to be said against her in his presence, and never gave up behaving respectfully. After the Incident of the Camel, one of the most severe tests of his life, he became sad, and described the grief he felt because he had been tested with Aisha.[464] When the two armies met as a result of ibn Saba's plotting, Ali became frightened. He had

---

[460] Zarkashi, *al-Ijaba*, 863-864.

[461] *Muslim*, Tafsir, 15 (3022); Ishaq ibn Rahuya, *Musnad*, 2:321 (847).

[462] Ahmad ibn Hanbal, *Musnad*, 1:86-87 (656); Hakim, *Mustadrak*, 2:165 (2657); Bayhaqi, *Sunan*, 8:180; Abu Ya'la, *Musnad*, 1:367 (474).

[463] *Bukhari*, Hayd, 20 (315).

[464] *Fathu'l Bari*, 13:55; Tabari, *Tarikh*, 3:61; Ibn Kathir, *al-Bidaya*, 7:246.

saved Aisha from being the target of the Hypocrites, and when he saw that Aisha's palanquin was the target of a downpour of arrows, he ran to her and risked his own life to protect her. He had his men pitch a tent for her and moved her to a safe place.[465] That day, Ali gave advice to Aisha's brother, Muhammad ibn Abu Bakr, who was in his army. He sent Aisha to Medina with her brother and his soldiers, along with forty women from Basra. He insisted his soldiers not harm anyone with Aisha.[466] He said, "Today, I hope that God Almighty will place all those who are able to control their feelings in Paradise," and led the Prayers for martyrs that day.[467]

This superiority did not only belong to Ali and Aisha. It was the same sensitivity seen in the attitudes of those in Ali's army as well.[468] Together, these proofs demonstrate that there was neither anger or offense between Ali and Aisha. It is impossible to assert that as a reason for Jamal.

---

[465] Tabari, *Tarikh*, 3:29; Ibn Kathir, *al-Bidaya*, 7:238.

[466] Bayhaqi, *Sunan*, 8:181.

[467] Tabari, *Tarikh*, 4:534; Ibn Haldun, *Tarikh*, 2:606.

[468] Nadawi, *Siratu's Sayyida Aisha*, 180.

# BIBLIOGRAPHY

ABDURRAZZAQ IBN HAMMAM, Abu Bakr as-San'ani, *al-Musannaf*, Edition critique by Habiburrahman al-A'zami, al-Maktabu'l Islami, Beirut 2003.

ABU DAWUD, Sulayman ibn Ash'as as-Sijistani al-Azdi, *Sunan*, Edition critique by Muhammad Muhyiddin Abdülhamid, Talik: Kemal Yusuf Hut, Daru'l-Fikr, Beirut, undated.

_____, *Aisha bint Abi Bakr as-Siddiq*, Edition critique by Abdulghafur Husayn, Daru'l-Aqsa, Kuwait, 1985

_____, *Sualatu Abi Dawud Li'l Imam Ahmad ibn Hanbal fi Jarhi'r Ruwat*, Edition critique by Ziyad Muhammad Mansur, *Maktabatu'l Ulum wa'l-Hikam*, First edition, Medina: 1414.

ABU HAYYAN, Asiruddin Muhammad ibn Yusuf al-Andalusi, *Bahru'l Muhit*, Daru'l Fikr: 1983.

ABU HAYYAN AT-TAWHIDI, Ali ibn Muhammad ibn Abbas, *al-Imta wa'l Muanasa*, http://www.alwarraq.com

ABU NUAYM, Ahmad ibn Abdillah al-Isfahani, *Hilyetu'l Awliya wa Tabaqatu'l Asfiya*, Daru'l Kitabi'l Arabi, Beirut: 1405 AH.

_____, *Musnadu Abi Hanifa*: http://www.alsunnah.com

ABU YA'LA, Ahmad ibn Ali al-Mawsili, *Musnad*, Daru'l Ma'mun li't Turas, Edition critique by Husayn Salim Asad, Damascus: 1984.

ABU'L FARAJ AL-ISFAHANI, *al-Agani*, Edition critique by Samir Jabir, Daru'l Fikr, Beirut.

ABU'L HASAN ALAADDIN ALI IBN BALABAN, *al-Ihsan bi Tartibi Sahihi ibn Hibban*, Edition critique by Yusuf Hut, Daru'l Kutubi'l Ilmiyya, Beyrut, undated.

AHMAD IBN HANBAL, Abu Abdillah ash-Shaybani, *al-Musnad*, Zayl: Shuayb Arnawut, Muassasatu Qurtuba, Cairo, undated.

AL-AJLUNI, Abu'l-Fida Ismail ibn Muhammad, *Kashfu'l Khafa*, Daru'l Kutubi'l Ilmiyya, Beirut: 1988.

ALI AL-MUTTAQI AL-HINDI, *Kanzu'l Ummal*, Muassasatu'r Risala, Beirut: 1989

ALUSI, *Ruhu'l Maani*, Daru Ihyai't Turasi'l Arabi, Beirut, undated.

AYNI, Abu Muhammad Mahmud ibn Ahmad, *Umdatu'l-Qari*, Daru Ihyai't Turasi'l Arabi, Beirut, undated.

AZIMABADI, Abu't Tayyib Muhammad, *Shamsu'l-Haq, Awnu'l-Ma'bud Sharhu Sunan-i Abi Dawud*, Daru'l-Kutubi'l Ilmiyya, Beirut, 1415 AH.

AZİMLİ, MEHMET, "Hazreti Âişe'nin Evlilik Yaşi Tartışmalarında Savunmacı Tarihçiliğin Çıkmazı", *İslami Araştırmalar*, Vol. 16, Issue 1, 2003.

BAGHAWI, Abu Muhammad Husayn ibn Mas'ud, *Sharhu's Sunnah*, Edition critique by Shuayb Arnawut and Muhammad Zuhayr Shawish, al-Maktabu'l Islami, Beirut: 1983.

BAYHAQI, Abu Bakr Ahmad ibn Husayn ibn Ali ibn Musa, *Sunanu'l Kubra*, Edition critique by Muhammed Abdulqadir Ata, Maktabatu Dari'l Baz, Mecca: 1994.

_____, *al-Madhal ila Sunani Kubra*, Matbaat'u Dairati'l Maarifi'n Nizamiyya, First Edition, Haydarabad, 1344 AH.

_____, *Shuabu'l Iman*, Daru'l Kutubi'l Ilmiyya, Beirut, 1410 AH.

BERKİ, ALİ HİKMET, OSMAN ESKİOĞLU, *Hatemu'l Enbiya Hazreti Muhammed ve Hayatı*, Diyanet İşleri Başkanlığı, Ankara: 1981.

BUKHARI, *al-Jamiu's Sahih*, İstanbul, 1401 AH.

_____, *at Tarikhul Kabir*, Daru Ihyai't Turasi'l Arabi, Beirut, undated.

_____, *Tarikhi Saghir*, Maktabatu Dari't Turas, Cairo: 1977

_____, *Adabu'l Mufrad*, Edition critique by Muhammad Fuad Abdulbaqi, Daru'l Bashairi'l Islamiyya, Beirut: 1989.

BURSEVİ, İsmail Hakkı, *Ruhu'l Beyan*, Darü't Tibaati'l Amire, Bulak, 1255 AH.

BUTİ, Muhammad Said Ramazan, *Aisha: Ummu'l Mu'minin*, Daru'l Farabi li'l Maarif, Damascus: 1997.

DARAKUTNI, Ali ibn Umar Abu'l Hasan, *Sunan*, Daru'l Marifa, Beirut: 1966.

DARIMI, Abu Muhammad Abdullah ibn Abdirrahman, *Sunan*, Daru'l-Kitabi'l Arabi, Beirut: 1407.

DHAHABI, Abu Abdillah Muhammad ibn Ahmad ibn Uthman, *Siyaru A'lami'n Nubala*, Muassasatu'r Risala, Ninth edition, Beirut: 1993.

_____, *Tarikhu'l Islam*, Maktabatu Qudsi, Cairo: 1367 AH.

_____, *Tazkiratu'l Huffaz*, Daru Ihyai't Turasi'l Arabi, Beirut, undated.

DOĞRUL, Ömer Rıza, *Asr-ı Saadet*, Eser Kitabevi, İstanbul: 1974.

FAWZI, Jihan Rafat, *as-Sayyidatu Aisha wa Tawsiquha li's Sunnah*, Maktabatu'l Hanji, Cairo, 2001.

FIRUZABADI, Abu't Tahir Majduddin Muhammad ibn Ya'qûb ibn Muhammad Shirazi, *al-Kamusu'l Muhit*, Matbaa-i Hasaniyya al-Mısriyya, Second edition, 1344 AH.

AL-GHAZZALI, Abu Hamid Muhammad ibn Muhammad, *Ihyau Ulumiddin*, Daru Ihyai'l Kutubi'l Arabiyya, Beirut, undated.

GÜLEN, M. Fethullah, *Emerald Hills of the Heart: Key Concepts in the Practice of Sufism*, Tughra Books, NJ, 2011.

_____, M. Fethullah, *Messenger of God*, Tughra Books, NJ, 2011.

HAFNA, Abdulmin'im, *Mawsuatu Ummi'l Mu'minin Aisha bint-i Abi Bakr*, Maktabatu Madbuli, 2003.

HAKiM AN-NAYSABURI, Abu Abdillah Muhammad ibn Abdillah, *al-Mustadrak Ala's Sahihayn*, Edition critique by Mustafa Abdülqadir Ata, Daru'l Kutubu'l Ilmiyya, Beirut: 1990.

HALABI, *as-Siratu'n Nabawiyya*, Daru'l Marifa, Beirut: 1400 AH.

HANNAD, *Zuhd*, Daru'l Khulafa Li'l Kitabi'l Islami, Kuwait: 1406 AH.

HATIB AL-BAGHDADI, Abu Bakr Ahmad ibn Ali ibn Sabit, *al-Jami' Li Akhlaqi'r Rawi wa Adabi's Sami'*, Edition critique by Mahmud Tahhan, Maktabatu'l Maarif, Riyad, 1403 AH.

_____, *al-Kifaya fi Ilmi'r Riwaya*, Edition critique by Abu Abdillah as-Sawraki and İbrahim Hamdi al-Madani, al-Maktabatu'l Ilmiyya, Medina, undated.

_____, *Tarikh Baghdad*, Daru'l Kitabi'l Arabi, Beirut, undated.

HAYTHAMI, *Majmuatu'z Zawaid wa Manbau'l Fawaid*, Daru'l Fikr, Beirut, 1412 AH.

_____, *Mawaridu'z Zam'an*, al-Maktabatu'sh Shamila, Daru's Sakafati'l Arabiyya, Beirut: 1990.

HAYTHAMI, Nuraddin and Harith ibn Abi Usama, *Musnad-i Harith*, Markaz-i Hidmati's Sunnah, Medina al-Munawwara: 1992.

IBN ABDILBARR, *Istiab fi Marifati'l Ashab*, Daru'l-Kutubi'l Ilmiyya, Beirut: 1995.

_____, at-Tamhid, Wizaratu Umumi'l Awqaf wa'sh Shuuni'l Islamiyya, Morocco: 1387 AH.

IBN ABDIRABBIH, *al-Iqdu'l Farid*, http://www.alwarraq.com.

IBN ASAKIR, Abu'l Qasim Ali ibn Husayn ibn Hibatillah, *Tarikh Dimashq*, Daru'l Fikr, Beirut, 1998.

IBN ABI'D DUNYA, *Makarimi'l Akhlaq*, Maktabatu'l Qur'an, Cairo, undated.

IBN ABI HATIM, *al-Jarh wa't Ta'dil*, Matbaatu Majlisi Dairatu'l Maarifi'l Uthmaniyya, First Edition, Haydarabad, 1371 AH.

IBN ABI SHAYBA, Abu Bakr Abdullah ibn Muhammad al-Kufi, *al-Musannaf fi'l Ahadith wa'l Asar*, Edition critique by Kamal Yusuf Hut, Maktabatu'r Rushd, Riyad: 1409 AH.

IBN HAJAR, Abu'l Fadl Shihabuddin Ahmad ibn Ali al-Asqalani ash-Shafii, *Fathu'l Bari Sharhu Sahihi'l Bukhari*, Daru'l Marifa, Beirut: 1379 AH.

_____, *Hadyu's Sari*, Daru'l-Marifa, Second edition, Beirut, undated.

_____, *al-Isaba fi Tamyizi's Sahaba*, Edition critique by Ali Muhammad Bujawi, Daru'l Jil, Beirut: 1412 AH.

_____, *Taqribu't Tahzib*, Dirasa wa muqabala: Muhammad Awwama, Daru'r Rashid, Fourth edition, Syria: 1992.

_____, *Tahzibu't Tahzib*, Daru'l Fikr, First edition, 1404 AH.

IBN HALDUN, *Tarikh*, Daru Ihyai't Turasi'l Arabi, Beirut, undated.

IBN HIBBAN, Muhammad ibn Hibban Abu Hatim al-Busti, *Sahih, Muassasatu'r Risala*, Edition critique by Shuayb Arnawut, Beirut: 1993.

_____, *as-Siqat*, Dairatu'l Maarifi'l Uthmaniyya, Haydarabad: 1973

IBN HISHAM, *as-Siratu'n Nabawiyya*, Daru'l Jil, Beirut: 1411.

IBN HUZAYMA, Abu Bakr Muhammad ibn Ishaq as-Sulami, *Sahihi Ibn Huzayma*, Edition critique by Muhammad Mustafa al-A'zami, al Maktabu'l Islami, Beirut, undated.

IBN ISHAQ, *Sira*, Konya: 1981.

IBN JA'D, Abu'l Hasan ibn Ubayd al-Jawhari, *Musnad*, Edition critique by Amir Ahmad Haydar, Muassasatu Nadir, Beirut, 1990.

IBN KATHIR, Abu'l Fida Ismail ibn Umar al-Kurashi Ad-Dimashqi, *Tafsiru'l Qur'ani'l Azim*, Edition critique by Sami ibn Muhammad Salama, Daru Tayba, Second edition, 1999.

_____, *al-Bidaya wa'n Nihaya*, Maktabatu'l Maarif, Beirut, undated.

IBN MAJAH, *Sunan*, Daru'l Fikr, Beirut, undated.

IBN MANDA, *Ma'rifatu's-Sahaba*, Köprülü Library, No: 242, Varak: 195b.

IBN MANZUR, Abu'l Fadl Muhammad ibn Mukarram ibn Ali al-Ansari Jamaluddin. *al-Ifriki, Lisanu'l Arab*, Daru Sadir, First edition, Beirut, undated.

IBN QAYYIM AL-JAWZIYYA, Abu Abdillah Muhammad ibn Abi Bakr, *I'lamu'l Muwakkian*, Daru'l-Jil, Beirut, 1973.

_____, *al-Manaru'l Munif fi's Sahihi wa'd-Daif*, Maktabu'l Matbuati'l Islamiyya, Aleppo: 1983.

_____, *Zadu'l Maad fi Hadyi Khayri'l Ibad*, Edition critique by Shuayb Arnawut Abdulqadir. Arnawut, Muassasatu'r Risala, Beirut: 1986.

IBN SA'D, *Tabaqat*, Daru Sadir, Beirut, undated.

IBN TAYFUR, *Balaghatu'n Nisa*, Daru'l Fadila, Cairo, undated.

IBNU'L ATHIR, *Usdu'l Ghaba fi Sahaba*, Daru'l Fikr, Beirut: 1995.

IBNU'L JAWZI, *Sifatu's Safwa*, Edition critique by Fahuri and Kal'aji, Daru'l Marifa, Beirut, 1979.

IBRAHIM MUSTAFA et al, *al-Mujamu'l Wasit*, Çağrı Yayınları, Istanbul: 1990.

ISHAQ IBN-I RAHUYA, *Musnad*, Maktabatu'l Iman, Medina: 1991.

JAHIZ, Abu Uthman Amr ibn Bahr, *al-Bayan wa't Tabayyun*, Daru Sa'b, Beirut: 1968.

JAWHARI, Abu Nasr Ismail ibn Hammad al-Farabi, *as Sihah Taju'l Lugha wa Sihahi'l Arabiyya* (Taju'l Lugah), Edition critique by Ahmad Abdulghafur Attar, Daru'l Ilm, Fourth edition, Beirut: 1990.

KALKASHANDI, Ahmad ibn Ali, *Subhu'l A'sha fi Sinaati'l Insha*, Daru'l Fikr, Damascus: 1987.

KANDAHLAWI, *Hayatu's Sahaba*, Haydarabad: 1959.

KAYRAWANI, *Zahru'l Adab*, http://www.alwarraq.com

LALAKAI, Hibatullah Abu'l Qasim, *I'tiqadu Ahli's Sunnah*, Edition critique by Ahmad Sa'd Hamdan, Daru Tayba, Riyad: 1402 AH.

MAHMUD SAID MAMDUH, *Is'afu'l Mulihhin bi Tartibi Ahadithi Ihya-i Ulumu'd Din*, Daru'l Bashairi'l Islamiyya, Lebanon: 1986.

MALIK IBN ANAS, *Muwatta*, Daru Ihyai't Turasi'l Arabi, Egypt, undated.

MAQDISI, *al-Ahadithu'l Mukhtara*, Maktabatu Nahda, Mecca: 1410.

MAS'UDI, *Muruju'dh Dhahab*, http://www.alwarraq.com

MIZZI, Abu'l Hajjaj Yusuf ibn Zaki Abdi'r Rahman ibn Yusuf, *Tahzibu'l Kamal*. Edition critique by Bashshar Awwad Maruf, Muassasatu'r Risala, First Edition, Beirut: 1980.

MUNAWI, Zaynuddin Muhammad Abdurrauf, *Fayzu'l Qadir Sharhu'l Jamii's Saghir*, Daru'l Kutubi'l Ilmiyya, Beirut: 1994.

MUNZIRI, *at-Targhib wa't Tarhib, Daru'l Kutubi'l Ilmiyya*, Beirut, 1417 AH.

MUSLIM, Abu'l Husayn Ibn Hajjaj al-Kushayri an-Naysaburi, *Sahihu Muslim*, Edition critique by Muhammad Fuad Abdulbaqi, Daru Ihyai't Turasi'l Arabi, Beirut, undated.

NADAWI, Sayyid Sulayman, *Hazreti Âişe*, translated by Ahmet Karataş, Timaş, Istanbul: 2004.

_____, *Siratu's Sayyidati Aisha Ummu'l Mu'minin*, Edition critique by Muhammad Rahmatullah Hafiz an-Nadawi, Daru'l Qalam, Damascus: 2003.

NASAI, Abu Abdirrahman Ahmad ibn Ali ibn Shuayb, *Sunanu'l Kubra*, Edition critique by Abdulghaffar Sulayman al-Bundari, Daru'l Kutubi'l Ilmiyya, First edition, Beirut: 1991.

_____, *Sunan*, Edition critique by Abdulfattah Abu Ghudda, Maktabatu'l Matbuati'l Islamiyya, 1968.

NAWAWI, *Tahzibu'l Asma*, Edition critique by Mustafa Abdulqadir Ata, al-Maktabatu's Shamila, undated.

NUWAYRI, *Nihayatu'l Arab*, http://www.alwarraq.com

QURTUBI, *Tafsir (al-Jami Li Ahkami'l Qur'an)*, Daru Ihyai't Turasi'l Arabi, Beirut: 1985.

RAGHIB AL-ISFAHANI, Abu'l Qasim, Husayn ibn Muhammad ibn Mufaddal, *al-Mufradat fi Gharibi'l Qur'an*, Edition critique by Safwan Adnan, Daru'l Qalam, Second edition, 1418 AH.

SAID IBN MANSUR, Abu Uthman ibn Shuba, al-Hurasani, *Sunan-i Said ibn Mansur*, Edition critique by Sa'd ibn Abdillah ibn Abdilaziz Al-i Humayyad, Daru's Sami'i, First edition, Riyad: 1993.

SAHAWI, Abu'l Khayr Shamsuddin Muhammad ibn Abdirrahman, *al-Maqasidu'l Hasana fi Bayani Kathirin mina'l Ahadithi'l Mushtahira Ala'l Alsina*, Edition critique by Muhammad Uthman al-Husht, Daru'l Kitabi'l Arabi, Second edition, Beirut: 1994.

SALAFI, Abu Tahir Ahmad ibn Muhammad, *Mu'jamu's Safar*, al-Maktabatu't Tijariyya, Mecca, undated.

SAM'ANI, *Adabu'l Imla wa'l Istimla*, Daru'l Kutubi'l Ilmiyya, Beirut: 1401.

SAMHUDI, *Hulasatu'l Wafa*, Cairo: 1908.

SAN'ANI, *Subulu's Salam*, Daru'l Kitabi'l Arabi, Beirut: 1987.

SAVAŞ, Rıza, "Hz. Aişe'nin Evlenme Yaşı ile ilgili Farkll Bir Yaklaşım,", *D. E. Ü. İlahiyat F. Dergisi*, Issue 4, Izmir: 1995.

_____, *al-Itqanfi Ulumi'l Qur'an*, Beirut, 1987.

SHALABI, Mahmud, *Hayatu Aisha*, undated

SHAWKANI, Muhammad ibn Ali ibn Muhammad, *Naylu'l Awtar min Ahadithi Sayyidi'l Abrar*, 6/170, Idaratu't Tibaati'l Mudiriyya, undated.

_____, *al-Fawaid-i Majmua*, al-Maktabu'l Islami, Beirut: 1407.

SUYUTI, Abu'l Fadl Jalaladdin Abdurrahman ibn Abi Bakr, *al-Jamiu's Saghir fi Ahadithi'l Bashiri'n Nazir*, Daru'l Kutubi'l Ilmiyya, Beirut: 1990.

_____, *ad-Durru'l Mansur fi't Tafsiri bi'l Ma'sur*, Daru'l Fikr, Beirut: 1993.

TABARANI, Abu'l Qasim Sulayman ibn Ahmad, *al-Mujamu'l Awsat*, Edition critique by Tariq ibn Iwadullah, Daru'l Haramayn, Cairo: 1415 AH.

_____, *Mujamu's Saghir*, Daru Ammar, al-Maktabu'l Islami, Beirut: 1985.

_____, *Mujamu'l Kabir*, Maktabatu'l Ulum wa'l-Hikam, Mosul: 1983.

TABARI, *Tarikhu'l Uman wa'l-Muluk*, Daru'l Kutubi'l Ihmiyya, Beirut: 1407.

TAHAWI, Ahmad ibn Muhammad ibn Salama ibn Abdilmalik ibn Salama Abu Jafar, *Sharhu Maani'l Asar*, Edition critique by Muhammad Zuhri an-Najjar, Daru'l Kutubi'l Ilmiyya, Beirut: 1399 AH.

_____, *Sharhu Mushkili'l Asar*, Shuayb Arnawut, Beirut: 1994.

TAHMAZ, Abdulhamid Mahmud, *as-Sayyidatu Aisha*, Daru'l Qalam, Damascus, 1999.

TANTAWI, *Abu Bakr as-Siddiq*, Daru'l Manar, Jeddah: 1986.

TAYALISI, *Abu Dawud, Musnad*, Daru'l Marifa, Beirut, undated.

TIRMIDHI, Abu Isa Muhammad ibn Isa, *al-Jamiu'l Kabir (Sunan)*, Tahqiq tahrij wa taliq: Bashshar Awwad Maruf, Daru'l Gharbi'l Islami, First Edition, Beirut: 1996.

ÜNAL, Ali, *The Qur'an with Annotated Interpretation in Modern English*, Tughra Books, New Jersey: 2008.

VEHBE ZUHAYLİ, *İslam Fıkhı Ansiklopedisi*, Risale Yayınları, Germany: 1994.

WENSBICK et al, *al-Mujamu'l Mufahras Li Alfazi'l Hadithi'n Nabawi*, Çağrı Yayınları, Istanbul: 1988.

YAQUT AL-HAMAWI, Abi Abdillah Shihabu'd Din ibn Abdillah, *Mujamu'l Buldan*, Edition critique by Farid Abdulaziz al-Jundi, Daru'l Kutubi'l Ilmiyya, Beirut, undated.

YÜCE, Abdülhakim, *Efendimiz'in Bir Günü*, Işık Yayınları, Istanbul: 2007.

ZAGHLUL, Abu Hajar Muhammad Said Abu Hajar Muhammad Said ibn Basyuni, *Mawsuatu Atrafi'l Hadithi'n Nabawiyyi'sh Sharif*, al-Maktabatu't Tijariyya, Mustafa Ahmad al-Baiz, Daru'l Fikr, Beirut: 1994.

ZABIDI, Abu'l Fayz Murtaza Muhammad, *Taju'l Arus min Jawahiri'l Qamus*, Daru'l Fikr, Beirut: 1414.

ZARKASHI, Badruddin, *al-Ijaba Lima Istadrakathu Aisha ala's Sahaba*, Maktabatu Mishkati'l Islamiyya, undated.

ZAYLAI, Abu Muhammad Abdullah ibn Yusuf al-Hanafi, *Nasbu'r Raya Li Ahadithi'l Hidaya*, Edition critique by Muhammad Yusuf al-Bannuri, Daru'l Hadith, Egypt: 1357 AH.

ZIRIKLI, *A'lam*, Daru'l Ilm li'l Malayin, Beirut: 1980.

## COMPUTER PROGRAMS AND WEB SITES

1. "Mawsuatu'l Hadithi'sh Sharif" 2.00, Sahr Company (Shirkatu Harf li Takniyati'l Malumat, Egypt.

2. "al-Maktabatu'sh Shamila" 2.11, http://www.waqfeya.net/shamela

3. "al-Maktabatu'sh Shamila" 1.5, http://www.waqfeya.net/shamela

4. "al-Jamiu'l Kabir Li Kutubi't Turasi'l Arabi wa'l Islami" 2.0, Turas Computer Services, Jordan, 2005.